Norse Fighting Heroes

Norse Fighting Heroes

Kings, Conquerors and Shield-maidens

Jamie Ryder

First published in Great Britain in 2024 by
Pen & Sword History
An imprint of Pen & Sword Books Limited
Yorkshire – Philadelphia

Copyright © Jamie Ryder 2024

ISBN 978 1 39903 890 4

The right of Jamie Ryder to be identified as
Author of this Work has been asserted by him in accordance
with the Copyright, Designs and Patents Act 1988.

A CIP catalogue record for this book is
available from the British Library

All rights reserved. No part of this book may be reproduced or
transmitted in any form or by any means, electronic or mechanical
including photocopying, recording or by any information storage and
retrieval system, without permission from the Publisher in writing.

Typeset by Mac Style
Printed in the UK by CPI Group (UK) Ltd, Croydon, CR0 4YY.

Pen & Sword Books Limited incorporates the imprints of After
the Battle, Atlas, Archaeology, Aviation, Discovery, Family History,
Fiction, History, Maritime, Military, Military Classics, Politics,
Select, Transport, True Crime, Air World, Frontline Publishing, Leo
Cooper, Remember When, Seaforth Publishing, The Praetorian Press,
Wharncliffe Local History, Wharncliffe Transport, Wharncliffe True
Crime and White Owl.

For a complete list of Pen & Sword titles please contact

PEN & SWORD BOOKS LIMITED
47 Church Street, Barnsley, South Yorkshire, S70 2AS, England
E-mail: enquiries@pen-and-sword.co.uk
Website: www.pen-and-sword.co.uk
or
PEN AND SWORD BOOKS
1950 Lawrence Rd, Havertown, PA 19083, USA
E-mail: uspen-and-sword@casematepublishers.com
Website: www.penandswordbooks.com

Contents

Acknowledgements vii
Author's Note viii
Introduction x

Chapter 1   The Dragon Slayer and The Allure of Ambition   1

Chapter 2   The Valkyrie and The Princess   8

Chapter 3   The Dynasty of Shaggy Breeches and Eternal Fame   19

Chapter 4   The Boneless Warlord and The Blood of Kings   28

Chapter 5   The First Christian King of Scandinavia   36

Chapter 6   The Queen Mother and the Ingenuity of Norse Women   43

Chapter 7   The Norse Alexander the Great   47

Chapter 8   The Warrior Poet and The Wisdom of Verse   54

Chapter 9   The Deep-Minded Matriarch and the Uncertainty of Starting Again   76

Chapter 10   The Vikings of the East and the Founding of a New Kingdom   82

Chapter 11   The Saintly Sinner and The Brave Pagan   88

Chapter 12   The Well-Travelled Voyager and The Mystery of Runes   95

Chapter 13	The Wanderluster and The Mediterranean Sojourn	99
Chapter 14	The Exile and The Discovery of a Lifetime	103
Chapter 15	The Siblings of Luck and Savagery	107
Chapter 16	The Hard Ruler and The Path to Greatness	113
Chapter 17	The Norman Conqueror and the Conquest of England	139
Chapter 18	The Crusader and The Holy Calling	152
Notes		160
Bibliography		166
Index		170

Acknowledgements

I'd like to thank several people for helping me bring this project to life. Thank you to my mum and dad for encouraging me to write from a young age and being curious about the world. Thank you to my partner Kim for putting up with all the random historical facts that you've listened to, the day-to-day neurotic writing habits that have been up and down and for being my sounding board when I've needed to come back to the present day. Thank you to Pen & Sword Books for publishing the book and to my commissioning editor Sarah-Beth Watkins for suggesting I write it in the first place. Thank you to all the scholars, academics and authors who've put out some incredible work on Viking studies and have helped to improve my knowledge of the subject. Thank you to Dr Alex Woolf for the enlightening interview and for helping me understand the complexities of a historical period that has so many different perspectives and avenues. Thank you to everyone who reads this book and if it's something you've enjoyed then please leave a review online where you can. Reviews are one of the best ways to help authors keep on writing, improving their craft and doing what they love.

Author's Note

The lives of the men and women in this book have been passed down to us through sagas and without those stories, we wouldn't know half of what we know of the ideals that the Norse embodied. Runestones, graves and artefacts have been left behind to fill in the facts of the societies from where these characters sprang. The melding of epic legendary fiction, of complicated heroes, warriors, gods and monsters, with the evidence of how the Norse *actually* lived thanks to the efforts of archaeologists and scholars, will continue to captivate people for years to come.

I feel compelled to mention the sagas of the people, organisations and businesses who are furthering the conversation of Viking lore today through various mediums. Let this book serve as a record of their contribution long after they've gone and that their work and output made an impact.

Dr Neil Price, archaeologist and specialist in the study of Viking Age Scandinavia; Dr Johanna Katrin Fridriksdottir, medievalist specialising in Old Norse history and historical consultant; Dr Cat Jarman, bioarcheologist, specialising in forensic techniques to chart the history of the Vikings as they came to British soil; Dr Jackson Crawford, translator of Old Norse and Scandinavian studies professor; Dr Alex Woolf, British medieval historian; Peyton Parrish, metal and rock band with several Viking-inspired songs (https://peytonparrishofficial.com/); Nidhoggr Mead (https://nidhoggrmead.co.uk/); Lancashire Mead (www.lancashiremeadcompany.co.uk/); Jorvik Viking Centre in York, England (www.jorvikvikingcentre.co.uk/); Horns of Odin, seller of drinking horns and other Viking merchandise (www.hornsofodin.com/); Norse Spirit, Viking merchandise seller (https://norsespirit.com/); The Viking Museum in Stockholm, Sweden (https://thevikingmuseum.com/): The Viking

Ship Museum in Olso, Norway (www.vikingtidsmuseet.no/); Midgard Viking Centre in Borre, Norway; Nordvegen History Centre in Avaldsnes, Norway; Birka Museum in Sweden (www.birkavikingastaden.se/); Northan Viking Silver, producers of Norse jewellery (www.northanvikingsilver.com/); History Time, a YouTube channel that offers well-researched content about the Vikings and other time periods (www.youtube.com/@HistoryTime); and The Viking Channel, a YouTube channel run by Dr Lena Elisabeth Norrman (www.youtube.com/@thevikingchannel9431).

> Disclaimer: Every attempt has been made to ascertain, locate and contact the copyright holders (or the personal representatives of their estates) of all photographs in the book and I request that any copyright holders make themselves known to the publisher so that they may be fully credited and acknowledged in any future reprint of this book.

Introduction

What does it mean to be a hero and what're the qualities of someone who's heroic? This question is worth asking because as human beings, we're hardwired to celebrate heroes and they come in all shapes and sizes.

There are superheroes like Marvel's Iron Man and Captain America, bombastic characters fighting against world-changing odds that we want to root for to save the day. There are down-to-earth heroes like Sherlock Holmes and Nancy Drew, characters that don't have any special powers and rely on their intelligence and adaptability to solve mysteries. There are everyday heroes like soldiers and firefighters who put their lives on the line. There are people you know that will have changed your life in a profound way and are worthy of being called a hero. All these archetypes are cut from a similar cloth. They are brave, strong, capable and we praise those qualities because we perceive them as inherently good. In our modern view, a hero is a righteous and morally virtuous figure that puts their own needs above others to serve the greater good. It's a black-and-white way of looking at the world, but if we look back at the origins of a hero, the truth is more complicated.

Hero comes from the ancient Greek word *heros* meaning 'defender' or 'protector'. To the Greeks, a hero was a person who performed extraordinary feats and went on epic quests – people like Hercules and Achilles who fought legendary battles and had the typical characteristics we associate modern day heroes with.

But many of these ancient heroes committed extreme acts of violence and barbarism in their quest to prove their strength. They killed and slaughtered in battle in pursuit of their honour (another word that's evolved over time and one we'll come back to) and were celebrated for their bloodlust.[1]

By our standards, mass killing and violence for the sake of proving who's the strongest isn't heroic at all. That term becomes even more complicated when you could be called a hero for raping, pillaging and enslaving those you came into contact with, just like the subjects of this book, the Vikings, revelled in.

Like the civilisations that came before them, the Vikings were active during a time in history when fighting, expanding and imposing their will on cultures they perceived as weaker made the difference between life and death. In the Scandinavian cultures of Norway, Denmark, Finland, Iceland and beyond, the warriors who went raiding were held as inspirations to their kinsmen. They were heroes because they embodied all the traditional values of their culture. And while there's truth in the popular image of Vikings as bloodthirsty killing machines, to only see them through this narrow lens is a mistake.

They were change-makers who transformed every territory they stepped into, introducing innovations that impacted the course of history. The Vikings had a rich, complex mythology that demanded they explore, adapt and connect with communities that were unlike their own. They were poets, farmers, craftsmen, rulers and politicians who lived their lives to the fullest and that is the heart of *Norse Fighting Heroes: Kings, Conquerors and Shield-Maidens*.

This book is about getting to the essence of some of the most (in)famous figures throughout Viking history, men and women who carved a space for themselves, defied odds, founded regimes, made mistakes, honoured their gods, loved, laughed, fought and died for any number of reasons; legendary warriors like the famed Ragnar Lodbrok, whose epic saga has been the stuff of the silver and small screen; fabled adventurers like Leif Erikson, who discovered America and his firebrand sister Freydis Eriksdottir; and silver-tongued poets like Egil Skallagrimsson who could charm with the power of his words. Although the title of the book is *Norse Fighting Heroes*, I've featured people from across Scandinavian cultures and lore. This is because the Vikings weren't a single ethnic group but a diverse cast of nations with their own idiosyncrasies and collective identities. With that said, 'Norse' is a recognisable term when referring to all the cultures associated with the Vikings and is used here for the layman. Other phrases used to refer to people of Scandinavian origin are 'Northmen' and 'Norsemen.' All these terms will be used interchangeably throughout. For the Anglo-Saxons, whom the Norse fought against, I've chosen to use the term 'English'.

The life of every character that appears is told in a mixture of essays, short stories and anecdotes. I've done this to honour the sources and sagas that have been written about them and to look beneath the stereotypes of Vikings as blunt instruments of destruction. This comes with the acknowledgement that I've written through my own subjective lens and I'm presenting a version of the Viking Age that differs in scope and perspective from other authors. Many of the chapters are written out of chronological order, i.e. they don't follow a historical narrative of the Viking Age that traditionally starts with the ransacking of the Lindisfarne abbey in England in 793 AD and ends with the fall of Harald Hardrada at the Battle of Stamford Bridge in 1066 AD. People of Scandinavian origin were migrating before and after those dates and the history of the Vikings is anything but linear. It goes back and forth, twists and turns across generations, families and continents. So, you can read each chapter like a short story, while still appreciating the undercurrent of history that weaves every event and motivation together, just like the Norns of Norse mythology who decided the fates of all.

For as the epic poem *Havamal* (Words of the High One), allegedly composed by Odin, king of the Norse gods, states, 'be a maker of shoes or a maker of spearshafts/But for yourself alone/If the shoe's poorly made, or the shaft is crooked/Then you'll gain the curses of men.'[2]

I interpret this stanza as writers and creatives needing to stand by their work. But it's also putting *in* the work to make sure they understand a topic and do it justice – to look at a narrative from multiple angles, to refine a product and put it out into the world knowing that it can stand up to scrutiny. It's also about being willing to take feedback on the chin and saying that any mistakes made are my own. Before we look at the individual heroes of the book, it's important to understand who the Vikings were and how their environment shaped who they would become.

The origins of Vikings

Two of the biggest misconceptions about Vikings is that they were a single race or nation and they wore horned helmets. Both are untrue. The word 'Viking' refers to an occupation and activity in Old Norse. The first is the noun *vikingr*, meaning raiders and warriors who travelled great distances by sea to seek their fortune. The second meaning is the verb *viking*, which is the act of travelling by sea and raiding – in other words, to go *viking*.[3] Both terms can be applied to men and women, as the latter also travelled far and wide to trade with new communities, even if they weren't battle-hardened fighters.[4]

The validity of the word is hotly debated among scholars and academics, with several origins given about where it comes from. One interpretation derives from the Old Norse *vik*, meaning bay or inlet. This brings to mind the longships Norse warriors used to travel between regions and make them a force to be reckoned with. Another theory is that the term is derived from the people who lived in the Viken region, defined in the Middle Ages as the strait between Norway and the southwestern coast of Sweden and the Jutland area of Denmark. There's also an interesting perspective on the word *vika*, meaning to turn or shift. This refers to oarsmen working in shifts aboard a longship. On long voyages, rowing was an integral part of ship movement, so the wayfarers who set out on these journeys would need to have tremendous strength and stamina to continue propelling a vessel through unpredictable weather and uncertain waters.[5] As for the horned helmets, this legend probably came about through the later depictions of Scandinavian artists wanting to create a distinct image for the raiders.

Archaeologist and author Dr Neil Price acknowledges that 'we will probably never speak the Vikings' secret name' but that we can understand them on a much deeper level by not relegating ourselves to only one area of study or a single strand of thought. Readers and students of Viking lore should spend time looking into 'archaeology, saga scholarship, philology, runology and the history of religions'[6] so we can see the bigger picture and appreciate the lives of individuals that lived in Viking Age Scandinavia.

Whatever the case, there's no denying the Northmen of the eighth century were restless and had an outward-facing mindset that compelled them to travel. In the context of the Early Middle Ages, the term 'nation' was a loose concept: modern countries like Norway, Denmark and Sweden were not unified but made up of disparate tribes with chieftains vying for power, which mirrored England, the place where the Norse would leave one of their most enduring marks on history. England wasn't a single country either and consisted of various kingdoms.

There are many reasons why the Norse chose to venture out into the world. For example, a shift in climate happened in the eighth century, which is known as the Medieval Warm Period. Temperatures were generally warmer than they are today and that opened new seafaring and trading routes for Scandinavian farmers and fishermen whose livelihoods were connected to the North Sea. This had a knock-on effect on greater land cultivation at home, societal changes and population increase. With these changes came increased conflict as Scandinavian chieftains claimed more and more territories, leading to less opportunity for others. There were also harsh winters and freezing temperatures to contend with so it's little wonder that more and more people chose to seek their fortune abroad.[7]

Viking ethos and ethics

Contrary to their identity as warmongering brutes, Norse societies promoted order and hierarchy. This would have likely seemed at odds with the chaotic warriors that people in England, Spain, France and Ireland saw running towards them with axes and shields. But if there was no order to the Norse then they would not have been able to carve out new kingdoms or assimilate into societies all over the world.

The social structure of the Norse was built on a foundation of function, status and money across three classes of people. At the top, there were the jarls, the kings and the chiefs that commanded and demanded the respect of their followers. In turn, they needed to give back to their warriors by extending their personal wealth. In some ways, the power of a jarl relied upon the loyalty of his men and if they deserted him, he could quickly find himself ousted.

Skalds (poets) and artists might also find themselves in the jarl class because of the importance of creativity and learning within Norse society.

The middle class, karls, were the largest group. As men and women who owned property, karls could have a range of occupations, running from farmer to merchant. This class enjoyed a great amount of freedom when compared to the eventual feudal system that dominated Western civilisation for centuries of serfs being bound to their lords.

Thralls made up the bottom of the societal ladder. They were slaves, indentured servants and vagrants and of the three, vagrants were the most reviled. This is because slaves and indentured servants still contributed to society, while vagrants had no ties to anything. Slavery was an unfortunate reality of the Viking Age and by our modern standards, it's an inhuman practice. Within the context of the time, slaves in Norse society were subjected to the same abuses as other slave cultures throughout history. In some instances, however, both male and female slaves could still achieve a higher status based on things like their craftsmanship and their physical attractiveness.[8]

While we wouldn't think of a society that normalises slavery as particularly just, the Norse were sticklers for the law and democracy. The most prominent example is the *thing*, where an assembly would gather to judge an accused and where freedmen in the community could have their say. The assembly would also be presided over by a lawspeaker who recited the law from memory and took part in the judgement. But if an assembly failed to resolve matters, there were other methods that an aggrieved could call upon like duelling.

The original form of Norse duelling was known as *einvigi*, unsanctioned single combat where there was no judge. Two parties fought with whatever weapons they had to hand. If one or either of the combatants died, their family could demand *weregeld*, (man-gold), money paid to the deceased's family as compensation for the death. As the custom evolved, *weregeld* became a part of the legislation and if the money wasn't paid then a family was legally obligated to retaliate with violence.

Over time, duelling became more ritualised to limit violence, evolving into *holmgang*. The rules and practices of this type of duelling varied from place to place, but generally there were common characteristics.

Two men would meet inside a roped-off area on an island with a sword. Accompanied by seconds who provided the fighters with a total of three shields, the duellists battled on cloaks within the ring and each man struck a single blow. Once every shield was broken and when one man's blood fell onto the cloaks, the duel ended. Witnesses made sure the fight was kept fair and put a stop to further bloodshed.[9] *Holmgangs* solved a couple of problems. First, warriors were able to keep their honour and save face because they had fought bravely in the duel. Second, neither fighter died, and it limited the chances of family blood feuds consuming a settlement. There were still strict rules to adhere to when preparing for and fighting in a *holmgang*. Both duellists were required to show up for the fight, otherwise they risked being branded as *nidingr* (people without honour) and being sentenced as outlaws.

In Norse politics, full outlawry was effectively a death sentence because the outlaw lost all his rights as a member of society. His property would be confiscated and he could be legally killed by anyone. In the eyes of his community, he was little more than a beast to be banished to the forest. A lesser form of outlawry existed, which involved the offender being banished for three years.[10] If these laws sound paradoxical, then it's a common theme within Norse ethics. Another example of this dichotomy lies in their perspective of theft: stealing was one of the worst offences a Norseman could commit on home soil, i.e. the taking of goods or the 'stealing' of another man's wife by way of adultery. It was tantamount to cowardice. But when warriors went *viking*, this was considered raiding. It's the proverbial case of 'might makes right' as Norsemen plundering an abbey would have seen themselves as demonstrating their strength. The monks they were raiding had the opportunity to fight back and if they were unable to overcome the raid, it was down to their own weakness. So, the taking of any possessions won through raiding was wholly justified in the Norse mindset.

An indication of how seriously the Norse took the distinction between stealing and raiding can be seen in a story from a saga. A Viking band had been captured but managed to escape with some of their plunder. But before they got back to their ships, an overwhelming sense of guilt shook them to the core. The loot they had won in battle was now being carried off by stealth, making them little more than thieves. To clear their conscience, the group went back to their captors and slaughtered them all.[11] In another instance, the poet Egil Skallagrimsson raided a farm with his men and as they were escaping into the woods, he thought they had acted cowardly. The farmer hadn't known of their deeds or that he'd been robbed. When he returned to the farmstead, Egil set it on fire and blocked the door so no one could leave. He slaughtered all inside and then, when he was satisfied, he went back to his men believing he'd shown himself to be courageous instead of a coward. What we can see from these laws is that great physical strength, cunning, adaptability and honour within context were all highly praised qualities in Norse society. As was faith in the gods.

Wanderers, tricksters, strongmen and fate-shapers

Norse mythology is undoubtedly one of the most fascinating aspects of Scandinavian cultures. There has been plenty written on the various stories of deities like Odin and Thor who were among the most important gods in the Norse mythos. In books that focus on Vikings, there's often a section dedicated to the Norse creation of the universe, Yggdrasil the world tree, the nine realms and all the mythical communities that live within each space.

All of it makes for fantastic reading, even though the sagas should be taken with a pinch of salt. For engaging modern retellings of these stories, I recommend Neil Gaiman's *Norse Mythology* and Neil Price's *The Children of Ash and Elm: A History of the Vikings*. As this book is about character studies, I'm focused on the motivations of the otherworldly beings the Northmen looked to in times of battle, uncertainty and merriment. I'm also interested in looking at the human characteristics that made the Norse gods both relatable and unrelatable to the people they inspired and why we're still talking about them today.

The price of wisdom

All-Father, Havi, Grimnir, Harbard, Oski, Vafud. There are just a few of the names attributed to Odin, king of the Aesir, one of the two divine families that make up the society of Norse gods. The other group, the Vanir, fought a brutal war with the Aesir until peace was made between them through a series of negotiations and hostage exchanges. When looking at the difference between the two families, the Vanir seemed to be tied to the earth, signifying the relationship between humans and their natural dependence on agriculture. Aesir like Odin were more individualistic and warlike (though that didn't mean Vanir like Freyja were any less violent).[12] Yet it's in Odin that we see the quintessential example of a figure displaying all the contradictions of godly and human nature.

On one hand, he was the god of war, poetry and wisdom, the name jarls and kings evoked when they needed to lead their people to victory. Odin sacrificed himself for knowledge by giving up an eye, when he sought out the wise Mimir at the Well of Urd. Found beneath Yggdrasil, the vast tree that connects all the realms of the universe, the well contained the secrets of the cosmos, secrets Mimir knew by drinking from it. When Odin asked for a draught, Mimir rebuffed him. Such knowledge should come with a sacrifice equal to the weight of it. Seeing what had to be done, Odin cut out his eye and offered it as payment. Then he drank from the well and took the gift of wisdom.

In this context, Odin sacrificed one form or perception for another. The eyes see the everyday and the mundane. By drinking from the Well of Urd, the All-Father acquired sight into the unseen, the deeper truths of the world that very few could interpret. This wouldn't be the last sacrifice he made.

Odin was aware of the Norns, who could see the past, present and future. They were able to read and manipulate runes, the mysterious symbols the Norse used to mark important events and wield magic. Determined to prove himself worthy, the Hanged God pierced himself with his spear and hung himself on Yggdrasil for nine days and nights. Throughout this time, he ordered that no creature should approach to give him food or drink or cut him down. At the end of the ninth night, Odin finally understood the runes which made him even more powerful.

As well as the god of wisdom, Odin acted as a patron to fallen warriors that hoped to appease him and go to his hall of Valholl or Valhalla, which is commonly mistaken as the Norse afterlife. It was one of several spaces the souls of the dead could travel to. Other realms included Folkvangr, the home of Freyja and Hel, the home of a Norse goddess of death.

Through his insatiable hunger for knowledge, Odin wandered the nine realms, looking for ways to improve his learning so he could be ready for Ragnarok. This was the apocalyptic prophecy of Norse lore that signalled the gods' end and led to chaos throughout the nine worlds. Odin would fight Fenrir, the great wolf that would ultimately be the end of him.

With this knowledge-seeking aspect of Odin, we can see why the Norse chose to travel the world and expand into new territories. Acquiring knowledge of new things is vital to growing as a person.

We also get a glimpse of the Norse perspective on fate. For them, Ragnarok was a certainty. It was bound to happen, just as death is inevitable. Fighting against what couldn't be controlled was a waste of energy, so going into battle and fighting courageously was a method of choosing how to respond to death. But to call Viking Age Scandinavians fatalistic would be to miss the point. Fate was a fluid construct, shaped by the Norns, beings who shaped fate, even Odin's. The Norns weaved the thread of every individual in a constant strand of evolution, which crossed over with the strands of everyone else you would meet over the course of your life. In other words, according to Price 'free will existed, but exercising it inevitably led to becoming the person you always really had been'.[13]

So, who was Odin really? In hunting for limitless knowledge, the darker side of the High One comes to light. In the sagas, Odin is a shapeshifter, liar, manipulator and murderer who does whatever it takes to achieve his goals. He's full of contradictions and a useful source for seeing this is the *Havamal* poem, which distils Odin's lessons. His advice ranges all the way from being a good host to strangers to then manipulating them to get what you want.

Through this lens, we see how the gods didn't serve just one function to the Vikings. Odin fulfilled several roles at once. He could be the din a warrior heard in battle and the fervour that he felt when he raised his axe to an enemy. He could be the words of wisdom spoken to a friend and the poetry written to celebrate a great victory.

A pattern that's held true of the nature of Odin and, to a greater extent, every other mythical being throughout the centuries, is how their stories and characteristics have been altered depending on the culture that's telling the story. In modern media, there have been several portrayals of Odin, emphasising his different aspects. In the Marvel Cinematic Universe's *Thor* series, the High One is mostly portrayed as a wise elder statesman and guide to his sons Thor and Loki. He has the bombast and superheroic qualities that are expected from a movie franchise that's consistently broken box office records. But this portrayal misses lots of the nuances and complexities of the Aesir king.

There are two other modern interpretations that are closer to the wily, unpredictable Odin that the Norse would've been familiar with. The first is from Neil Gaiman's *American Gods*, the character of Mr Wednesday. This version of Odin is as a grifter who's focused on regaining his power of old by any means necessary. The second and perhaps most faithful portrayal is from the *God of War* gaming series. In *God of War: Ragnarok*, Odin isn't a jacked-up behemoth like the Viking stereotypes that are rampant in TV and cinema. He's an unassuming, frail-looking old man who seems very agreeable when father–son protagonists Kratos and Atreus meet him for the first time. Eventually, the High One reveals his true colours as a master manipulator and shyster who charms with false words and then ruthlessly destroys anyone who gets in his way. *God of War*'s Odin is essentially a mob boss in charge of a crime family, manoeuvring the Aesir and Vanir around like chesspieces. This is a useful analogy of how classical sources tell us the Norse gods operated: they were a dysfunctional family who seemed to involve themselves in human affairs on a whim, for entertainment or when they had the most to gain.

The embodiment of strength

If Odin was the god of kings and jarls, his son Thor was a god for all, from the most important politician down to the humblest of farmers. The god of strength and thunder, Thor represented all that was good in the Viking mindset: courage, physical might, stalwartness and indomitable will. With his enchanted hammer Mjolnir, Thor embodied the fighting spirit of the Norse and on his many adventures he enjoyed slaying all kinds of creatures, especially the *jotunn* (giants). The giants and Aesir were entangled in a complicated symbiosis. When they weren't fighting each other, they were having sex with each other and Thor himself may have been half-giant. His mother Fyorgyn is identified as either a giant or the personification of Earth.

Despite his parentage, Thor was the bane of all giants. There are two Old Norse stories that attest to the god of thunder's giant-killing abilities. The first involved a battle with a giant called Hrungnir, a fight manipulated by Odin. He and Hrungnir had got into a contest about whose horse was faster. Odin's steed Sleipnir had eight legs. Odin became so confident that no horse could outrace his own that he bet his head. Provoked into action, Hrungnir mounted his horse Gold Mane and the two raced across the land. In the end, Odin beat the giant back to Asgard and the Aesir invited him to drink with them in the spirit of good cheer. Disgruntled by the loss, Hrungnir drained drinking bowl after drinking bowl, becoming more belligerent by the minute. He began to boast that he would destroy all Asgard and take the goddesses Freyja and Sif home with him. Bored of the giant's rants, the Aesir called in Thor, who raised Mjolnir, ready to kill the drunken fool on the spot. Hrungnir accused the thunder god of cowardice for saying he would kill an unarmed guest of the High One himself. If he was a man of honour, Thor would meet him for a duel. Always ready to prove his honour and strength, Thor accepted. When the two met for battle, Hrungnir was dressed in stone armour and brandished a massive whetstone as his weapon of choice. As soon as he saw Thor arrive, the giant tossed the whetstone at him. In a bellow of rage, Thor launched Mjolnir and the hammer smashed through the whetstone, crushing Hrungnir's skull. But Thor would not escape the duel unscathed. A piece of the whetstone lodged itself deep into his brow, which stayed with him until Ragnarok.

The second story is about Thor's fishing trip with the giant Hymir. It all started when the Aesir rocked up in the hall of Aegir, the most powerful of the sea giants. They demanded to be fed and Aegir chose to accommodate them. His one condition was that they brought him a cauldron large enough to brew beer for them all. Knowing they didn't have such a cauldron, Aegir didn't have to put on a banquet for the gods. Mighty Thor asked all the Aesir for advice on where to find such a cauldron and he gained wise counsel from Tyr, god of war. Tyr told Thor that his stepfather, Hymir, king of the giants, had a cauldron that was three miles deep. So, Thor and Tyr ventured to Hymir's realm, where they were greeted by Tyr's grandmother and mother.

On hearing the arrival of her husband, Tyr's mother told them to hide under her kettle, for Hymir was often in a bad mood and tended to treat his guests badly. Thor and Tyr should only come out of hiding when Hymir had settled down. The giant king raged, smashing various objects until the giantess told her husband that their son had come for a visit and he'd brought his friend Veor.

'Thor?' Hymir rumbled. 'Enemy and killer of our people?'

'Veor,' his wife explained, 'is a giant and a friend to our son. An enemy of your enemy so there's no need to fight.'

Now calm, Hymir lifted the kettle to see his stepson and the man called Veor. The giant king said they should stay for dinner and several of his prized oxen were brought in as food. The meat was stirred in Hymir's legendary cauldron and once it was ready, Thor helped himself, devouring two oxen.

'That was meant to feed us for several days, Veor. I'd never known a giant to eat so much so quickly,' Hymir grunted, feeling put out.

'I was hungry.' Thor shrugged. 'Anyway, I heard you are quite the fisherman. Why don't we go out tomorrow and we can catch some food together?'

Hymir became prideful about his fishing skills and agreed. The next day, he and Thor left to prepare. Wanting to catch something extraordinary, Thor needed a certain kind of bait. So, he went into the giant's pastures and found an ox and ripped its head off. Eating two oxen so brazenly the night before hadn't been the best start to Thor and Hymir's relationship. Killing another would only add to the growing tension. Out at sea, Thor dismissed all of Hymir's fishing spots and demanded they go out into the deepest water possible. The duo found themselves in the vastness of the ocean, with Hymir casting the first line and pulling up a few whales. Thor had a bigger prize in mind. He wound the ox head to his fishing rod and plunged it into the depths, right into the hungry mouth of Jormungandr, a serpent so large it wrapped around the entire world. And so, a tug of war began between Asgard's strongest warrior and the great snake. The sea broiled and rocked, with Thor getting angrier and angrier that he couldn't reel in his prize. But with each tug, the god of thunder brought the world serpent closer to the surface and when its monstrous head finally reared, Thor was seized with battle ecstasy. Grabbing Mjolnir, he began to strike Jormungandr. Hymir, in a moment of fear and adrenaline, recovered long enough to cut the fishing line, freeing the world serpent and bringing the apocalyptic battle to an end. Other versions of the story say Jormungandr was able to break free by itself but the ending is the same: Thor and Hymir finally came to blows and Odin's son slayed the giant in rage.[14]

In the legends, Thor comes off as a brute and a bully by our modern standards. It's a far cry from the heroic, noble version that exists in Marvel comics and the Marvel Cinematic Universe. In the Norse mind, these stories of Thor were part of a wider oral tradition of how one forged a life worth living where physical strength was the greatest virtue. In keeping with the importance of family and community in Scandinavian cultures, Thor was a family man. He loved and protected his wife Sif ferociously and had complicated relationships with his daughter Thrudr and sons Modi and Magni. Thor's familial relationships are handled with nuance in *God of War: Ragnarok*, where he's portrayed as a drunken, hot-blooded brute who seeks vengeance for the death of his sons at the hands of the main character Kratos. While acting as Odin's enforcer and blunt instrument, Thor also cares deeply for his wife and daughter, doing what he feels is best for them.

The light of honour and vengeance

As the end times in Norse lore, Ragnarok is characterised by cruel winters, darkness and chaos and the dying of the light. This extinguished light was another of Odin's sons, Baldr. A god associated with beauty and brightness, Baldr was said to be the most beloved of the gods and that nothing could physically harm him. Interestingly, while the other Aesir are famed for their warmongering, Baldr is described as the gentlest and his death was mourned by everyone in Asgard. Except for a certain trickster that we'll come to shortly.

The events that led up to Baldr's end began with him having nightmares about his death. Deeply disturbed by her son's dreams, the goddess Frigg went out into the nine worlds to get an oath from every living thing and object that they would never harm Baldr. Odin too went on a journey to prevent his son's death. Travelling to Hel, Odin summoned the spirit of a seeress to make sense of the dreams. What he found was troubling.

Meanwhile, Frigg had been successful in getting the sworn oaths of all that Baldr would be unharmed. Feeling secure in this knowledge, the gods put on some games and practised throwing axes and shooting arrows at Baldr to test his invulnerability. The trickster god, Loki, didn't participate in the games. Instead, he disguised himself as an old woman and went to Frigg to ask her if there was truly nothing that could harm Baldr. Thinking nothing of it, Frigg mentioned mistletoe, a thing so young and harmless that there hadn't been any need to get its oath.

Armed with this knowledge, Loki went to a mistletoe bush and made a dart out of a branch. He returned to find the gods had moved on to throwing missiles at Baldr. All except for Hodr, the god of light's blind brother. Giving Hodr the chance to take part in the sport, Loki gave him the mistletoe dart and guided his hand to throw it. The dart pierced Baldr's skin and killed him instantly, fulfilling the prophecy Odin had gleaned from the seeress in Hel.

He and the rest of the gods were devastated – perhaps no more than Frigg, who begged her family to bring Baldr back from Hel. Another of Odin's sons, Hermodr, rode the eight-legged horse Sleipnir down to Hel to rescue Baldr's soul. In the land of the dead, Hermodr beseeched Hel, the goddess of death, to release his brother. She was willing to release him on the condition that every living and dead thing in the world would cry for Baldr. If any failed to weep, the god of light would never return to Asgard.

The Aesir sent messages out to all in the nine realms to shed a tear for Baldr and they did cry for him – every man, animal, stone and metal. Everything except for a giantess called Tokk, who coldly dismissed Baldr and said, 'Let Hel hold what she has!' This was none other than Loki in disguise and so the trickster god had the last laugh. Baldr remained in the cold of Hel, his light forever lost to the world.[15]

What can we learn about the Vikings from this story? One might be tempted to search for a softer side to the Norse in the notion that Baldr was the gentlest of the gods. But this would be a romantic lie, as we've already established the life of a Northman intent on making his way in the world was one of violence, status, power plays and complex family dynamics. Baldr's death provides insight into the Norse perspective of honour and avenging one's family. However, the gods did wreak vengeance on Hodr and Loki. The former was killed by Vali, a son sired by Odin for the sole purpose of avenging Baldr, and the latter was captured and tortured by being bound into the entrails of his children and having the venom of a snake dripped onto his head until the coming of Ragnarok.

The evil of dishonour

In religions like Christianity, there's a black-and-white perspective of good and evil. God and Jesus are figures of absolute morality and virtue, while the Devil is the personification of darkness and corruption. In the Norse worldview, this would have seemed foreign and strange. Because what they saw as good and ethical involved proving your strength and conquering weaker foes in battle. For an idea of what the Norse saw as unethical and wrong, we must look at Loki.

While seen as the god of trickery and lies, Loki may not have been a god at all. The stories claim he was a giant adopted by the Aesir and depending on his mood, he could play tricks on either the gods or the giants. Often, he was the source and solution to the problems of the gods, flitting from harmless prankster to malicious backstabber that brought on Ragnarok.

One aspect of Loki is his wit, intelligence and comedic timing. This is shown in a story called Thor's wedding. One night, while the god of thunder slept, a giant snuck into his bed and stole his hammer Mjolnir. The next morning, Thor woke up enraged and realised he needed someone with brains to help him recover his lost hammer. So, he called on Loki, who called on Freyja to lend him her magical cloak. Wearing the cloak,

Loki turned into a hawk and flew to Jotunheim, the realm of the giants, where he met Thrym, king of the *jotunn*. When Loki asked him if he'd seen the hammer, Thrym announced that he'd been the one who stole it and had buried it eight miles under the ground. The only way he would return Mjolnir was if Freyja agreed to marry him.

Returning to Asgard, Loki relayed the giant's demands to Thor, who felt like it was a reasonable request. He and Loki visited Freyja and the thunder god said, 'Freyja, you need to wear a bridal veil. Put on a pretty cap, a magnificent dress with flowers and fine gems and let your wonderous necklace Brisingamen shine. The king of the giants, Thrym, took my hammer and buried it eight miles deep. There's no other solution but to marry him. You must do this for me because the gods always help each other in their time of need. Remember to smile for it's your wedding day.'

But Freyja didn't smile. She snapped back at Thor that she refused to marry a giant and lashed him with Brisingamen and told him he should start digging for his hammer until the other gods intervened. The keen watcher Heimdall, who could see the future, told Thor that he must dress up in the bridal veil and wed Thrym. Exploding in rage, Thor refused and the rest of the Aesir laughed at his predicament. But Loki stepped in and convinced Thor it would be the best trick to get Mjolnir back. Otherwise, it was only a matter of time before the giants came to Asgard and wielded the hammer against them.

Swallowing his immense pride, Thor agreed to put on a dress and cap and Freyja helped to clothe him. She even gave him Brisingamen, as proof that it would indeed be she who showed up to be wed on the day of Thrym's choosing. Loki, disguising himself as a bridesmaid, accompanied Thor to Jotunheim. Thrym put on a huge wedding feast; it surprised him when his bride-to-be devoured a whole ox, eight salmon and downed three barrels of mead. Quick-witted as ever, Loki explained to the king of the giants that Freyja was so excited for the marriage that she hadn't eaten anything in eight days.

Believing the lie, Thrym then asked Freyja for a kiss and as he pulled up the veil, Thor's eyes blazed with fury. Stepping in once again, Loki claimed Freyja was heatedly passionate because she hadn't slept in eight days. This pleased Thrym and so he called for Mjolnir to be brought out so the wedding could be blessed. As the mighty hammer was placed in Thor's lap, he ripped off the veil and beat Thrym to death with it. Thor then went on a rampage and killed every other giant at the wedding. Finally satisfied, he returned to Asgard with Loki.[16]

Another story that showed Loki's mouth getting him into and out of trouble was the building of the great wall around Asgard. Once, when Thor was away fighting trolls, the home of the gods was undefended. Odin suggested that a wall be built, a barrier so tall that not even the biggest giant could climb over it, a fortification so dense that not even the hardiest troll could smash through it.

When the gods all agreed on this plan, a tall man showed up in Asgard. He wore the clothes of a smith and brought a big grey stallion with him. The smith said he'd heard that the Aesir needed a wall built and that he could build them a structure so tall and wide that it'd last for a thousand years.

Loki remarked, 'This wall would take a long time to build.'

But the smith was confident. 'For an average builder, it surely would. I am something of a specialist. All it would take is three seasons and as tomorrow is the first day of winter, it'd only take me a winter, summer and another winter to get the job done.'

'What do you want in return?' Odin asked.

'Not much. Only three things. First, to be wed to the beautiful Freyja.'

The All-Father snorted. 'What you ask is not so easily done and Freyja will have her own opinion on the matter. What are your other demands?'

The smith flashed an arrogant smile. 'The sun that shimmers in the sky and the moon that waxes and wanes in the night. All three things you'll give me once I build your wall.'

All looked to Freyja, whose pale face and pursed lips held a deep anger that boiled beneath the surface. Odin told the smith to wait outside. He complied but not before asking for food and water for his stallion, Svadilfari, a name that meant unlucky journey. No doubt a harbinger of discord.

Odin asked the gods for their opinions and they all squabbled. No one's opinion was louder than Freyja's, who demanded that the smith be beaten for his arrogance and thrown out of Asgard. Still, they were able to reach an agreement: that Freyja, the sun and the moon were far too important to be given away to some cocksure stranger. As Odin was deciding the best action to take, a cough echoed through the hall and all looked to Loki.

'Might I point out that you're all overlooking something very important.'

'We aren't overlooking a damn thing, trickster.' Freyja snarled.

Loki continued, 'What the smith has proposed is to build a wall in eighteen months. It's an impossible task to build it to the dimensions he claimed in the time he stated. Not even a god could do this, never mind a mortal man. I'd bet my life on it.'

Most of the gods saw the soundness of Loki's logic. Everyone except Freyja. 'All of you are idiots. And you are the biggest idiot of all Loki for thinking yourself cleverer than you are.'

The trickster persisted. 'I swear to you all that what the smith proposes is impossible and my solution is this: agree to his demands on the condition that he accept strict rules. He can't have any help building the wall and rather than three seasons he has one. If even a section of the wall isn't finished on the first day of summer, then he gets nothing.'

The Aesir were sceptical and so Loki continued to explain. 'The smith will build the wall for six months as an unpaid labourer. After those six months, we can drive him away however we like and what he's built we'll use for our own plans and add to. He's so arrogant that he'll agree to whatever challenge we put to him.'

At last, the gods were sold on Loki's plan. They brought the smith back into the hall and told him of the conditions, personally delivered by Loki. The smith thought long and hard. Then he shrugged. 'Those terms are agreeable. My one ask is that you allow me to use my stallion to haul the stones to build your wall. I don't think that's unreasonable.'

The gods agreed that it wasn't and so oaths were sworn by Aesir and smith – oaths that couldn't be broken. When morning came, the smith set to work and began to dig the trench that would hold the first stones. The Aesir noted how fast and deep the smith was digging. Loki wasn't worried. To dig a trench was one thing. To travel many miles to the mountains and carry stones, to pile them high on top of each other, was another thing entirely.

At sunset, the smith mounted his horse, which had an empty stone boat and sledge attached to it to haul rocks. He set off for the mountains and in his absence, the Aesir feasted and made merry, expecting him to be back in a week. In the middle of the night, Heimdall, the far-seeing god, told his compatriots that the smith was back. On the horse's sledge, heavy granite stones weighed the apparatus down, though the stallion dragged them along as if they were as light as air.

As the Aesir grumbled, Loki still wasn't worried. 'The horse seems strong, but it will tire soon enough. It won't be able to do that day after day and winter is coming. The path to the mountain will be treacherous. Mark my words. There is naught to fear.'

Day after day, the smith went to the mountain and returned with granite stones. The wall got higher and higher, and Odin called the gods together for another meeting. They concluded that the smith was no ordinary man. He must be a giant in disguise. Loki soothed their worries, believing that even the most powerful giant couldn't complete the task in the time that had been set. The days became longer, and the smith and his stallion Svadilfari continued to gather rocks and build the wall as the snow melted and the earth churned up with mud.

'The horse won't be able to keep on dragging stones through all that mud.' Loki insisted. 'They'll sink and it'll be stuck.'

Yet the horse never lost its footing. The smith never stopped in his mission. On the contrary, he went about his work with good humour and laughter. He hauled rocks hundreds of feet high and dropped them into place, building layer upon layer.

The last day of winter approached, and the wall seemed completed. The gods despaired that they would have to give away the sun, the moon and Freyja. The fertility goddess spoke with venom in her voice. 'Should I be given to the giant and married off to him, I ask one thing from all of you. That you kill the fool that put all of this in motion. That is a fair trade.'

Loki butted in. 'Who knows who was to blame? We all agreed to make the deal together …'

'It's your fault we're in this mess,' Freyja hissed. 'You should be the one to pay with your head.'

Loki tried to protest, but Odin shut him down. 'Freyja speaks true. Your bad counsel put us in this position, and you've continued to give poor advice ever since.'

The wisdom god stroked his beard. 'The smith must lose, but we can't break our oath. You will fix this mess, Loki. Otherwise, your death will be long and painful.'

'Fine. I'll see what I can do.' The trickster departed.

Meanwhile, the smith had almost finished the wall. All that remained were twenty more stones to layer in. He called out to Svadilfari, who always came on the first whistle. This time there was no response. The smith tried again and this time he heard hooves rumbling towards him. But as he gazed across the meadow, the smith realised that there were two horses nearby. Svadilfari was chasing after a chestnut mare, an elegant creature that seemed to always be one step ahead of the stallion. No matter how many times the smith called to his horse, Svadilfari ignored him. Soon, the smith got tired of all this and chased after them. The mare brushed up against the stallion and they ran towards the woods, out of sight.

Cursing the lust of his horse, the smith had no choice but to carry on without the animal. He went to the mountain, dragging the stone boat with him to collect the last twenty stones. By dawn, he hadn't returned. It was only when the sun was high in the sky that he came back to Asgard with ten rocks. As he was filling them in, Freyja observed the smith needed twice as many to make good on his promise. The other gods watched the progress too, calling out and heckling the smith that his horse was gone and that he wasn't going to get anything.

'You damned cheaters,' the smith bellowed, driven to the brink of exhaustion.

'We haven't cheated any more than you have.' Odin replied. 'Do you believe we'd have let you build our wall if we'd known you were a giant?'

His deceit revealed, the smith smashed the rocks and grew. He stood fifty feet tall, face twisted in anger. 'Oath breakers and liars all of you,' the mountain giant boomed. 'I was so close to building your wall and it would've happened had I still had my horse. Freyja would be mine and the sun and moon would have lit my days and nights.'

'We've broken no oaths,' Odin retorted. 'But now we will make a final one for you. This is your end.'

Roaring in defiance, the mountain giant gripped two jagged chunks of rock and rushed the Aesir. Thunder boomed and lightning rattled in the sky. Thor, having returned from the East, launched his hammer at the giant which crushed his skull. Following the giant's death, the gods finished building the wall, though it took them weeks to haul and cut the remaining ten blocks. This hard labour was made brighter by Thor's presence. The thunder god had thoroughly enjoyed slaying the giant and appreciated that his fellow Aesir had brought some entertainment for his return.

No one knew where Loki had gone. It was strange that the trickster hadn't been around to boast of his own hand in stopping the mountain giant. A year later, Loki returned to Asgard with a grey foal. But this foal was different from others: it had eight legs and it took to Loki like a son to its mother. The foal, named Sleipnir, was given to Odin as a gift. This was the tale of how Odin received the fastest, hardiest horse in all the nine realms and how the wall of Asgard came to be.

Loki's dark side

In other stories, Loki acts maliciously, such as when he cut off the golden hair of Thor's wife Sif. This could've been done for many reasons – to humiliate the thunder god and his family, so Loki could entertain himself and sow discord among the gods. Thor threatened to kill him and the demands of the Aesir compelled Loki to fix the problem by visiting the realm of the dwarves. While visiting the dwarves, Loki flattered the sons of Ivaldi into making him various wonders. The first was a wig of spun gold that Sif could wear. The second gift was Skidbladnir, a mystical ship that could be folded up into one's pocket and would forever have favourable winds to guide it to the right destination. The third gift was Gungnir, the deadliest of all spears that Odin took as his primary weapon.

Not content, Loki decided to stir up further discord by visiting the brothers Sindri and Brokkr. Showing off the three gifts from the sons of Ivaldi, the trickster taunted them. They couldn't possibly make three items equal to the power and wonder of the wig, the ship and the spear. Loki was so confident that he even bet his head and the brothers accepted the wager.

As the dwarves began to work, Loki changed into a fly and stung Sindri's hand. This messed up his rhythm and the first thing he pulled from the fire wasn't a golden wig but a living boar with golden hair called Gullinbursti. The boar glowed in the dark, ran faster than any horse and could move through water and air.

Next, Sindri set another gold slab onto the fire, while Brokkr worked the bellows. Loki, still in fly form, bit Brokkr on the neck. From the forge he pulled the ring Draupnir, which could multiply itself. Every ninth night, eight new rings dripped from Draupnir of equal size and weight.

For the final challenge, Sindri put iron into the forge and told his brother that they needed to be extremely careful. One wrong move would cost them more dearly than their previous creations. Loki knew this too and stung Brokkr on the eyelid. Blood dripped from the wound, blocking his vision. But the brothers carried on and they pulled a mighty hammer from the forge that always hit its target and could be called back to its owner. They called it Mjolnir. Yet the weapon was flawed. The handle was too short. Nevertheless, Sindri remained confident that their gifts were more than a match for the sons of Ivaldi and they left for Asgard to claim their due on Loki's head.

The god of mischief hurried back to Asgard ahead of the brothers and presented all the wonders he'd gained. To Sif, he gave the golden wig. To Thor he gave Mjolnir. To Freyr, the twin brother of Freyja, he gave Gullinbursti and Skidbladnir. To Odin, he gifted Gungnir and Draupnir. In return for the marvels, Loki was forgiven for his transgressions by the Aesir. But he wasn't out of the woods yet.

When Sindri and Brokkr came to Asgard, the gods concluded that Loki still owed the dwarves his head. After all, the quality of their gifts was undeniable. Thinking on his feet, Loki found a loophole. Technically, he'd offered the brothers his head, not his neck, which needed to be cut through, so their pact was voided. Sindri and Brokkr agreed that this was a good point, but that they would be content to sew Loki's mouth shut because he talked too much. And so that's what they did.

Later, Loki would fix his mouth and there would be no forgiveness for him after the death of Baldr. The gods trapped him in a cave and left him to rot with a snake forever pouring venom onto his head. Loki's dutiful wife Sigyn stayed by his side and used a bowl to catch the venom when it dripped down, but even she couldn't hold back the torture. During the times when the poison coated his face, Loki writhed in pain, causing earthquakes throughout the world, his bitterness and rage towards the Aesir growing until he would finally be released to lead giants and monsters against the gods at Ragnarok. In the stories, Loki is the ultimate betrayer, a coward that uses subterfuge and trickery. It's these attributes that the Vikings found to be unethical and dishonourable because they were the antithesis of a true warrior.

The nuance of gender roles

No story of the Norse gods would be complete without referencing Frejya and the role she played across all strata of Viking societies. A member of the Vanir, Frejya came to live with the Aesir as part of the pact that brought peace between the two families. Depending on the perspective, she may have been the same goddess as Frigg, Odin's wife and the mother of Baldr. Or she may have been an aspect of a multifaceted deity that represented motherhood and fertility.

What's consistent across all interpretations is that she was a complex figure that embodied the agency of women, sexuality, independence and war. To dismiss her as simply a kind of Norse version of the Greek/Roman goddess of love Aphrodite/Venus would not do the stories about her justice. For one thing, Freyja was evoked on the battlefield. Contrary to the stereotype of all Viking warriors going to Odin's Valholl, a portion of them found a place in Freyja's hall of Sessrumnir. She also taught the All-Father everything he knew about magic, pointing towards her role as a powerful sorceress with ambitions to forge her own destiny.

Her fiery spirit is displayed in stories like Thor's Wedding, where she refuses to be married to Thrym, the king of the giants. She also has a prominent role in Thor's confrontation with Hrungnir. To bide time until the god of thunder's return to Asgard, Freyja fills his cup with alcohol and has the patience to deal with the giant's drunken rants. Her sexuality is another defining trait, with the rest of the gods regularly slut-shaming her for having affairs with various people, most prominently in the poems *Hyndluljod* and *Lokasenna* in the *Poetic Edda*, one of the main collections of Norse myths.

However, as Johanna Fridriksdottir points out in *Valkyrie: The Women of the Viking World*, Freyja was often cast in a misogynistic light and is more often 'accused of having extramarital sex than actually having it' but is 'typical of the way Norse authors sketched their characters: women, no less than men, are complex figures, often admirable, sometimes flawed, but whether sympathetic or not, they are conceived of as individual subjects with considerable agency'.[17]

A typical instance of Frejya being accused of infidelity comes from the story of how she acquired her necklace Brisingamen. One day, she noticed four dwarves crafting the most beautiful necklace she'd ever seen and wanted it for herself. Freyja offered silver and gold but the dwarfs each wanted to spend a night with her in exchange for Brisingamen. So, Freyja fulfilled her part in the deal and once done, she took the necklace and went home.

Loki found out about her trysts and told Odin about it. The king of the Aesir tasked Loki with bringing the necklace to him and when the trickster tried to break into Freyja's house, he found that the door was locked. To get inside, he turned into a fly and buzzed around the house until he slipped through a tiny hole in the roof. There he found a sleeping Frejya, Brisingamen glistening around her neck. The only trouble was that the clasp was at the back of her neck. To overcome this obstacle, Loki changed into a flea and bit the goddess on the neck, forcing her to turn over. Freyja awoke with a start while the mischief-maker hid himself until she'd gone back to sleep. Now he could undo the necklace and take it to Odin.

In the morning, Frejya realised her necklace was gone and went straight to Odin, demanding that he give it back. With everything involving the All-Father, there was a catch. He'd return the necklace, providing his wife worked her *seidr* magic on two great kings in their fight for eternity until they were killed by Christianised men. These two kings, Hogni and Hedinn, fought each other across generations for 143 years until the Christian king Olaf Tryggvason stepped in to end the battle with his Christian followers.

Another interpretation of the story is that Loki decided to steal Brisingamen for himself and hid it away on a skerry. He guarded the necklace in the form of a seal and when Freyja found out, she sent Heimdall to retrieve Brisingamen. Becoming a seal himself, Heimdall clashed with Loki until he could take the necklace back to Freyja. Both versions of the story put the emphasis on Freyja's sexuality and promiscuity. It's a characterisation of Christian writers who point towards unvirtuous behaviour, whereas the pagan Norse who actually worshipped Freyja probably saw her through the lens of fertility and birth.

Gender roles in Norse society will be discussed in depth throughout the coming chapters with Freyja a gateway to understanding the varying identities women could take up depending on their circumstances. But an intriguing point to mention on gender comes from the nuanced perception of what we could term the soul in the Norse mind, which comes in four parts:

1. *Hamr*: The shell or shape i.e. the body. A container for other portions of the person, which could change in specific circumstances e.g. shapeshifting or altered moods.
2. *Hugr*: The authentic essence of a person and the closest thing that we can describe as a soul.
3. *Hamingja*: The personification of a person's luck and an integral part of their success. This could also be an independent being that chose to leave the body which is the literal interpretation of someone's luck running out.
4. *Fylgja*: A female spirit within every human regardless of gender. A kind of guardian and link to one's ancestors and family.[18]

The last part really flips the hyper-masculine Viking warrior stereotype on its head: that every man could've had a sliver of Frejya or a womanly spirit inside of them to govern their decisions. It's another reminder that the civilisations we call Vikings were far more otherworldly and unique than we'll ever be able to put into words. But the stories of the people who lived during the Viking Age and beyond are enduring landmarks that echo through the ages. With that in mind, let's venture onwards and hear the stories of the Norse fighting heroes, real and mythical, who etched their names into legend.

Chapter 1

The Dragon Slayer and The Allure of Ambition

On a windswept heath, a young man shovelled dirt. Every motion, from the rippling of his broad shoulders to his breath's ragged patter, came with a purpose – a duty that kept him digging in the cold and bleak landscape. Bit by bit, he made his pit deeper until his muscles ached and burned. The young man's name was Sigurd and today he was going to kill the great dragon Fafnir that jealously guarded a treasure trove of gold.

Climbing out of the hole, Sigurd looked down at his handiwork, pondering if it was deep enough. He considered all the events of his life that had led him to this moment. The avenging of his father King Sigmund and the slaying of his killers. The actions of his foster father Regin, who'd been at his side through all the years, only to abandon him in fear on this lonely, fire-ravaged heath. The destruction of Fafnir walled him in from every side, the blackened earth churned up by the tracks of the dragon on the way from his lair to the river below. Sigurd turned his attention to the mouth of the cave higher up the trail, watching for any signs of the beast's approach.

The sound of footsteps broke his concentration and Sigurd gripped Gram's hilt, the sword passed on from one father and remade by another. Squinting in the gloom, Sigurd saw the outline of a man and he called out, 'Regin?'

But it was not Regin. An old man, grey-bearded, wearing a broad-brimmed hat, strode towards him. Sigurd sensed there was something familiar about the noble way in which the man walked. It unearthed a childhood memory of a wise wanderer guiding him to choose Grani, the most reliable and steadfast of horses, by the river Busiltjorn.

The old man stopped at the edge of the pit, silently inspecting it. Then he acknowledged Sigurd and said, 'It is unwise to have only one pit. The dragon's envenomed blood will kill you once it's spilt. Dig more pits so the blood runs off into them and position yourself so you can strike at its heart.' The old man disappeared without another word and Sigurd considered the counsel. He realised the terrible mistake he could've made and so dug more pits and a pathway between them.

When he was done, Sigurd camouflaged each pit as best he could and sat down in his main dugout to wait for his foe's arrival. Then, in the blackness of the pit, Sigurd felt the ground shake and his heartbeat boomed like Thor's hammer. Giant claws scratched the dirt and the sweat gathered on Sigurd's brow. Grunts and heavy breathing filled the world above with poison and Sigurd gripped Gram tightly. He was the son of the Volsungs, the most legendary and courageous of all families. He would not let fear overwhelm him.

When he felt the dragon's weight atop him, he struck upward, piercing through the left shoulder, towards the heart. Sigurd buried Gram so deep that it went in up to the hilt and for a split second he feared that his blade would be trapped in the hardened scales. But then the sword came loose; Sigurd dashed through a passage, chased by the pained roar of Fafnir and the gush of toxic ichor that filled the pit.

Standing in the next pit, Sigurd saw Fafnir struggle to get his bulk out of the hole. Writhing and bellowing, the serpent glared hatefully at him and unleashed a wall of fire from his maw. Sigurd threw himself to the ground, narrowly avoiding the torrent of flames that scorched the air. He felt the heat against his back and hair, a cloying, acrid stench in his nose.

Crawling through another passage, Sigurd outflanked Fafnir and thrust his sword through the dragon's neck. Rearing back in rage and agony, tearing up rocks and debris, Fafnir threw his weight down, wanting to eviscerate and rend flesh. Again, Sigurd disappeared into his warren and the loud thud and shallow breathing of his foe signalled that Fafnir was in his death throes. Stepping out from the pits to watch the end, Sigurd locked eyes with the dragon.

'Who are you to have been so reckless and foolish as to bring weapons against me? Tell me your name. I am owed it in my death.' Fafnir growled.

'I am Sigurd. Son of Sigmund. My courage made me do it, my strong arm helped and this sharp sword got the job done.'

'You are but the instrument of another's will,' Fafnir retorted. 'I smell the stink of my brother on you. Regin caused my death and I laugh knowing he'll be the cause of yours too. He's lusted for my gold since the day it was handed to our father Hreidmar by the Aesir for the death of our brother Otr. I killed Hreidmar because I was strong enough to take the gold for myself as only the strongest should take such a prize worth having. So, go to my lair and find the gold. It will be enough for all your days, and it will kill you and everyone else who owns it.'

Mulling over the dragon's words, Sigurd answered, 'If it were in my power and if I knew that I would never die then I would leave the treasure alone. But every bold man seeking his fortune in this world wants to be in control of his wealth until his final day. Yours has come, Fafnir. Lie in the broken pieces of your life and go to Hel.'

With Fafnir's death, Sigurd wiped the blood and gore from Gram. He heard the rattle of hooves and saw Regin riding up the trail on his horse Grani. 'What a victory, my lord! You have done what no other man has been able to do. They will call your Sigurd Dragon-Slayer from this day forth and sing your name for all of time.' Then, he went quiet, gazing at the motionless hide of the dragon and muttered, 'You have murdered my brother, but I am not innocent in the deed.'

'There's blood on both our hands. You who ran away and left me to fight alone, and I who bested Fafnir with strength and will,' Sigurd replied.

Feeling his anger grow, Regin grunted, 'It was I who reforged your father's sword. Without it, you would not have stood a chance.'

'In the midst of battle, it's the strength of the arm that wields the sword and the brave heart to swing true that brings victory,' Sigurd retorted, standing his ground against the rage of the man who'd taught him all he knew. 'Your counsel has been a gift from the All-Father all these years and I ask for it again with what must be done next.'

Mastering his emotions, Regin replied, 'As I said I'm not innocent in the death of my brother and your victory was well fought. Come, my lord. What you must do is cut out Fafnir's heart, roast it and allow me to eat it. This will help me provide all the answers you seek.'

So, Sigurd followed Regin's instructions. Cutting out the dragon's heart, he put it on a spit and grilled it. As blood boiled out of the organ, Sigurd pressed his finger to the juices and tasted to see if the heart was ready. Suddenly, he heard a racket from the trees above him and he looked up to see a group of birds. It took him a few moments to realise he could understand their language.

One bird said, 'There stands Sigurd, slayer of Fafnir. He should be the one to eat the heart. It'll make him the wisest man alive.'

A second bird chittered, 'Over there is Regin. The man he trusts and the man who'll betray him.'

Another bird chimed, 'He should cut off Regin's head before his own is. Then all the gold will be his alone.'

A fourth bird agreed. 'He'd be wise to take your advice. Then once he's taken the gold, he should ride to Hindarfjall and awaken the sleeping Brynhild. From her he'll learn great wisdom.'

A fifth bird wanted his say, 'Sigurd isn't wise at all! He's planning on letting one brother live free when he's killed the other. Not wise at all.'

A sixth bird chattered back, 'Yes. Much better if Sigurd killed Regin and be the only one with the gold.'

Hearing the birds' gossip, Sigurd remembered the dying words of Fafnir and made up his mind. He wouldn't be deceived or meet with such a poor fate. He unsheathed Gram and beheaded Regin with a single cleave of his sword. Picking up the heart of Fafnir, Sigurd ate a part of it and saved the rest. Then he mounted Grani and travelled to the dragon's cave, which flowed with treasure. Among the riches was the sword Hrotti, a magnificent golden suit of armour and the Helm of Terror, which struck fear into the hearts of the bravest of men.

There was so much gold that Sigurd believed he needed at least three horses to get it all out. He gathered as much as he could and stuffed the gold into two chests. Afterwards, Sigurd tied them to Grani and rode away, carrying with him fame and fortune for the ages.[1]

The structure of a saga

The story of Sigurd the Dragon Slayer is part of the wider Volsung saga, a rich tableau of warriors, kings and queens across seven generations.

Themes of duty, greed, ambition, betrayal and transformation wind through the history of the Volsung family whose exploits have inspired countless stories, ranging from Tolkien's *Lord of The Rings* to Wagner's *Ring Cycle*. It begins with the story of Sigi, a son of Odin who was outlawed for killing another man's slave and goes all the way down to Ragnar Lodbrok and the accomplishments of his sons.

Through the lives of the Volsungs, we see the classic shaping of a Norse saga. A long-form style of storytelling, 'saga' comes from Iceland and was used to recount the histories of legendary heroes and myths. While there have been several forms of saga writing, the two most often connected to Vikings are the Icelandic family and legendary sagas.

Written in the 1200s and 1300s, the Icelandic family sagas focus on the settlement of Iceland and the motivations, hopes and desires of an individual e.g. *Egil's Saga*, which is the life of the poet Egil Skallagrimsson, his family history and accomplishments. These literary portraits mix the supernatural and the spiritual against the evolving backdrop of Iceland as a free republic. The legendary sagas include fantastical elements of heroes, gods and monsters and narratives that go back centuries before the Viking Age. Iceland isn't always the main setting – locations can jump around Europe and into the East. The Volsungs belong to the legendary saga tradition as part of the *Poetic Edda*. A collection of mythological poems written by several authors, the *Poetic Edda* is one of our chief sources on Norse legends, gods and hero stories. While many stories in the *Poetic Edda* contradict each other, due to being composed at different times, the author of the Volsung saga did a good job of stringing the material together into a united narrative. It was likely written in 1250 AD and is very much set in the Norse world of family honour, revenge and fated encounters, even though the story was written in Christian Iceland. Because of Iceland's isolation from the rest of Scandinavia and Europe, the country maintained independent practices that carried over into the literature.[2]

Bound by fate

Independence runs through the blood of all the Volsungs and Sigurd is perhaps the greatest example of everything the Norse saw in a cultural hero. The son of King Sigmund and Queen Hjordis, Sigurd grew up in the court of King Alf, who took Hjordis into his care after Sigmund fell in battle.

The blacksmith Regin raised Sigurd to have all the qualities of a high-born noble until he pointed out that Sigurd had created very little wealth of his own. It prompted Regin to tell his foster son about Fafnir and his gold and set everything in motion that would turn Sigurd into the greatest hero in the land. Sigurd is tested in battle by Fafnir and overcomes his enemy with bravery and strategy (qualities the Vikings prized). Sigurd then kills Regin before he can be betrayed and takes the gold for himself, which is said to be cursed. Even though Sigurd goes on to become a famous king and respected warrior, the curse follows him throughout the rest of his life and the prevailing message of his story is that he's bound by fate. He achieves his destiny by slaying Fafnir, winning great renown, which later leads him towards his death through a web of betrayals and trickery. Another aspect of Sigurd's story is his relationship with Odin, who interferes in his life at several points, guiding his actions. Odin appears many times throughout the Volsung saga, manipulating events so he can gather the souls of the slain in the prime of their lives. This is done to bring them into his army for the coming of Ragnarok.

Yet like Sigurd, Odin is trapped in his fate, destined to fall with the rest of the Aesir as their journeys intersect in the acquirement of knowledge. After drinking the blood of Fafnir, Sigurd can hear the speech of the birds, gaining new insight into the world. Odin sacrificed his eye to drink from the Well of Urd to gain enlightenment. Other similarities occur with Odin constantly shapeshifting to achieve his own ends, while Sigurd changes appearance when caught in a complicated love triangle between the two princesses Brynhild and Gudran, whom we'll meet in the next chapter. But though Sigurd and Odin both gain great knowledge, it's debatable as to whether they ever become truly *wise*. Despite all his schemes and machinations, Odin is undone at Ragnarok. Despite all his strength and new insight, Sigurd succumbs to the manipulation of others and both god and man meet their fates.

There is something to be said about the price of ambition in Sigurd's and Odin's stories. As the poet Robert Browning wrote, 'A man's reach should exceed his grasp/Or what's a heaven for?'[3] Ambition certainly isn't a bad thing, but it's all relative to the amount of wisdom that's applied on the path to achieving one's goals. Many Norse rulers had high ambitions that helped them forge their own legacies and the price they paid often came in blood because they were following the values of their culture. But if ambition isn't tempered, it can become a destructive force that consumes everything around it; we must all exercise our own best judgement.

Chapter 2

The Valkyrie and The Princess

A woman named Brynhild slumbered in battle sleep atop the mountain Hindarfjall. Although she couldn't move, she could dream of past glories. She dreamed of iron and steel, the clash of two kings, a battle favoured by the All-Father. She dreamed of her hand in the battle and Odin's retribution upon her.

Brynhild went on dreaming until she could finally open her eyes again and the first thing she saw was a man looming over her, a tall, good-looking man with flowing chestnut hair whose armour shimmered gold and whose sword had cut through the chainmail that had clung to her body like skin and left her naked. Brynhild had never met this man before and yet she *knew* him. She had seen him in her dreams.

'You've been sleeping long enough,' the man said, sheathing his blade.

'And who is this that is powerful enough to break my chainmail? It can only be Sigurd Sigmundsson, slayer of the dragon Fafnir,' Brynhild replied, moving her shoulders, working the stiffness from her body after years of inertia.

A look of surprise crossed the dragon slayer's face. 'I was told of your wisdom and insight as well as your beauty and that you are the daughter of a mighty king. Is this true?'

Brynhild confirmed that it was true and then told Sigurd how she'd come to be here. Telling the story was as much for herself as it was for him. 'I was once a valkyrie of Odin, a chooser of the slain. One day, there was a battle arranged between two great warrior-kings named Hjalmgunnar and Agnar. I swore an oath to Agnar and slew Hjalmgunnar in this battle. He had been chosen by the High One and for my transgressions Odin commanded that I should marry. I refused and swore a new oath: that I would marry no man except one who knew no fear. Odin took revenge and stung me with a sleep-thorn. His final words were that I would never again have victory in battle.'

Sigurd listened intently and asked her to share the wisdom that she knew. Grateful for her awakening, Brynhild poured the dragon slayer a drink and told him of many things. She told him to learn wave-runes to carve on boats that would stop them from sinking, speech-runes to prevent the hand of vengeance, life-saving runes to spare a woman in childbirth, limb-runes to heal the gravest of wounds and mind-runes to be wiser still.

She told him to avoid being seen with fools in public. They are louder than they realise and to be associated with them is to be branded a coward. Never indulge in the conversation of drunken men. Their wits are always gone, and it only leads to sorrow. Be sure to fight enemies face to face and don't wait for them to burn you in your hall. Never swear a false oath because the worst punishment comes to oathbreakers.

'Never have I met a wiser or more beautiful woman,' Sigurd said. 'I swear that I will marry you and that there will be no other who will have my heart and strong arm.'

Brynhild thought deeply about the proposal, about everything she'd seen in her dreams and had yet to see. Fate followed the young man before her, as watchful as Odin's ravens flying through the nine worlds gathering knowledge. Here she was bearing witness to her own fate, and she knew from this moment onwards that hers would be forever bound to Sigurd's. 'I would choose you over all other men,' Brynhild answered and the two swore oaths together that they would be married.

Brynhild and Sigurd went their separate ways, aware there was still much for them both to accomplish. She returned to the home of her foster-father Heimir, where in a high tower she set about weaving a magnificent golden tapestry of all of Sigurd's great deeds. Scenes of his fight with Fafnir came to life, as did the capture of the treasure and the killing of Regin. The more Brynhild sewed, the more of his life path she saw until one day she noticed a hawk sitting by her window. In her heart, she knew the hawk belonged to Sigurd and that their day to be reunited had finally come.

Soon enough, Sigurd came to her room, and they shared drink and conversation, which stoked the dragon slayer's loins. He embraced and kissed her, whispering, 'The greatest day of my life would be the day I had you.'

But Brynhild had seen the future. She knew what was coming and that their days would not be filled with the happiness they both yearned for. 'We are not fated to live together. I am a shield-maiden, sworn to fight alongside kings and prove my mettle.'

Stung by the response, Sigurd insisted, 'The pain of your words cuts deeper than the sharpest blade. But know this. We would be happiest if we lived together and shared the rest of our years.'

Brynhild shook her head sadly. 'You will marry Gudrun, the daughter of Gjuki and I will summon armies.'

Clasping her hand into his, Sigurd declared, 'I will not be tempted by any other princess or woman. You alone are in my thoughts, and I swear before the gods that you will be my wife and I will be your husband.'

Brynhild understood that she would never be able to dissuade Sigurd from his path. Their life threads, for better or worse, were forever entangled. All would happen as it was meant to happen. She agreed to Sigurd's request, and he gave her a gold ring called Andvaranaut as a promise. Their oaths renewed, even though the cost would be great.[1] Little did they know, this ring would be their undoing. For Andvaranaut was a cursed ring passed down from a dwarf called Andvari. Once, it'd made him rich beyond his wildest dreams until the day the trickster Loki stole away the ring and Andvari's treasure. In vengeance, the dwarf cursed the ring to bring misfortune and chaos to anyone who possessed it. Loki quickly passed on the ring to the dwarf king Hreidmar and Andvaranaut was thus taken by his son Fafnir and hoarded until the day Sigurd had killed the dragon and taken it for himself.

An exploration of valkyries

Brynhild is the classic example of a valkyrie and shield-maiden, two cliched tropes in Viking narratives that represent liberated warrior women. In Norse mythology, valkyries are servants of Odin that carry the souls of the dead to either his hall Valholl or Freyja's Sessrumnir. Within literature, they've run the gamut from robotic order takers to beautiful, fiery women who have affairs with mortal men. The images of valkyries as sexy, barely clothed fighters are pure fiction, the invention of Christian writers who had their own fantasies and positioned them as chivalric heroines.[2] To a certain extent, this is how Brynhild is portrayed in the Volsung saga. She's introduced as a beguiling warrior-goddess stripped of her powers who tragically falls in love with a human man. To the Norse consciousness, this image would've been nothing like the terrifying, demonic spirits that were unleashed on the battlefield to personify the brutalities of war.

An example of this comes from the famous Icelandic saga, *The Story of Burnt Njal*, which depicts several blood feuds and in one instance a man named Dorrudr watched a group of valkyries decide the flow of combat during the Battle of Clontarf in 1014. Dorrudr observed twelve women standing around a warp-weighted loom. The warp and weft were made from human entrails and the weights were kept taut with human skulls. Each valkyrie weaved their gory fabric with swords and arrowheads, chanting gleefully about the din and carnage of conflict.[3] These valkyries were bloodthirsty agents of death, not guardian angels who swept down from the heavens to carry souls gently off to their final resting place. The valkyries represented various aspects of fighting, storming and raging through a fray. We can see their violent nature reflected in their names. There is Gondul (War-Fetter), Geirahod (Spear-Battle), Teeth-Grinder, Battle-Weaver, Shield-Destroyer and many more descriptive titles for the sounds of death and war.[4]

It's worth applying the same level of scrutiny to the shield-maiden. We imagine an armoured, ferocious woman in the thick of a shield wall. Or perhaps she's brandishing an axe or sword and a superior level of skill, tactics and favour from the gods has helped her overcome a bigger, stronger opponent. Again, we should be extremely wary of such romanticism and ground our understanding in the context of Viking Age Scandinavia.

The debate as to how much of a role Norse women played in warfare is influenced by a mixture of literature, folklore and archaeological evidence. Let's start with a literary example of the kings' sagas, which looks at the lives of famous Scandinavian rulers. There is hardly any reference to women being a part of raiding parties or wielding weapons in open combat. Mostly, women are portrayed as instigators of violence, inciting their husbands and relatives to go to war. An outlier of these sagas is a character called Aud, who wounds her ex-husband with a sword in vengeance for him divorcing her through trickery.[5]

Remember that many literary interpretations of the Norse came from the Christian perspective of their victims or Christianised Scandinavians who had their own subjective view of the past. That same kind of embellishment would extend to Norse women in battle and can hardly be taken as historical fact, despite how engaging the prose may be. The twelfth-century Danish theologian Saxo Grammaticus is a good case study for engaging fiction (which he probably considered historical truth in his own time) about shield-maidens in his *History of the Danes*. He records several battle-hardened women who fight in legendary skirmishes, like Rusla, whose nickname Red Woman comes from her bloodthirsty reputation. In Saxo's work, Rusla quickly rises to power as a war leader, rebelling against a king called Omund and defeating her brother Thrond. While Saxo writes with an admiring tone about shield-maidens, he also states that they're far removed from everything that's natural and have dislocated from their true selves and gender.[6]

The idea of being 'unsexed' brings up some interesting questions as to whether women dressed as men to fight in battle and a deeper conversation about crossdressing, transgender identities and gender fluidity within Norse society.

For this discussion, we can now look at archaeological finds. In 1878, a body was uncovered in a cemetery in Birka, Sweden. The corpse, labelled Bj.581, was dressed lavishly and buried with a full weapon set and two riding horses. These are all the markers of a warrior with high status and for decades, Bj.581 was assumed to be a man. But in 2017, new genomic research identified the body as a woman, carrying XX chromosomes. This exciting discovery highlights that the possibility of Norse women taking up shield, axe or sword wasn't an *impossibility*. And through another lens, Bj.581 may have identified as transgender or non-binary within the context of how they perceived themselves; as Neil Price observes in *The Children of Ash and Elm*, 'there are other possibilities too. But the point is that they must all be recognised as possible Viking Age identities while crucially not assuming this must be the case.'[7] We can only speculate on how the people of this period chose to identify themselves down to an individual level. Rather than paint the Vikings with a generalised brush, we can recognise that every life experience was different. It recalls the Norse view of the *hamr* (body) and how the perspective of humans and gods being able to shapeshift into animals suggests the Norse could possibly see more than one body shape. Now that we've explored connections between gender and taking up arms in Norse society, we can see how a figure like Brynhild emerged and her story interweaves with another influential woman in the Volsung saga.

The yearnings of a princess

South of the Rhine, a king called Gjuki ruled. He had three sons called Gunnar, Hogni and Guttorm and a daughter called Gudrun. A fair and beautiful woman, Gudrun dreamed of things at night that both overjoyed and terrified her. She understood those feelings, but she didn't understand what the dreams meant. Gudrun longed for clarity and so one day she told one of her serving women that she'd dreamed of a majestic hawk with golden feathers.

The woman told her it was a sign of good things to come. The hawk represented a noble hero who would come and ask for her hand in marriage. Gudrun replied that she could think of no better man than this hawk and that it frustrated her that she didn't know his identity. But she knew someone who might.

Dressing in the finest jewels and clothing, Gudrun journeyed to the hall of Brynhild, who greeted her warmly. The two princesses talked of battles and warriors, valorous deeds and adventures. Swept up in the conversation, Gudrun asked, 'Who do you think is the mightiest and foremost of all kings?'

Brynhild replied, 'It is the sons of Hamund, Haki and Hagbard. Their feats are legendary.'

'That's all well and good. But why haven't you talked of my brothers? Many now consider them to be the greatest of all warriors,' Gudrun commented.

Brynhild admitted Gunnar, Hogni and Guttorm all came from a good family, but their mettle had yet to be tested. With a wistful gleam in her eyes, she spoke of Sigurd and everything he'd accomplished. The more she listened to Brynhild talk about this Sigurd, the clearer it became to Gudrun that it wasn't simple admiration. It went deeper and a complex swirl of emotions welled up inside of her.

'From the way you talk about the man, it sounds like you love him. But I came here to talk of my dreams and how they've made me miserable.'

Gudrun heard Brynhild say something, but she didn't register. She needed to unburden herself. 'I dreamed of seeing a big stag and his hair was made of gold. But I wasn't alone. There were other women with me, and we chased this beautiful creature through the forest and only I was able to catch him. I was so close that I could run my hand through his hair. But then the stag died in front of me, pierced by *your* arrow. The most awful grief filled me. It was as if you had pierced me with another arrow. But you didn't. You gave me a wolf pup and it drenched me with the blood of my brothers.'

Gudrun looked to Brynhild for any kind of insight. In the woman's eyes, she saw sadness, resignation and resolve.

Then Brynhild said, 'Here's what will happen: Though I've chosen Sigurd to be my husband, it will be you who marries him. Your mother Grimhild will poison him with cursed mead and cause a conflict that will end only in blood. You will lose Sigurd and be married once more. Then you will lose your brothers and you will kill your new husband.'

Although hearing this prophecy filled her with great sorrow, Gudrun knew Brynhild spoke the truth. And alongside this sorrow came a giddy, guilty joy that she would have the man who haunted and enriched her dreams.

Indeed, the prophecy came to pass, and Sigurd stayed in her father's kingdom for two and a half years. In this time, Gudrun and Sigurd were married. He and her kin Gunnar and Hogni swore oaths to each other, so they were brothers in bond and blood. Gudrun felt overwhelming happiness with Sigurd. They had a son together called Sigmund. One night, her husband even shared the heart of Fafnir with her to eat. Gudrun gained great knowledge, but she also became crueller and pettier. The ominous words Brynhild had spoken became a distant memory, the words of another life. But this would not be the end of their relationship. Gunnar married Brynhild and the two women became sisters.

One day, Gudrun and Brynhild bathed together in the Rhine. Brynhild waded away from her and Gudrun wondered why she was being so distant lately.

'Why would I act as if you are my equal?' Brynhild sniped. 'My father is more powerful than yours and my husband has accomplished feats far greater than yours.'

Unable to hold the anger that had been building up for some time, Gudrun snapped, 'You're a fool to mock my husband. There has been no better man in all this world, and you only show your envy for no longer having him for yourself. Sigurd is the slayer of Fafnir and the man who rode through the fire that surrounded your hall when you thought it was my brother. He was the one who lay with you and took the ring Andvaranaut. Here's the proof.' Gudrun proudly showed the gold ring on her finger and Brynhild turned ghostly pale. This was the beginning of the end.

The downfall of Sigurd, Brynhild and Gudrun

Context is key here. Brynhild had declared that she would only marry a man who had no fear and set up a challenge for Gunnar to ride through a ring of fire to claim her. Only Gunnar was actually Sigurd in disguise thanks to a magical spell taught to him by his mother-in-law Grimhild (who'd also tricked him into drinking cursed mead that made him forget his oath to Brynhild). After successfully jumping through the fire, Sigurd slept with Brynhild and conceived a daughter Aslaug. Believing Sigurd to be Gunnar, Brynhild agreed to marry Gunnar and by the time Sigurd remembered his oaths to his first love, it was already too late.

The argument between Brynhild and Gudrun sets off a chain of events that escalates in death and misfortune. Brynhild goes on the warpath, attempting to kill her husband, but is put in chains. Sigurd goes to see her and they have a bittersweet reunion where Brynhild declares that although she still loves him, she can't break her oath to Gunnar as his wife.

Either she would die or keep her oath. There was no in-between and here we witness the iron-clad bonds of honour that held up the societies of the Northmen. Stung by betrayal and grief, Brynhild convinced Gunnar to murder Sigurd, who found it difficult to act because he had sworn a blood oath to Sigurd. So, he and Hogni directed their younger brother Guttorm to kill the dragon slayer because he hadn't sworn any oaths.

Guttorm crept up on Sigurd and Gudrun while they were asleep in bed. After some hesitation, he stabbed Sigurd with his sword, but not before the man retaliated by throwing his blade at Guttorm and cut him in half. Then Sigurd died in Gudrun's arms and she screamed in agony and loss.

When she heard the scream, Brynhild laughed and then wept and for the former valkyrie it was time to put her affairs in order. She ordered all her gold and worldly possessions be brought to her and invited people to take what they wanted. She prophesied the future and asked Gudrun to build a great bonfire for her and Sigurd. When the funeral pyre was built, Sigurd and his son Sigmund, along with the remains of Guttorm, were placed on top of the pyre. Brynhild went last, burning with the man she loved. Sigurd and Brynhild's lives might have ended but their legacy lived on through their daughter Aslaug. Gudrun's life went on too, mostly for the worst, hardly for the better. After Sigurd's death, she was forced to marry the powerful King Atli (who was supposedly Atilla the Hun) and their marriage wasn't a happy one. Atli coveted the riches of Gudrun's brothers and eventually killed them, an act that caused further strain on Gudrun's psyche.

In revenge, Gudrun killed their sons by cutting off their heads and feeding them to her husband. Their skulls were used for drinking cups, their blood was mixed with wine and their hearts were cooked on a spit. Then she killed Atli with the help of her nephew and burned his hall down. With her revenge completed, Gudrun tried to end her own life by throwing herself into the ocean. Instead, the waves carried her to a place with another king called Jonakr and they were married. Gudrun raised her daughter with Sigurd, Svanhild, in Jonakr's court and had three sons: Hamdir, Sorli and Erp.

If Gudrun was hoping for any peace, it wouldn't last. Svanhild married a king named Jormunrek, who killed her because he suspected her of having an affair. Naturally, Gudrun wanted vengeance and coerced her sons into fighting Jormunrek. She cast a spell on the armour of her sons so that they couldn't be pierced by iron. As a caveat, her sons couldn't injure stone or other large objects, otherwise, they wouldn't be shielded anymore. So, Hamdir and Sorli asked Erp for help and when they interpreted that he didn't plan to do anything, they killed him. Then they rode to Jormunrek's realm and cut his hands and feet off. Surrounded by their opponent's men, they fought on, unable to be harmed by the iron of swords and arrows. Odin appeared on the scene and advised Jormunrek's men to kill the sons of Gudrun with stones. And that's what they did. The stones came flying and Hamdir and Sorli died.

Reflecting on Gudrun's journey, we see a woman marked by tragedy and experiencing various losses through the machinations of greedy, powerful men. We also see a child murderer willing to sacrifice everything to gain her vengeance and appease her tarnished honour. The Volsung saga may paint a picture of Norse women like Brynhild and Gudrun being instigators of violence, even revelling in the decisions that allow them to carve out some expression of power and catharsis, but that viewpoint is limiting. It's important to note that the sources didn't glorify the sacrifice of children for the sake of honour or that there's an implication Viking parents didn't love their children.

This can be seen in an eddic poem called *The Whetting of Gudrun*, where Gudrun breaks down in tears after sending Hamdir and Sorli off to avenge their sister. It's implied that Gudrun understands that she's changed for the worse, but that she's also accepted her fate.[8] The poem provides insight into the difficulties that many parents within a society of rigid honour codes must have faced with balancing bloodshed and love for their children. The struggles Norse women went through day to day in Viking Age Scandinavia are summed up by Carol J. Clover in her essay *The Politics of Scarcity*. She argues that there were two kinds of power that women had access to. The first was the structural power of the law and the rights that came with it, where the women were bound within specific gender expectations. The second was dyadic power, i.e. the power held within personal relationships.[9] This is where women could influence their position in society by directing their husbands, brothers and relatives to act in violent or non-violent ways. It's a trope that did exist and is very much a part of Brynhild and Gudrun's stories. In no way does it diminish them as literary characters or as examples of the strength, intelligence and resilience of Norse women in the harsh realities of their environments.

Chapter 3

The Dynasty of Shaggy Breeches and Eternal Fame

A pleasant, summer breeze blew across the sea and the waves rocked peacefully. It was good sailing weather for the fleet of ships that cruised through the water on the way to the island of Gotland. The head of the fleet, a man named Ragnar, gave thanks to the sea goddess Ran and her daughters for guiding his ships with good fortune.

A tall, strong man, Ragnar stood out for more than just his physique. He wore a shaggy cloak and shaggy pants boiled in pitch. Some of his men wondered why he dressed in such a fashion, and they nicknamed him Lodbrok. But it didn't change the way they saw him. He was the greatest warrior they had ever seen, and they would follow Ragnar into Hel if it came to it. The ships docked in a fjord at nightfall and the next morning, Ragnar woke up and put on his shaggy cloak and his shaggy pants. He picked up a large spear and left his fleet without telling anyone. Going down to a beach, Ragnar rolled around in the sand and then took the nail out of his spear that held the shaft to the point. Prepared, Ragnar journeyed to the realm of jarl Herrud, whose beautiful daughter Thora was guarded by a great dragon. Ragnar had heard that the jarl would marry Thora to anyone who could kill the serpent and it was exactly the kind of challenge he was looking for to prove his mettle.

Arriving at Thora's cabin, Ragnar surveyed the obstacle in front of him. A large, sleeping serpent coiled around the building, its scales glimmering in the dawn. Slowly approaching the beast, Ragnar moved stealthily, probing for weak spots, waiting for the right opportunity. The size of the damned thing was awe-inspiring, the head being able to touch the tail and eat itself if it so chose. When he was close enough to smell the dragon's breath, Ragnar stabbed the beast through the back and yanked the spear away. He thrust again quickly, striking even deeper in the same spot. Ragnar twisted the spear so violently that the spearhead came loose and stayed embedded into the monster's hide.

By now, the dragon had wakened and writhed about, poisonous blood leaking from the wound, splashing Ragnar's shoulders. But his clothes protected him from the venom and he stayed out of the dragon's reach until it stopped squirming, roaring and shaking the earth and finally died.

All this commotion woke Thora and she rushed outside to see a tall, shaggy-cloaked man striding away from the corpse of the serpent that had encircled her for so long. She called out to him for his name and where he was going. Turning to face her with spear shaft in hand, Ragnar told her who he was. He was fifteen years old. He'd risked his life to kill the dragon and it'd been worth the risk to see her. Then he left and Thora wondered if she was dreaming and if the young man who'd spoken to her was human or some god in disguise.

In the morning, she realised it hadn't been a dream. The dragon lay dead and the spearhead that felled it remained in its hide. Her father, jarl Herrud had the spearhead taken out and on the suggestion from his daughter arranged a meeting for any man to come forth who'd killed the dragon. For whoever slew the beast would still be carrying the spear shaft with him.

Ragnar came to the meeting with all his men and listened to the speech Herrud gave about rewarding the owner of the spearpoint. Every man who carried a spear shaft was examined and when the jarl's forces came to him, Ragnar showed his spear shaft and the point fitted.

From that day onwards, Ragnar achieved great fame throughout Scandinavia. He and Thora wed and had two sons, Eric and Agnar. Content with his family, Ragnar ruled Denmark wisely and happily for a time until the day Thora became ill. When Thora died, it devastated Ragnar and he no longer wanted to rule. So, he asked his men and sons to rule in his stead while he took to the seas once again, raiding and taking victory wherever he went.

On one such adventure to Norway, Ragnar rested his ships near a place called Spangarheid. Ragnar's servants needed to make bread and so went to the nearby farm to ask for help. At the farm, they found an old woman named Grima who identified herself as the lady of the house.

'We would like it if you could help us with our tasks,' the servants asked of her.

'My hands are stiff from age, but I have a daughter named Kraka who will help you,' Grima said.

When Kraka returned home, the servants were awestruck by her beauty. They found it odd that a woman as ugly as Grima could give birth to such an enchanting girl but carried on with the tasks at hand. They directed Kraka to make bread and her beauty was so intense that all the men forgot about making their own loaves and burned the bread. Ragnar wasn't pleased to have this terrible food served to him for breakfast and he demanded to know why the bread was so awful. His men answered that they hadn't been able to concentrate because they'd seen the most beautiful woman in the world. Scoffing at such a claim, Ragnar said there was no way that the woman could be as beautiful as his Thora. The servants insisted the woman wasn't any less beautiful and from this, Ragnar hatched a plan.

'Very well, I'll send those of you who have the best eyesight. If it's as you say, your laziness will be forgiven. But if the woman isn't as beautiful as my Thora, then you'll suffer the consequences.'

But the men couldn't be dispatched because of strong winds and so Ragnar changed tack. 'If this woman is as beautiful as you claim, tell her to visit me. But I don't want her to be naked or clothed, fed or starving. I don't want her to come alone, though she can't come with any other person.'

The men delivered their king's message to Kraka. Her mother thought the request to be impossible, yet Kraka thought otherwise. 'I will come to him. But not today. Tomorrow morning, King Ragnar will see me and his request will be fulfilled.'

Then Kraka went to her father Aki to ask for his help. 'I need your fishing net to wrap around myself, so I won't be naked. I'd like to have one of your onions to chew on. As it's only a little food, it cannot be said that I've eaten or that I'm starved. I must also have your dog follow me so that I won't be alone, but no person has come with me.'

In the morning, Kraka visited Ragnar and when he saw her for the first time, he found her both beautiful and clever for the way she'd handled his request. He took her back to his quarters and said that he wanted her to stay the night with him. The king gave her a gold-sewn shirt that had been worn by Thora. Kraka refused twice, saying that she couldn't wear the garments of a queen when she lived among peasants. She could not stay the night or come with him because he might feel differently when he returned from his next raid.

Ragnar told her his mind wouldn't be changed and they reached an agreement. He sent Kraka home and went on his raid, which proved successful. Soon, he returned and sent messengers to fetch the woman who had captivated him. Before leaving for the ship, Kraka confronted Aki and Grima. 'I've always known you killed my foster-father Heimer and there is none more deserving of vengeance. But I will not have anything cruel happen to you because you raised me all the same. Here are my parting words: every day will be worse than the last and your final days will be the worst of them all.'

That night, Ragnar asked Kraka to sleep with him in the same bed and she agreed only on the condition that they marry. Ragnar honoured her words and they were married in Denmark. After much celebrating and feasting, the king moved to have sex with his new wife. Again, Kraka hesitated. 'We must live in the hall for three nights and make a sacrifice to the gods. Otherwise, a curse will be placed on our son and he will have no bones.'

Ragnar sniped, 'Neither of us possesses second sight. All I see is the woman whose beauty cannot be put into words. The woman I married.' And so the king had his way that night.[1]

A Danish legend

Ragnar Lodbrok is one of the most famous names in all Viking lore and his adventures are connected to the Volsung saga through his marriage to Kraka aka Aslaug aka the daughter of Sigurd and Brynhild. While written by a different author, the saga of Ragnar Lodbrok and his sons features similarly epic deeds and legendary fighters as the Volsung mythos. It's not hard to imagine why the person who spliced these two sagas together could believe they connected one family together.

The lore surrounding Ragnar blurs fact and fiction. One interpretation is that he was a composite figure of several different people, early explorers who raided in places like England and who may have been present at the Lindisfarne raid in 793 AD. Another interpretation was that he was a real-life figure, with sources like Saxo Grammaticus attempting to give him a factual existence. From Saxo's perspective, Ragnar was born in Zealand, an island off Denmark, to King Siward. His father's throne was eventually usurped by a traitor called Ring. Other sources reverse the roles and have Siward as the traitor and Ring as Ragnar's father.[2]

A consistent message emerges of Ragnar's personality across the sagas. Even at a young age, he was known for his courage, craftiness, fighting prowess and flamboyancy. We see this in his nickname of Lodbrok (shaggy breeches) that refers to the clothes he wore when fighting the dragon that guarded his first wife Thora. Picture leather chaps that have been coated in a substance that's not quite liquid or solid, hardens in cold weather and is similar to asphalt or tar. This unique shielding protected Ragnar against the venom of the dragon, indicating a mind for strategy and tactics that challenges the stereotype of Vikings as unrefined brutes.

This also raises some interesting questions about Norse clothing and fashion choices. The Muslim traveller Ahmad ibn Fadlan gave a detailed account of the Scandinavians he saw in the East. 'I have never seen more perfect physical specimens, tall as date palms, blond and ruddy; they wear neither tunics nor caftans, but the men wear a garment which covers one side of the body and leaves the hand free.'[3] This garment Fadlan refers to was probably a cloak and Scandinavian men who had a decent amount of wealth may have worn an undertunic made of wool or linen. A long-sleeved shirt with a wide neck opening would've been worn over the top. Their bodies were adorned with various jewellery, including arm rings, finger rings and heavy neck chains of gold or silver. Based on grave finds, men likely wore tight trousers fastened with belts and extra bindings for insulation. In Ragnar's case, his trousers may have been made using a weaving technique called *roggvar*, which produced a tufted, furry effect on the leggings – perhaps a bold fashion choice for the time which required a flair for the dramatic and ample charisma to pull off.[4]

Another aesthetic choice a man of Ragnar's status may have engaged in is teeth filing. Remarkable discoveries have been made of Viking males having grooves cut into the front teeth with either multiple lines or single lines on a tooth. The grooves could have been filled in with resin that appeared red. Why Viking men did this is open to speculation. Maybe it was an intimidation tactic during raids where teeth were borne into a bloody grin. Maybe it signified a certain set of accomplishments or a rank.[5]

While Ragnar's appearance would certainly have contributed to his legend, his deeds are the most crucial factor for understanding the kind of person he was, along with the traits that epitomised the Viking ethos. One such legendary feat is the raid of Paris in 845 AD, where Ragnar is meant to have played a decisive role. As the story goes, Ragnar served as a vassal to Horik, a king of Norway. Discontent to wait around and seize glory, Ragnar led 120 ships into Francia and took advantage of the poor leadership of King Charles the Bald, the grandson of Charlemagne. The king had split his forces across both banks of the River Seine so he could defend the nearby abbey of Saint-Denis.

Ragnar concentrated his attack on one of the banks, taking 111 Frankish prisoners and then hanging them in sacrifice to Odin. The onslaught carried on into Paris, with the raiders capturing the city. To get Ragnar and his men to leave, Charles bribed them with a big cash playout called a *danegeld* (Dane yield or tribute).[6] Ragnar's victory set a standard for many more *danegelds* to come in the next two centuries from kingdoms that fell to the Northmen with their versatile dragon boats, strategic fighting tactics and ruthless drive.

Glory runs in the family

The story of Ragnar Lodbrok can't be fully appreciated without the feats of his family. His second wife Aslaug is an important figure and was just as cunning and courageous as her husband. The daughter of Sigurd and Brynhild went through a few transformations in her life. First, she was known as Kraka (Crow) and forced into obscurity by the slayers of her foster father. Even when she married Ragnar, she still didn't reveal her heritage until Ragnar potentially thought of marrying the Swedish princess Ingibjorg. Aslaug admitted her true parentage and Ragnar broke off his engagement, which angered the father of Ingibjorg, King Eystein, and led to a feud that would be taken up by the sons of Ragnar.

The dynamic between Ragnar, Aslaug and Ingibjorg is revealing of the importance of status and wealth within Norse society. Before Aslaug showed her true self, she was only a farmer's daughter chosen by a king. Ingibjorg was superior to her in rank and status as the daughter of a king. But even that paled in comparison to being the child of two of the most famous Norse heroes and Aslaug wasn't afraid to follow in the footsteps of her parents onto the battlefield.

After her stepsons Eric and Agnar were killed in a skirmish against King Eystein, Aslaug emboldened her sons to take revenge on Eystein and accompanied them into the fight. To mark her leadership, she changed her name to Randalin (warrior-shield) and fought beside her sons to defend the family honour in Ragnar's absence.

Speaking of the sons of Ragnar, they are another vital part of his legacy. There was Ivar the Boneless, Bjorn Ironside, Sigurd Snake-In-The-Eye, Halfdan, Ubba and Hvitserk, men who all went on to become legendary folk heroes in their own right and eclipse their father. And how did Ragnar react to the glory and fame that his children won? Of course, he had to try and outdo them all.

Ragnar's last stand

Ragnar had a plan. A plan so ambitious it would trump the feats of his sons and be the greatest offering he'd ever made to Odin. He ordered every man in his kingdom to prepare for war and news travelled across many kingdoms and lands. Every lord and ruler who heard the news warned their soldiers to keep watch for any sign of attack.

One night, Ragnar sat before the fire in his hall, watching the flames flicker and splutter like the infernos of Muspelheim. If he stared long enough, Ragnar could swear he saw the fires twist into visions of the battles to come in both life and in Valholl when he finally took his place within the hall of the High One. Randalin came into the room and sat beside him.

'Where do you intend to travel, husband?'

With his gaze still on the flames, Ragnar answered, 'To England with no more than two large new ships and as many men as they can carry.'

'This seems like an unwise journey,' Randalin replied. 'It would be wiser to take smaller ships and a lot more of them.'

Finally looking her in the eye, Ragnar hummed, 'There is nothing special about men conquering lands with many ships. But it's unheard of for a place such as England to be conquered by only two ships. Yet if I'm defeated it will be just as well that I didn't take all our ships away from our land and leave it undefended.'

Randalin continued to insist that it was a fool's errand to take so few ships and that it wouldn't take much more to build more longships. Also, it was difficult to get to England and if any of the vessels were lost then so were the men. If a great army descended on the raiding parties, then they would be outnumbered by overwhelming force.

Ragnar wouldn't be deterred. He spoke with a clear mind and a clear heart, 'If a man wants his men's loyalty, he shouldn't spare his gold. It's better to have a great following than great wealth. Only a fool stands in the middle of a battle with golden rings – I've known plenty of rich men to die while their treasure outlasted them.'

And so the King of Denmark prepared his two ships and before he left, Randalin went to the harbour to bid her husband farewell. She gave him a long shirt, blessed by the gods, a shirt that would protect him against the bite of swords and the piercing of arrows. Ragnar accepted the gift and they parted ways.

Choppy waters and harsh winds dogged Ragnar on the voyage. As he drew close to England, the weather wrecked his ships and all his men were driven ashore in full armour and weapons. With every farm, church, castle and settlement Ragnar came across, he emerged victorious.

Soon, a king named Aella caught wind of Ragnar's path of destruction. He put together a great army and the two forces met on the battlefield. Aella's fighters outnumbered Ragnar's raiders and the latter lost many of his troops. But wherever Ragnar went, he cut through Aella's army, wearing the shirt Randalin gave him. In his hand, he wielded the spear that had killed the dragon so many years ago and turned him into a living legend. Ragnar fought recklessly, bravely, relentlessly, stabbing and cutting a bloody swathe through the men who dared to face him. In the end, Ragnar stood alone, hemmed in by shields on all sides and was captured.

The Dynasty of Shaggy Breeches and Eternal Fame

King Aella demanded Ragnar speak his name so he could know who this final defiant invader was. But Ragnar remained silent.

'As this man won't tell me his name it means he must have been through tougher trials than this. Throw him into a pit of snakes and then we'll see how loose his tongue becomes,' Aella ordered.

So, Ragnar was thrown into a pit teeming with serpents of different sizes where he sat without being bitten. Murmurings, both fearful and astonished, rippled around the pit. Here was a great warrior, a man who might not even be human, who defied even snakes.

Aella silenced the whispers by demanding Ragnar's shirt be removed and then the serpents sunk their fangs into him. And Ragnar finally spoke, letting his voice carry despite the pain of the bites and the poison infesting his veins. He declared himself the killer of many men, the fighter of glorious battles and reflected on death coming when a man is least prepared for it. His final words echoed, 'How the piglets would squeal if they knew what the old boar was going through.' With that, Ragnar breathed his final breath.[7]

Ragnar's death in a snake pit provides a full-circle moment that goes back to the slaying of the dragon that guarded his first wife and which has been retold many times throughout history. Another modern depiction is in the *Vikings* TV series that was originally created for the History Channel. The Ragnar of this historical drama is every bit as complicated and hard to pin down as he is in the sagas. A young upstart who rose to the highest pinnacle of Norse society. An adventurer who desired to carve out a new piece of the world for his people. A father and husband torn by honour, ambition and a yearning to be remembered. A defiant warrior who struggled against and accepted his fate. A man who died knowing who he was.

Just like the dragon he killed in his youth, just like Jormungandr the world serpent, Ragnar circled his own world and ate his tail many times. It's a universal truth that we all must come face to face with. We're born, we decide what to do with our lives and go through a series of cycles that inevitably bring us back to where we begin and end. On your journey, only you can choose what to make of it.

Chapter 4

The Boneless Warlord and The Blood of Kings

The din of battle raged, shields shattering, swords singing, axes whistling, men panting, growling, yelling, spluttering, a cow mooing, which was the most terrible sound of all, for it came from the war cow Sibilja. Her bellows caused the very air to shake, breaking through the shields of even the hardiest of fighters. Every man who heard the bellowing went insane, attacking their brothers in a blood-soaked frenzy. From far behind the battle lines, the Swedish King Eystein watched with a smile on his face as his cow devasted his hated enemy, the Ragnarssons.

On the other side of the battle-scarred landscape, Ivar the Boneless, son of Ragnar, also watched the cow and its path of destruction. He'd already told his men to cause a huge ruckus with their weapons and shouting to drown out the cow's dreaded noise. To the warriors who carried him, he said, 'Make me a long bow and get me close to the cow. I'll tell you when to throw me onto her.' While his bow and arrows were being prepared, Ivar pushed his warriors forward, demanding that they bellow and scream so the All-Father would hear them in his hall, that they were louder than the valkyries screeching through the fray to take the dead, that they were more terrifying than any beast of the nine realms. With his long bow and arrows in hand, Ivar was carried in front, towards the cursed bovine and the ear-splitting bellow that caused fresh insanity to spring among his forces and defile their *hugr*.

The men carrying Ivar saw him pull back on his great bow and nock two arrows before the bowstring snapped louder than they had ever heard a bowstring snap before. The arrows flew straight and pierced the cow in both eyes. Sibilja tumbled headfirst to the ground. Picking herself up, the cow charged towards Ivar and when she was close enough, he ordered his men to throw him onto her back. Landing shakily onto the cow, Ivar struggled with the beast, determined to hang on. Eventually, Sibilja fell dead and Ivar called his men to pick him up again. His voice carried across the battlefield and the warriors who'd been fighting each other wakened from the curse that had been placed upon them. Rallying to Ivar's cry, the warriors of the Ragnarssons overwhelmed the Swedes. Ivar's brothers, Bjorn and Hvitserk, fought harder than anyone and none could stand in their way.

The battle ended with the death of King Eystein and but a handful of his men left. The sons of Ragnar spared those who were alive and seeing that there were no longer any rulers to conquer in this land, Ivar said, 'We should go somewhere where we'll find more of a challenge.'[1]

A leader among leaders

Killing a mystical cow is only one of many accomplishments in a parade of legendary feats by Ivar the Boneless. While this fanciful story is told in the saga of Ragnar Lodbrok, there is historical evidence to suggest that Ivar was a real person and his raiding career took him across the British Isles, where he made a name for himself.

There's been much debate about where Ivar's nickname came from as the sagas and stories have described him as having no bones or only having cartilage where the bones should have been. A popular perspective is Ivar may have been born with osteogenesis imperfecta, or brittle bone disease. Perhaps Ivar experienced muscle weakness in his legs and uncontrollable fractures that made it difficult to walk. This is suggested in the fight against King Eystein, with Ivar's men helping him move and carrying him around on their shields. Some scholars have rejected this view on the grounds that the Norse would never follow someone into battle who couldn't even move under their own power. But it isn't impossible to think that someone physically disabled in Norse society wouldn't receive care and respect depending on their status and family. As we've already discussed, the *hamr* or shape of a person was not nearly as important as the *hugr* or spirit in the Norse mind. Deeds and actions carried weight. The interesting thing about Ivar in the sagas is that there isn't a lot of emphasis on his condition. Instead, his tall height, cunning and battle prowess are front and centre, suggesting that either a physical impairment wasn't obvious, or he'd proven his worth so many times with his victories that he'd transcended any kind of categorisation.

There's also the opposite take that Ivar was so flexible and fast that to his opponents it might have seemed like he had no bones at all. If so, he could've been born with the rare Ehlers-Danlos syndrome, which causes extreme elasticity in the joints and bones. Whatever the case of his physical attributes, Ivar gained a reputation for his brutality and strategic mind with his battles in Ireland and England. While we don't know the exact course of his life, his birth is generally stated to be 794 AD. He's also referred to as Ingvar and Imar in English and Irish sources. Through the Irish lens and his identity as Imar, Ivar is meant to have been the founder of Dublin and a dynasty that ruled the Irish Sea and York into the tenth century. However, this birthdate doesn't line up with the historical record as the man known as Imar was first mentioned in the 850s.[2] As with historical sources, there are always contradictions, but the fragments of Ivar's life put together a clearer picture of who he was.

Earlier in his life, it was said that he raided in Ireland with another future king of Ireland, Olaf the White, and when Ivar heard about the death of his father Ragnar at the hands of King Aella, he and his brothers plotted revenge. What follows is the retelling of this grand plan according to the Ragnar Lodbrok saga.

Ivar the Patience

Ivar returned to Denmark after many successful raids. There he found his brothers, who had their own stories of conquest to tell. The Ragnarssons put on a feast to regale each other and their followers of all they had seen and done in their voyages. During the feast, messengers of King Aella arrived to inform the Ragnarrsons of their father's death.

Sigurd Snake-In-The-Eye and Hvitserk had been playing a board game and stopped to listen intently. Bjorn Ironside stopped shaving the point of his spear, leaning on his weapon. Ivar asked the messengers to explain every detail of their father's end and when they revealed the final words of Ragnar – 'how the piglets would squeal' – the silence in the hall became oppressive. Bjorn gripped his spear so tightly his knuckles turned white and he snapped the shaft in two. Hvitserk, with a game piece he'd captured in hand, squeezed so hard that blood oozed from his fingernails. While he'd been listening to the story, Sigurd Snake-In-The-Eye had been trimming his nails with a knife. So intense was his focus that he was cutting himself to the bone and felt nothing.

Ivar's face changed colour, from purple to red as he continued to ask for the details of the battle between Ragnar and King Aella. Hvitserk interrupted, declaring vengeance should be swift and terrible upon Aella and should begin with the killing of the messengers.

'That's not going to happen,' Ivar spoke calmly. 'These men will leave here unharmed and return to their king.'

After the messengers had left, the sons of Ragnar held a meeting as to how they would claim vengeance. Calm as ever, Ivar said, 'I won't have any part in this foolish fight. What happened to Ragnar was his own doing and is often the fate of prideful men. He was unprepared and had no business fighting King Aella. I will accept money as compensation for Ragnar's death if the king would grant it.'

His brothers flew into a rage when they heard such cowardice. They refused to let their father's name be disgraced and by extension themselves – even if Ivar so chose. They would gather a large army from across Denmark and meet Aella with every man who could raise a weapon. Still, Ivar refused to change his mind, contributing no men or ships to the cause. When it became known Ivar would spare no aid to the expedition, the Ragnarssons' forces were smaller than they had anticipated, but they set sail for England all the same. After the Norse armies arrived in his kingdom, Aella fought and beat back the sons of Ragnar, without Ivar present.

While Aella was busy pushing his brothers back, Ivar decided that he would stay in England and see whether the king would meet him face to face and accept his terms of payment. He bid his siblings farewell and told them to send him money when he requested it later. Ivar met Aella at his court and spoke respectfully. 'I've come to arrange a settlement on behalf of my brothers for the death of our father. I'll accept whatever honours you're prepared to give as this is preferable to the loss of more of our men.'

Aella told the one they called Boneless that the word of a Ragnarsson was difficult to trust.

'I will ask of you very little and swear to never stand against you,' Ivar stated.

When the king asked him what he wanted, Ivar asked to be given only as much of Aella's land that a steer-hide would cover. Outside of it, he would also be permitted to create the foundations of a building.

The king found this payment acceptable, and Ivar swore an oath that he'd never shoot an arrow at Aella or give advice in any way that would lead to harming him. In exchange, Ivar would receive a plot of English land that was as big as the biggest steer-hide he could find to cover it. Crafty Ivar fetched hide from an old bull and ordered for it to be stretched and softened three times. He had it cut into thin strips and had the hair-side split from the rest. What remained was a string much longer than anyone had anticipated, which Ivar placed across a vast plain big enough to build a city on. Outside of the land, he marked the foundations of a fortress to be built and he set about creating his vision.

After Ivar had built his city, he spread the rest of his money around the country, giving advice, gold and wisdom gladly. He became a friend to many, settled every dispute that came to him and kept his word to Aella. Once Ivar had established himself as a wise friend, he sent messages to his brothers to send him a large sum of gold and silver. The other sons of Ragnar didn't know what Ivar's plan was, but they trusted him and sent him everything requested.

Ivar gave this wealth to the greatest lords in England, taking support away from Aella. Fat with riches, every lord swore they would not intervene and would keep the peace even if Ivar moved an army through their territories. With the first phase of his plan complete, Ivar contacted his brothers again and told them to raise an army from across Gotland, Denmark and all the other lands where their names held power. The ranks of this Great Army swelled and the sons of Ragnar came back to England with a renewed sense of purpose.

When Aella heard of this news, he desperately tried to gather a counterforce. But he was unable to find many fighters because Ivar had removed his support. Stepping in to help the king, Ivar swore his oath again. 'I will keep the promise I've made to you. But I can't control what my brothers do. I'll go to them to see whether I can stop their army from marching here.'

So, Ivar went to his brothers and egged them on to cause as much chaos as possible. Then he returned to Aella and shook his head. 'My kin are too wild to be reasoned with. They rejected my offer for peace on your behalf. Still, I'll hold true to my oath and not fight against you with my men. But the quarrel between you and them will happen.'

When the two armies clashed, the sons of Ragnar cut through the opposition, fighting with everything they had until Aella's soldiers were in retreat and the king was captured. Satisfied with his plan coming to fruition, Ivar joined his brothers at their camp. He scrutinised the wounded and defeated king, the man he'd manoeuvred into meeting his end. 'Remember how he had our father killed,' Ivar told his siblings. 'Aella should be given the same kind of treatment. Have a man cut an eagle into his back and make it red.'

A man was chosen to carry out the task and Aella was horribly mutilated before he left the world. Now that the death of Ragnar had been avenged, the Ragnarssons felt they could return home. Ivar gave spoils to his brothers and claimed England as his own.[3]

Personality traits

There are plenty of revealing details of Ivar's personality in this tale. The first thing is his guile, as he plays a long game with King Aella to bring about his downfall and emphatically avenge his father. He wisely makes alliances with other lords and goes about his plan through a combination of patience, gift-giving, ruthlessness and extreme violence. The ultimate symbol of his violence is the so-called blood eagle that's inflicted upon Aella after he's captured. This grisly death supposedly involved severing the victim's ribs from the spine, pulling bones and skin out and removing the lungs to form 'wings.' Whether the blood eagle was a real-life execution method or a literary trope to play up the barbarity of the Norse is an ongoing debate. A possible depiction of the ritual killing is thought to be a part of the Stora Hammars image stones found in Gotland. In the image, there is a person who is seemingly about to have their back carved open with a bird of prey symbol.

To investigate the practicalities of the rite, a research project was conducted that involved using anatomical modelling software to see how a blood eagle would have been carried out. These constructs were paired with historical and archaeological data and there was a suggestion that the Norse may have used spears and shallow hooks to peel the ribs from the spine. The findings indicated that the victim would have died quickly from suffocation or blood loss, long before the full blood eagle was completed.[4]

The alternative view is that the blood eagle was a literary invention and some insight into this perspective comes from the fact that the rite becomes increasingly graphic across different texts. Historian Roberta Frank points out that authors like Saxo Grammaticus saw the rite as only carving the image of a bird of prey into the back. But other stories deliberately ramped up the horror, positioning blood eagling as an elaborate ritual to Odin and adding other gory details to show the savagery of the Norse in all their pagan heathenry against Christian morals.[5] We may never know the truth of this kind of death, but Ivar's name repeatedly comes up as one of the main arbiters of the blood eagle punishment. An undisputed fact is that the grand army he and his brothers brought to England *was* real, though the Ragnarssons' level of involvement is up in the air.

The Great Heathen Army as it was called landed in England in 865 AD and swept through the kingdoms of Northumbria, Mercia and East Anglia, occupying all three and establishing a presence in places like Jorvik (York), before moving against King Ethelred and Prince Alfred of Wessex. According to the sagas, Ivar split from the army with his own troops while his brothers, either Halfdan or Ubba, and another king named Guthrum waged war on Wessex. Ivar reunited with his old friend Olaf the White and attacked Dumbarton in the Scottish kingdom of Strathclyde, taking many slaves and loot. From there, he returned to Ireland and eventually settled down and established the city of Dublin. While it isn't known how he died, his death is generally placed at 871–873 AD and depending on the story he was either buried in Dublin or England.

Ivar the Boneless is undoubtedly one of the fiercest and most violent figures of the Viking Age and any physical disability didn't prevent him from rising to the top of the pile. As warlike as he was, he balanced his violent tendencies with a keen mind that helped his people settle and shape the future of lands beyond their own. In a modern context, there's something to be said about what we're all capable of regardless of physical impairments, for better or worse.

Chapter 5

The First Christian King of Scandinavia

A longship cruises across the North Sea, heading to the newly formed nation of England. But the warriors aboard the ship aren't coming to raid or fight as many of their kinsmen have done before them. They have crossed the sea on a diplomatic mission, a mission that could well decide the future of Norway.

Aboard the ship, a boy peers over the deck, towards the dark and rocky shores of a land that he's only ever heard of in stories brought back from across the sea. His name is Hakon and he's the son of Harald Fairhair, King of Norway. A boy bound by his father's will and a destination that he's uncertain of. All he can be certain of is the name told to him by his father and bandied about by the men he's travelling with – King Athelstan, a name that stirs mixed feelings whenever it's spoken. A harbinger of The White Christ and strange customs that were so different from the wisdom of Odin and the strength of Thor.

Days later, Hakon arrives at the court of King Athelstan and the boy is left in his care. Becoming his foster son, Hakon learns at the King of England's side, seeing how he rules, how he embraces his faith. He learns about his foster father's family, how his grandsire Alfred fought harder than anyone for his kingdom of Wessex, for the spirit of Christianity that permeates the land. Hakon learns all the values that are expected of a good Christian, values he takes to heart and commits to under Athelstan's guidance.

But even after all his years in England, he doesn't forget where he comes from, or the words of the gods that reveal themselves in ways he cannot express publicly but holds within himself. As he gets older, he hears rumours that come out of his homeland about the fate of his father and brothers. One name above all continues to be spoken and Hakon recalls the experience he had on the ship about how names take on a life of their own, regardless of the truth of things. The name is Eric Bloodaxe, his older brother, a man of pure savagery, a man who slaughters all in his path and rules Norway with an iron fist. Although young, Hakon knows what he must do. The virtues he's been taught in England all these years light the way to clarity and he prepares to return home.

King Athelstan sees his foster son's cause as righteous and gifts him ships, men and all the resources he needs to complete his holy mission. Arriving in Trondheim, Hakon meets with jarl Sigurd of Hlader, the most honourable jarl in Norway. After forging an alliance, Sigurd arranges a *thing* and many chieftains come to the assembly to see if the rumours of a son of Finehair returning are true.

With all eyes upon him, Hakon addresses the chieftains and the state of their country. He speaks of the bonds that have been placed on the jarls by his brother and promises to restore ownership of their lands, to return the rights of Norway to its people.

Hakon speaks passionately and eloquently, a rallying cry that rumbles through the hall and spreads through every man who hears it. The chieftains hail Hakon as their king, a 15-year-old who walks between the worlds of the gods and The White Christ. News spreads like wildfire and Hakon brings his message to more and more ears. In him, the people don't see another Finehair or Bloodaxe, grasping, ambitious men who live only for their own glory – they see a king willing to serve for the good of all.

At every *thing* he speaks at, Hakon wins support until eventually even Eric's sons, Trygve and Gudrod, come to him to voice concerns about their father. Hakon gives his nephews land and titles, but has men rule in their stead until they come of age. Hakon gains so much support that his army far outmatches his brother's and Eric flees to England, where he eventually rules as the King of Northumbria. In the end, Eric dies fighting in the Battle of Stainmore.

With Eric gone, Hakon becomes the uncontested king of Norway and resolves to make good on his promises, keeping peace between the jarls. Since coming home, he's been unable to deny the ways of his ancestors, the blood of the Norse coursing through him. He takes to the sea with his men, raiding and plundering across Denmark and Gotland, living as his father and brothers had. But he cannot deny the call of his childhood, of the Christian teachings instilled within him.

Wishing to spread Christianity throughout his country, the king attends a festival held by his friend jarl Sigurd. Here he delivers another grand speech. 'I come before you to declare that jarl or thrall, man or woman, young or old, poor or rich to accept Christianity into your lives. To be baptised in Christ, to believe in the one true God. To no longer sacrifice to the old ways, to fast on the seventh day and keep it holy.'

The leaders in attendance shout in uproar, accusing the king of trying to take away the very essence of who they are. They refuse to accept a faith so unlike their own, to surrender freedom. Murmurs spread through the assembly of Hakon being no better than his father and brother before him, binding them to his will.

Ever a shrewd man, jarl Sigurd addresses the crowd and says the king will make a sacrifice to the gods to bring a good year of harvest. Then he takes Hakon aside and counsels him to accept the will of the people. Agreeing with his friend, Hakon takes part in a sacrificial celebration to Odin, though he chooses to make a sign of the cross over his drinking horn.

'Why does the king do this?' One man grumbles.

Sigurd replies, 'Our king does as we all do. Putting our trust in strength and power. He's making the sign of the hammer over the drink in Thor's name.'

On the next day of the celebration, the attendees press Hakon to eat horse flesh, which he refuses. They press him to drink soup and he refuses. They press him to taste the gravy and he refuses. Sensing a brawl about to break out, Sigurd steps in again and directs the king to hold his mouth over the kettle to where the fat smoke of the horse meat has settled. Hakon wraps the handle in a cloth, does as suggested and returns to his high seat. Yet tension remains in the air.

In time, Hakon comes to accept that keeping the people's favour rests on giving them the freedom to worship as they wish. He continues to practise Christianity in private, invites bishops and monks from England to establish churches in Norway. Some accept the religion, while others keep to the ways of the gods. But whatever bright future Hakon has for

Norway, it cannot escape the darkness of the past and the vengeance of old foes.

The sons of Eric Bloodaxe, restless and eager to prove their mettle, strike against their uncle several times through the years. The first is at the Battle of Avaldsnes, where Hakon pits his forces against the warriors of Guthorm Ericsson. Hakon slays Guthorm and emerges victorious. The next attack, led by Gamle Ericsson, requires strategy over brute force.

Realising that Gamle's ships outnumber him twenty to nine, Hakon sends a message to dictate the place of battle. He chooses Rastarkalv on the island of Frei and asks the Ericssons to come by land. Then Hakon has his men place ten standards across a low ridge spaced apart. When Gamle sees the standards flowing over the ridge, he believes there is an army on two sides and he directs his soldiers to flee. Capitalising on his ruse, Hakon gives chase with his forces, cutting down every man in his vicinity until the enemy is pushed back into the sea and Gamle drowns.

In the twenty-sixth year of his reign, Hakon is ambushed by the last of the surviving sons of Bloodaxe. Led by Harald Ericsson, the army surprises the king at his home in Fitjar, though Hakon is quick to respond. Selecting the bravest of men to join him, Hakon charges out to meet the threat and fights as hard as any man who serves him. He fights on and on, his infantry pushing back the Ericssons once again.

Out of nowhere, an arrow pierces him below the shoulder, one of many flying in the melee of spears, swords and projectiles that turn the snowdrift red. Hakon pushes on until his rivals are overwhelmed and escape. With the day won, the king can finally take a moment to breathe. Returning to his ship and having his wound bandaged, he feels light-headed as blood continues to seep from his wound. He witnesses the thread of his life unravelling before him. With his strength failing him, Hakon directs his men to take him north to his home. He doesn't get very far and his men set him down at Hakonarhella Hill. With what strength remains in his body, the king finds resolve in his faith. He calls his friends to hear his final requests. His lands should go to the last of his brother's sons, who have fought well even in all these years of opposition. And then with his last words he says, 'Should fate extend my life, I will leave Norway and go to the Christian land and do penance for all the sins I've made against God. Should I die in my homeland, give me the burial you see fit.'

King Hakon dies soon after and his friends take his body to North Hordaland, where he is buried as a true Norse, in full armour and his best clothes. The people wish him to speed to Valholl and from that day forward he will always be remembered by the way he acted in life. Hakon the Good.[1]

Christianity in the Viking world

The story of the tenth-century king of Norway, Hakon the Good, is one of countless instances of different faiths crossing over and clashing with each other in the Viking age. Christianity had a slow infiltration into Scandinavia, dating back to roughly the eighth century, when a missionary known as Willibrord of Northumbria came to Denmark, but was unable to find much success. He did manage to take some local boys back with him to learn more about Christianity. A more successful attempt came a century later when Ansgar, the first archbishop of Hamburg-Bremen, converted the first Christianised Danish king, Harald Klak. In context, Klak didn't convert because he believed in the religion. An exile, Klak had been taken in by the Frankish ruler Louis the Pious as the Dane was looking for political support. Klak agreed to be baptised in exchange for Louis' support and returned to Denmark to seize the throne. Ansgar came with him on this journey and baptised many across the North.

The theme of Viking rulers converting to Christianity as a political strategy crops up several times throughout history. Following Harald Klak, other rulers like Harald Bluetooth agreed to be converted to consolidate his power and bring on forced change within his kingdom of Denmark. There's also the story of Guthrum, one of the leaders of the Great Summer Army, agreeing to be baptised to negotiate peace between his forces and Alfred the Great in England. This suggests Norse rulers saw plenty of advantages in paying lip service to Christianity, like being able to collect tax more efficiently through the establishment of dioceses and parishes.[2]

Hakon seems to have been an exception to this political manoeuvring, at least in terms of his faith. Being raised in the court of King Athelstan from a young age would've impacted his perspective of Christianity and made it much easier to internalise its teachings compared to an adult Norseman who'd known only the practices of the Norse pantheon.

According to his saga, Hakon was a practising Christian and did attempt to convert Norway through what appears to be non-violent reforms. We must take care with the historical reliability of the saga, as Hakon's life forms part of the wider Icelandic sagas written by Christian authors like Snorri Sturluson. It would be to the author's advantage to paint a Christian ruler in a positive light and create a narrative where Hakon lived up to all the ideals of the faith and limited bloodshed. On the other hand, Sturluson doesn't shy away from depicting Hakon's violent raiding, his ferocity in battle and with little hesitation in killing. There is nuance in Hakon's portrayal and we see a man trying to navigate between two worlds.

A notable character trait is his speaking ability, as he is able to rally many powerful rulers to his cause while still a youth, a teenager by modern standards. Yet his penchant for speeches in the sagas becomes a double-edged sword. In his speech to convert Norway to Christianity, he faces opposition from the same leaders who'd first rallied behind him and his pontificating backfires. It's only with the shrewdness of his friend jarl Sigurd that Hakon can placate the riled-up chieftains. By taking Sigurd's advice, Hakon shows a willingness to compromise and allow the people of Norway to worship freely, even though he continues to adhere to Christian beliefs in private, which indicates a level of tolerance and open-mindedness that may have contributed to his long reign as king.

We also see a good head for strategy in his battles with the sons of Eric Bloodaxe. Each time they attack Norway, Hakon outmanoeuvres them through a combination of guile and tactical genius. Coupled with courage on the battlefield, Hakon demonstrates the characteristics of what his followers may have considered a *drengr*. This word is one of high praise in Old Norse and can be associated with the kind of person we see as a badass. It implies a warrior who's courageous, sometimes reckless, but always possessing a sense of honour and fair play.[3] Hakon demonstrates his forgiving nature in his dying moments when he directs his lands to be given to his surviving nephews. Despite all the carnage and battles, Hakon still acknowledges the fighting spirit of the last sons of his brother and wants the line of his father Harald Finehair to continue with strong leaders.

Hakon's burial offers a fascinating insight into what the Norse thought of an afterlife. The king reveals that he's at peace with his dual faiths and is willing to enter Christian heaven or hell or go to Valholl. His followers choose to give him a Norse burial, indicating they see him as a true warrior. It also reveals a lack of prejudice to different faiths coexisting side by side and there's no reason to think that Scandinavian families couldn't have both Christian and Norse mythology believers living together. That's not to say there wouldn't have been opposition either, but it highlights another facet of a society that didn't just go raiding and slaving across the world. There was spiritual flexibility that came down to independent thought and experience, which Hakon the Good exemplified in his life.

How can this attitude be applied to our modern lives? Being open-minded about other people's faiths and beliefs is worthwhile for several reasons. It allows us to hear a different perspective but we don't have to agree with what we hear. It broadens the mind to a worldview that we never understood until we took the time to listen. It teaches us that we're all more than one thing and we don't have to be defined by what we believe in.

Chapter 6

The Queen Mother and the Ingenuity of Norse Women

In the Norwegian countryside, a woman guided her steed relentlessly, riding like her life depended on it. Since leaving Sweden, she'd raced past glittering fjords, over hills and through sprawling woodland, single-minded in her destination and purpose.

Her name was Astrid, daughter of Swedish King Olaf and the fate of her country lay in the balance. She was on her way to meet the King of Norway, Olaf Haraldsson, and make him an offer he couldn't refuse. Not for the first time did she curse her father's stubbornness for reneging on the marriage proposal between her sister Ingibjorg and the Norwegian king. Now, with the threat of retaliation and war looming on the horizon, it was up to her to take matters into her own hands.

The closer she got to her destination, the more Astrid's emotions shifted and churned like a choppy sea. Giddiness brought her up as anxiety weighed her down. Confidence broke her fear as uncertainty slipped through the cracks. Astrid whipped the reins of her horse to move faster, pushing through, trusting in the soundness of her plan and the will of the gods.

By dusk, she had reached the home of King Olaf and when the guards saw this beautiful, wild-eyed woman charging towards the gate they thought her to be the goddess Freyja.

Presented to the king, Astrid bowed low before Olaf and stated her case. She spoke of his greatness and strength, of his dedication to the Christian faith. She spoke of the short-sightedness of her father and the fact that there was more to gain in a feeling of peace between their kingdoms. She spoke of offering herself in marriage to bring prosperity. Moved by the wisdom, tactfulness and sense of her proposal, King Olaf agreed to marry Astrid and peace did indeed flow between Norway and Sweden for a time.

Astrid bore Olaf a daughter called Wulfhild and she ruled at her husband's side, supporting him even through the backlash of their subjects as he struggled to unite Norway as Harald Finehair had before him and his ongoing war with King Cnut of England and Denmark. Olaf bulldozed through the country, attempting to convert through strongarming and threats. The king estranged all the nobles so much that they were willing to throw their lot in with Cnut.

At the battle of Stiklestad, Olaf died while fighting alongside his younger half-brother and future king Harald Hardrada. Astrid was made a widow. Returning to Sweden, Astrid pledged support to her stepson Magnus for him to assume the throne of Norway. Before an assembly of Swedish lords, Astrid declared the legitimacy of her stepson and convinced her countrymen to back him in retaking Norway. With the support of Swedish troops, Magnus ascended the throne, becoming known as Magnus the Good for his restraint. To her dying day, Astrid was well-liked and respected for her diplomacy, leadership and forthrightness.[1]

A princess who took what she wanted

The life of Astrid Olafsdottir of Sweden provides an instructive window into the experiences of upper-class Norse women and the role of marriage. Firstly, her identity as a king's daughter makes her unique among the traditional perspective of Scandinavian men having all the power to arrange marriages and the sagas highlight her being the one to propose to King Olaf.

This same agency was unlikely to be available to girls from poorer families, who would've been forced to marry the men chosen for them. Within Norse society, marriage acted as a business transaction, with women being used as a kind of reproductive capital along with a dowry given to the family of the groom. In exchange, the family of the bride could receive increased political influence and other perks. So, marriage in the Viking world wasn't simply down to husband and wife. It was

The Queen Mother and the Ingenuity of Norse Women 45

a contract between the extended families, with rights and inheritance divvied up between generations.

The importance placed on tradition can be seen in the method in which marriage proposals were conducted. Usually, a man approached the woman's legal guardian and was accompanied by his father or uncle. If the suitor was considered worthy by the guardian, both parties agreed on the money they would put towards the wedding and the amount of property brought into the wider family relationships. All of this was usually done without the woman's knowledge and she was expected to accept the arrangement without any fuss. The one exception to her being able to refuse a marriage was if she was a widow and her father was dead.[2]

With Astrid, we can't assume that she genuinely did propose to Olaf and that her circumstances were any different than many Norse women, even with her increased privilege as the illegitimate daughter of a king. Her story is recorded in the *Heimskringla*, a thirteenth-century history of the Norwegian kings by Snorri Sturluson. As we've already established, the sagas can't be taken as historical fact, but as a queen, it's not hard to imagine that Astrid would be afforded more political power and sway than the average farmer's daughter and could impact the decisions of her realm.

Work that can be taken to be more historically accurate[3] is the poetry of Sigvatr, which heaps tremendous praise upon Astrid. The court poet of King Olaf and the godfather of Magnus, Sigvatr would have known the queen well and his poetry is perhaps the most praiseworthy of any woman in the *Heimskringla*. He writes, 'We will repay splendidly/with our praise Olaf's daughter/to whom the most victorious stout prince was married/for an abundance of bright treasures/ … She, a deeply decisive woman/has helped her stepson/in such a way as few others would/I make true words to the lady's glory.'[4]

In the poem, Sigvatr proclaims that Astrid led an assembly, which was traditionally a masculine affair and suggests a certain amount of influence for being able to lead it and be listened to by high-ranking men of Sweden. There's also a lot of detail about her political acumen and diplomatic skills that convinced the noblemen to lend their support to Magnus and that's an important point here. While composing his verse,

Sigvatr was likely trying to educate his godson that he owed Astrid for all the good fortune she would bring to his rule.

The dynamic between Astrid and Magnus also reveals much about her character. Astrid willingly helped her stepson become king – the sagas don't mention that she was trying to do it to advance her own position (though we can imagine that would still have been part of the reason). Both stepmother and son were born illegitimate too, which may have contributed to Astrid's fondness for the boy. The queen could have also had a strong influence on how Magnus chose to rule when he ascended the throne. With the combined counsel of her and Sigvatr, Magnus could've chosen not to take revenge on the killers of his father and put his energy into other pursuits.

What emerges from the sources is a picture of a woman who wasn't afraid to take fate into her own hands, a woman who could not only manoeuvre through the restrictively gendered world of Norse politics but thrived and impacted the history of two countries. Astrid shows that Norse women didn't have to be shield-maidens or great warriors to carve a place in society. If anything, she shows a more realistic interpretation of how people born into a position of power can affect their environment and that it's a conscious choice of how that position is managed.

Chapter 7

The Norse Alexander the Great

On a sunny day, King Cnut of England stood by the River Thames, watching the water flow. Surrounded by his courtiers and entourage, the king had been standing in the same position for some time, waiting for the right moment. And now, he'd found it. Ordering his throne to be set down by the shore, Cnut reclined back and cast his hand out to the tide as it began to rise. 'You are part of my kingdom and the ground that I'm seated upon is mine and for as long as I've reigned, none have disobeyed my orders. I order you not to rise upon my land, to not wet the clothes and feet of your king and to stay far away.'

The water gave no care to Cnut's decree and carried on its way, soaking his feet and legs. Satisfied with the response, the king nodded and looked to his subjects, who seemed nervous about how he would react. But Cnut's expression was serene, vindicated. 'Behold. Let this be proof that the power of kings is vain, trivial and fleeting. None is worthy of the name of king but He who rules in the heavens and the earth and sea obey only his laws.'

This story of a Scandinavian king literally trying to turn the tide comes from the historian Henry of Huntingdon in his *Historia Anglorum*. Written around a century after the reign of Cnut, the tale is often misrepresented as a ruler who was so prideful and arrogant that he believed he could bend the laws of nature to his will. If this event were to have actually happened, the opposite is far more likely. Cnut demonstrated his humility and piety by showing his sycophantic courtiers that only God had the power to command the world and any man who thought himself to have absolute power was a fool.

Given that Cnut ruled over England and Scandinavia as one of the most powerful Western kings in history, it's unlikely that he got to where he was by being delusional. Indeed, the story of Cnut is that of a survivor who outlasted all his competition to create an empire that etched his name into the history books and shows how the Norse were able to assimilate into other cultures and influence the course of Western civilisation.

Growing up in the school of hard knocks

The exact date of Cnut's birth is unknown, but his parentage is clearer. Born to the Danish prince Sweyn Forkbeard and a Polish princess, Cnut descended from a legendary Scandinavian line of heroes supposedly dating all the way back to Sigurd Snake-In-The-Eye, son of Chapter 3's Ragnar Lodbrok. His grandfather, Harald Bluetooth, had forcibly converted Denmark to Christianity and used the faith to consolidate his power for years. Some sources claim that Bluetooth's heavy-handed ambitions eventually led to his own son leading a rebellion against him and Sweyn seized the throne for himself.[1]

A formative experience for the young Cnut would have been hearing the news of the St Brice's Day massacre. King Ethelred the Unready of England had ordered the slaughter of all Danes within his territories, undoing decades of peace between the Norse and English that had been established with the Danelaw – a collection of territories in England under the control of the Norse that had been agreed between Alfred the Great and King Guthrum years before. Within the massacres, Cnut's aunt and Sweyn's sister Gunhilde and her husband were killed. This led to Sweyn's retaliation: he and his forces invaded England. To join his father in the raiding, Cnut would have needed to have been brought up in the ways of warfare; according to the thirteenth-century Icelandic manuscript *Flateyjarbok*, he spent his childhood training under Thorkell the Tall and the legendary order of the Jomsviking.

An elite unit of Norse warriors, the Jomsviking were said to be strict adherents of the old gods, though faith didn't stop them from fighting for the person who paid them the most. Life as a Jomsviking was harsh, with members between the ages of 18 and 50 needing to pass various tests to prove their bravery and strength. As sworn brothers-in-arms, a jomsviking was forbidden to speak ill of one another and were required to avenge the deaths of their brothers in blood feuds.[2] As a feared and respected commander, Thorkell put Cnut through his paces, creating a mentor–student relationship that would become more complicated as Cnut rose in power and standing. Whatever training he received, Cnut entered battle as a teenager and may have been a part of his father's armies as they raided England and fought against Ethelred.

By 1013, Cnut was ready to join his father in a full-scale invasion of England to avenge the deaths of his kinsmen during the St Brice's Day massacre. Landing at Sandwich, Sweyn's army swept through East Anglia and Northumbria, rallying support until they were ready to strike against London. In a twist of fate, Thorkell the Tall had defected to King Ethelred's side and held London against his fellow Norse. But the overwhelming force and Sweyn and Cnut's army were too much and Thorkell retreated. In the aftermath, Ethelred also fled to the Isle of Wight and sent his sons to Normandy.

Sweyn was crowned the King of England, but his reign would be cut short. Only a few months after coming to power, he died, throwing the court into chaos and creating a power vacuum that needed to be filled.

Becoming King of England

In this uncertain space, Cnut's brother Harald was elected King of Denmark, while the Norse of England called for Cnut to be made King of England. Meanwhile, the English aristocracy recalled Ethelred from exile in Normandy, who mustered an army led by his warrior son Edmund Ironside against Cnut's forces. Caught unawares, Cnut's troops were beaten back to their longships and they fled to Denmark.

Licking his wounds, Cnut went to his brother Harald for support. The King of Denmark eventually agreed to give his brother ships and manpower for another attack on England, so long as he didn't press his claim for the Danish throne. Returning to England at the head of a Viking army from across Scandinavia, Cnut dedicated all his energy and resources against Ethelred and his family. Joining Cnut was his old mentor Thorkill and his Jomsviking, who'd witnessed how his student waged war and rededicated himself fully to Cnut's side. Another defector,

Eadric, the ealdorman of Mercia, betrayed Ethelred in the wake of Cnut seizing Wessex.

In 1016, Ethelred died, leaving Edmund to defend England against the bloody advance of Cnut. But the man nicknamed Ironside gave as good as he got, directing his troops to block and harry the Scandinavian invaders wherever he could. One such bloody encounter came at the Battle of Sherston, where Thorkill put his Jomsviking on the frontline, embodying the Viking spirit of a berserker. A berserker was a warrior imbued with great rage and battle fury, who went into the fight without armour as a psychological tactic against his opponents. Thought to have the animal-like qualities of a bear or wolf, these warriors would have struck terror into the English who saw bare-chested maniacs running at them without any care for their own safety. Any number of reasons could be given for the state of a berserker or *ulfhednar* (wolf-skin) – a combination of alcohol and hallucinogens, a desire to win Odin's favour and a chance for eternal glory.[3]

Yet Edmund's men were no pushovers. They fought valiantly in the name of the warrior-prince who represented the highest virtues of the land, even in the face of deceit by the weaselly Eadric and the ferocity of the Norse. According to the sources, the battle was so bloody and violent that neither side won, and Cnut and Edmund came to the mutual decision of calling the fight off.[4]

The fate of England would ultimately be decided during the Battle of Assandun. Again, Eadric betrayed Edmund, withdrawing his soldiers and giving the Norsemen the advantage. With Edmund and the English in retreat, Cnut could've pressed his advantage and slaughtered his foes. Instead, he took a diplomatic approach. In Edmund, he saw a worthy rival and a ruler cut from the same cloth. There was more to be gained by reaching an agreement than the continued deaths of Scandinavians and English. So, Cnut and Edmund met to sign a peace treaty and reached an accord: Edmund would rule over Wessex and all land south of the Thames, while Cnut would reign over the North. On the day that either man died, they would claim all the country as their own. A few weeks later, Edmund either succumbed to his wounds or was assassinated, leaving Cnut as the sole ruler of England.

A reign of strategy, ruthlessness and piety

Crowned in London in 1017, Cnut started his reign pragmatically. To ensure that no one could oppose his ascension, he ordered the death of Edmund's brother Eadwig: his association with the treacherous Eadric had come to an end, as the ealdorman had argued that he deserved more power for the decisive role he had played in toppling Edmund. Cnut replied that a man who was ready to betray one master was as likely to betray another. From behind, Eadric's head was cut off by a battle axe.

Cnut continued to consolidate his power by marrying Emma of Normandy, the widow of Ethelred. Enchanted by her beauty and family connections, Cnut wed Emma and denounced his previous marriage to Aelfgifu of Northampton. In the marriage, Cnut and Emma acted in partnership and she was present for many of the king's acts at court. Together they had three children: Harthacnut, Gunhilda and a daughter whose name has been lost to history. Even after her husband's death, Emma continued to have a strong influence over English politics by trying to place Harthacnut or her older son, Edward the Confessor, on the throne.[5]

Cnut also had the issue of all the Scandinavians he'd brought with him to conquer England. This was in the context of him being a devout Christian and many of his followers adhering to the old ways. So, he collected a colossal *danegeld* of £82,500[6] to reward his soldiers and sent most of them home. The king retained forty ships and levied an annual army tax to be paid to his men to maintain their loyalty.

Even in the early days of his reign, Cnut gave generously to the Church and maintained the Christian faith. But he was also tolerant of the faiths of men like Thorkill the Tall, who continued to serve in his army, and he recognised that this was a crucial part of maintaining the loyalty of his Scandinavian followers. The nuances of faith and Cnut's role as king of both England and Scandinavia demonstrate the complexities and limitations of the Viking label, a debate that came up in a conversation I had with historian and scholar Dr Alex Woolf, who said, 'the Viking Age as it's presented starting with the raid of Lindisfarne and ending with the Battle of Stamford Bridge is Anglocentric. It's really all about

English history and has nothing to do with Scandinavian history. I'd argue that eleventh-century invaders like Cnut and Harald Hardrada are national kings. They're Christians leading national armies and have more in common with rulers of the Hundred Years' Wars than those early raiders on Lindisfarne.'[7]

Indeed, Cnut was an international monarch who shed his Viking identity – raiding in his youth in England – and used his acclaim as a springboard to become the most powerful man in more than one country. He put a stop to more *vikingr* attacks on England by his countrymen, showcasing his allegiance to Christianity and his subjects across the land. This led him into conflict with other Norsemen, particularly King Olaf of Norway and his dynasty.

In 1018, Cnut travelled to Denmark to claim the Danish crown in the wake of his brother's death. But after he'd extended his influence back in his homeland, Olaf started raiding Denmark and ultimately Cnut put him down, becoming the ruler of Norway and installing Hakon Ericsson to govern in his absence.

Once his control over Scandinavia was firmly established, Cnut could turn his attention towards Rome. Receiving an invitation to witness the ascension of the Holy Roman Emperor Conrad II, Cnut visited Rome in 1027. He travelled as a repentant pilgrim with his retinue, giving gold and silver to the monasteries he passed on the way. He also made the lives of the poor easier by reducing the tax on fellow pilgrims and used his political skills to gain further tax cuts for the English from the Pope himself. While attending the emperor's coronation, Cnut saw the magnificent crown placed upon Conrad's head as a display of power and religious commitment. Cnut's visit to Rome was probably done for political and genuinely religious reasons. By appearing before Conrad, he could further his relationship with a powerful Southern ally, demonstrate his piety towards foreign powers and seek repentance for the recent violence of the Scandinavian wars. On returning to England, Cnut even had a crown fashioned like the one Conrad wore to showcase his respect and admiration for the emperor.

In 1035, Cnut died from natural causes, leaving behind a fragmented North Sea Empire. His heirs squabbled and wrestled for control, though ultimately England fell into the hands of Edward the Confessor, advancing Norman interests within the country that cultivated the rise of William the Conqueror and the full Norman takeover three decades later.

During Cnut's reign, he ushered in an era of unprecedented peace between England and Scandinavia, arguably surpassing the prosperity that had been made during the time of Alfred the Great. Much of this had to do with Cnut controlling the forces that raided from across the seas and his ability to placate Christians and Norse alike. He was a ruthless and pragmatic king that eliminated all threats against his dynasty, balanced by a far-seeing perspective and shrewdness that looked beyond physical threats and strongarming. On the one hand, Cnut gave generously to his subjects, allies and foes who'd earned his respect and embodied Christian charity. On the other, the king armed himself with Norse practicality against internal and external threats, always ready to unleash his full might on those who attempted to harm him or his interests. Like the famed Alexander who conquered the known world by the age of 30, Cnut truly earned the moniker of 'the Great' attached to his name.[8]

Chapter 8

The Warrior Poet and The Wisdom of Verse

What do you picture when you think of a poet? Maybe a romantic who writes epic verses? Perhaps a wordsmith that reels off quotes by heart? Or a nice, non-threatening kind of person that just really likes writing? To get an understanding of the Norse view of poetry, let's start with a story about the gods.

At the end of the war between the Aesir and Vanir, the gods sealed their peace treaty by spitting into a large vat. From their saliva, a being formed called Kvasir, who became known as the wisest man alive. He was so wise that there wasn't anything he didn't know, and he travelled the nine realms, spreading his knowledge to whoever would listen.

One day, Kvasir was invited into the home of the dwarves Fjalar and Galar. Wanting Kvasir's precious wisdom for themselves, they murdered him and poured his blood into a vat which they mixed with honey to make mead. Whoever drank this mead of poetry would be gifted with Kvasir's silver tongue and the dwarves drank greedily. When the gods questioned them about what had happened to Kvasir, they answered that he'd choked on his intelligence.

Fjalar and Galar continued their murdering spree by killing a giant called Gilling and his wife. They took Gilling out to sea and sank his boat. On passing on the sad news to his wife, they got tired of her weeping and dropped a millstone on her head. This had consequences for the duo.

Gilling's son, Suttungr, heard about his father's murder and confronted the dwarves. Dragging them out to sea and dropping them on a reef at low tide, Suttungr threatened to drown them. The dwarves begged for their lives and Suttungr agreed to spare them in exchange for the mead of poetry. Coveting the wisdom for himself, Suttungr hid the mead deep in his chambers and instructed his daughter Gunnlod to watch over it.

But there was someone in the nine worlds even more starved of wisdom than Suttungr. This was Odin, whose hunger for knowledge was insatiable and when he heard about the mead being hoarded, he vowed to claim it for himself. Disguising himself as a farmhand, Odin travelled to the residence of Suttungr's brother, Baugi. There he found nine slaves cutting hay with their scythes and he offered to sharpen the scythes with a whetstone he took from his cloak. The whetstone worked like a charm and each slave asked to buy it from Odin. Agreeing to sell his marvellous product, Odin gave one condition: they must pay a high price. And so he threw the whetstone up in the air and in the struggle to take it, the slaves slashed each other's throats with their scythes.

Then The All-Father went to Baugi's door and said, 'Hello there, sir. I hope you'll permit me to have a moment of your time. I am but a simple wanderer and while I don't relish the thought of delivering bad news, I see it as my sworn duty to do what others turn away from. My name is Bolverk and I regret to tell you that as I was passing by your farm, I saw your thralls slaughter each other over a disagreement. I don't know how it started. What I do know is that I'm capable of filling in to do their work, and in exchange, all I ask for is a draught of your brother's mead. I've heard it's a wonderous drink and have travelled far to learn more about it.'

Baugi answered that he had no power over his brother's actions and that Suttungr was a notorious miser. But if Bolverk could truly perform the tasks of nine men then he would travel with him and see if he could persuade his brother to part with some mead.

So, that summer, Bolverk toiled in the fields and by winter, his promise to Baugi had been fulfilled. When they went to Suttungr, the keeper of the mead refused to provide a single drop. Undeterred, Bolverk convinced Baugi to help him get access to the mead in Gunnlod's chamber. The giant took Bolverk to a place in the mountain stronghold nearest the chamber and gave him a drill to bore a hole into the rock.

After Baugi drilled through the wall and announced he was done, the High One blew into the hole to check. Rock-dust blew back onto him and he realised the giant was trying to trick him. Bolverk demanded Baugi finish what he had started and the giant drilled all the way through. With the job done, Odin cast off his disguise, turning into a snake and slipping through the hole. Seeing that he'd been deceived, Baugi tried to kill the god with the drill, but he was too slow.

Now inside the chamber, Odin disguised himself as a handsome young man. He met Gunnlod and managed to seduce her. A bargain was struck. Three nights of sex for three sips of mead and so Odin spent his time in Gunnlod's bed. But every time he went for a swig of mead, the All-Father drained the vat as much as he could.

When he had what he came for, Odin transformed into an eagle, flying from the wrath of Suttungr, who'd discovered the deceit. The giant also transformed into an eagle and gave chase. Odin soared back to Asgard and when he was near, the other gods set out vessels at the ready. Flying into Asgard in the nick of time, Odin puked up the mead into the containers.

But Suttungr had been so close that in fear and haste, Odin shat out some of his precious mead and these paltry drops of poetry fell to Midgard below. Mankind could drink this sullied portion, but they would only ever be bad poets and unoriginal creatives. But the true greats, those poets and storytellers who could make their audience feel something, were given their gifts by Odin. He shared his original batch of mead with them personally.[1]

Types of Norse poetry

This tale of how Odin stole the gift of poetry from the giants indicates the value of creativity in Norse society. The ultimate expression of poetry was personified by a skald. Identified as court poets, skalds were in the service of rulers who relied on having their great deeds transmitted throughout Scandinavia. Reputation was key to how jarls and kings spread their influence and the job of a skald was to compose praise poetry so that the king would be remembered.

More than that, poetry was a way to pass down information in cultures where there were no written manuscripts and only runic carvings to express ideas. Skalds recorded battles, contributing to the tradition of oral storytelling that helped to create later works like the *Prose* and *Poetic Edda* and the Icelandic sagas. Without poetry, we wouldn't know nearly as much as we know about the actions and personalities of important Viking Age rulers or the events that shaped their worlds.

Generally, Old Norse poetry is divided into two types: eddic and skaldic (although there are always exceptions). The former refers to ballad narratives in the vein of the *Poetic Edda*, where the authors of the poetry are anonymous. Skaldic poetry is usually attributed to named authors and shows the dynamic between the poet and the patron, capturing the bravery, strength, battle prowess and generosity of their patron. The most elaborate of these skaldic poems is the *drapa* (long poem) and in exchange for immortalising their patron, the skald would be paid and given a respectable status in a community.[2]

Another fascinating aspect of Norse poetry is the penchant for complex word rhymes, wit and flair captured in kennings. This poetic device involved replacing a noun with a figure of speech as a metaphor or clever turn of phrase to showcase the creativity of the skald. For example, raven-feeder means warrior or river-steed means ship. In battle, a warrior became a literal raven-feeder through the bodies he left behind for scavengers with the association of death, ravens and Odin. A longship could be steered like a horse across water.

There were skalds that did live up to the classic ideals of a poet like Sigvatr. Others chose to embrace all the violence and bloodshed of battle like the hero of this chapter, Egil Skallagrimsson.

A man of many contradictions

Egil is the total antithesis of an attractive, romantic poet. He's a warrior, farmer, killer and family man described as having a 'wide forehead, bushy brows and a nose that was not long but extremely broad. His upper jaw was broad and long, and his chin and jawbones were exceptionally wide. With his thick neck and stout shoulders, he stood out from other men. When he was angry, his face grew harsh and fierce'[3] in the saga dedicated to his life. (Doesn't sound like the archetypical kind of poetic beauty, does it?)

At odds with his violent character is his ability to compose epic, creative verses that made him one of the most accomplished skalds of his generation. Let's take just one of his poems as an example: 'The god of the armour hangs/a jangling snare upon my clutch/the gibbet of hunting-birds/the stamping ground of hawks/I raise the ring, the clasp that is worn/on the shield-splitting arm/on to my road of the battle-storm/in praise of the feeder of ravens.' In context, Egil has composed a praise poem in honour of King Athelstan of England, who's given him an arm ring and other gifts as compensation for the death of the poet's brother Thorolf. Egil is highly descriptive with his language, using alliteration to create a word flow and using several kennings like 'jangling snare' for ring and 'rod of the battle-storm' for sword.[4] This same man who could bend words so masterfully and work magic tore a man's throat out with his teeth, made his first kill when he was 7, burned down homes and projectile-vomited onto people for fun. Naturally, it makes for a compelling narrative.

The author of *Egil's Saga* is unknown and it may or may not contain actual verses written by the historical Egil passed down through oral traditions or Icelandic written sources like *The Book of Settlements*. What the author constructed is a generational epic starting with Egil's grandfather Kveldulf and the move from Norway to Iceland to escape the machinations of King Harald Finehair. This struggle is paralleled by Egil's resistance against Harald's son Eric Bloodaxe and his wife Gunnhild. Here I've retold Egil's story across those generations.

Wolves in wolves' clothing

The story of Egil Skallagrimsson is a story of wolves, beginning with a man called Ulf. A clever, wise and capable farmer, Ulf tilled his fields and offered advice to those who asked during the day. Come nightfall, he became bad-tempered and wild and people called him a shapeshifter. He became Kveldulf, Night Wolf.

Kveldulf married Salbjorg Karisdottir and they had two sons, Thorolf and Grim, but their children were like day and night. Thorolf grew into a generous, energetic man who won friends easily and was favoured for his looks, which he got from his mother, who was fair in complexion and cheerful with all. Grim took after his father. Dark-eyed, dark-haired, dark moods and a desire to venture beyond the farm and seek his fortune. In time he would earn the name Skallagrim.

Eventually, Kveldulf and his sons were called upon by King Harald Fairhair to serve him and win great renown. Kveldulf rebuffed him. This irritated the king and so the Night Wolf's brother-in-law Olvir stepped in to mediate. He convinced Harald that Kveldulf would send Thorolf in his place and serve in the king's army when he returned from raiding in the summer. Kveldulf continued to have doubts about his family throwing their lot in with a man like Harald and he told Thorolf as much when he returned. But his fair-haired son would not be dissuaded and left to join the king with a crew of reliable men.

Under Harald's service, Thorolf proved himself to be a well-liked and capable fighter. But as his reputation grew, so did the list of people who grew envious of his acclaim. One such family poured poison into Harald's ear, whispering of how Thorolf planned to overthrow him. Harald sipped this poison like it was fine mead and consumed it as the truth. Over time, the rift between Harald and Thorolf became too great to ignore and Harald finally gave the order to have Thorolf killed. Confronting his subject personally, the king set fire to Thorolf's farm and delivered the killing blow to the man as he fought a losing battle.

When he heard about the death of his son, Kveldulf was overwhelmed with grief and became bedridden. He sent Skallagrim to speak with Harald to accept compensation for Thorolf's death. Arriving in the court with the strongest and boldest men he knew, Skallagrim came before Harald to hear his offer.

'Serve me as your brother did and in time you will be compensated for his death. But you must take more care in my service than he did,' said the king.

Skallagrim replied, 'Everybody knows that Thorolf was far more capable of serving you than I. For he had certain qualities that I lack. I also don't have the luck to serve you in the way that you deserve or that I would want.'

Reading between the lines, Harald's face turned blood-red and Olvir, who'd acted as chief negotiator between farmers and king for all this time, told Skallagrim and his men to leave quickly. Getting back into their ship, the group sailed away in the nick of time, as Harald had sent a large band of warriors out to kill them for the slight he'd suffered.

Returning home, Skallagrim told his father of what happened, and they reached an agreement: it was time to leave Norway. They would never be free from Harald's wrath in a country shackled by his tyranny and so they made plans to travel to Iceland. This was a land where farmers could live free and claim territory that wasn't coveted by a grasping ruler.

In the spring, Kveldulf and his family set sail for Iceland and along the way, Skallagrim spied the ship that had once belonged to Thorolf. It'd been seized after his death and put into the possession of Hallvard Travel-Hard, a man who served Harald. Seeing the opportunity to finally avenge their family, Kveldulf and Skallagrim made plans to take the ship back.

Father and son manned two boats between them and rowed until they found where the ship was moored. Watchmen saw the boats coming and roused Hallvard and his crew from slumber and all Hel broke loose.

Old Kveldulf, wielding a giant double-bladed axe, recalled the fury of his youth, unleashing the beast within. He cut through every man in his path, commanding his own to sever the awnings and pegs that held his son's ship captive. Skallagrim fed off his father's rage, ravaging the deck like hungry Fenrir, eager to spill blood. Kveldulf fought his way to Hallvard and swung his axe with such force that it cut through his helmet and head, buried up to the shaft. With a mighty bellow, the Night Wolf swung the man from his axe and hurled him over the side of the ship.

In the aftermath, only three survivors remained and Skallagrim told them to send word back to King Harald of what had happened that day. 'You will repeat this verse,' spoke the son of the Night Wolf. 'The warrior's revenge/is repaid to the king/wolf and eagle/stalk over the king's sons/Hallvard's corpse flew/in pieces into the sea/the grey eagle tears at Travel-Hard's wounds.'[5]

With the day won, Kveldulf and his family took the ship and its cargo and carried on to Iceland. But the battle had come at a price. Kveldulf's berserker rage had taken its toll on him and left him weak and exhausted. Bed-bound, his health continued to decline; he spoke his wishes, 'If I'm to die, make a coffin for me and put it overboard and if my son Grim is to make it to Iceland, tell him to make a home for himself.' Kveldulf passed away and his crew did as he'd instructed. They placed his body in

Yggdrasil from Oluf Olufsen Bagge's The Mundane Tree. (*Public domain via Wikimedia Commons*)

Odin with his wolves Geri and Freiki and his two ravens Huginn and Muninn. (*Public domain via Wikimedia Commons*)

Thor fighting giants, a painting by Marten Eskil Winge. (*Public domain via Wikimedia Commons*)

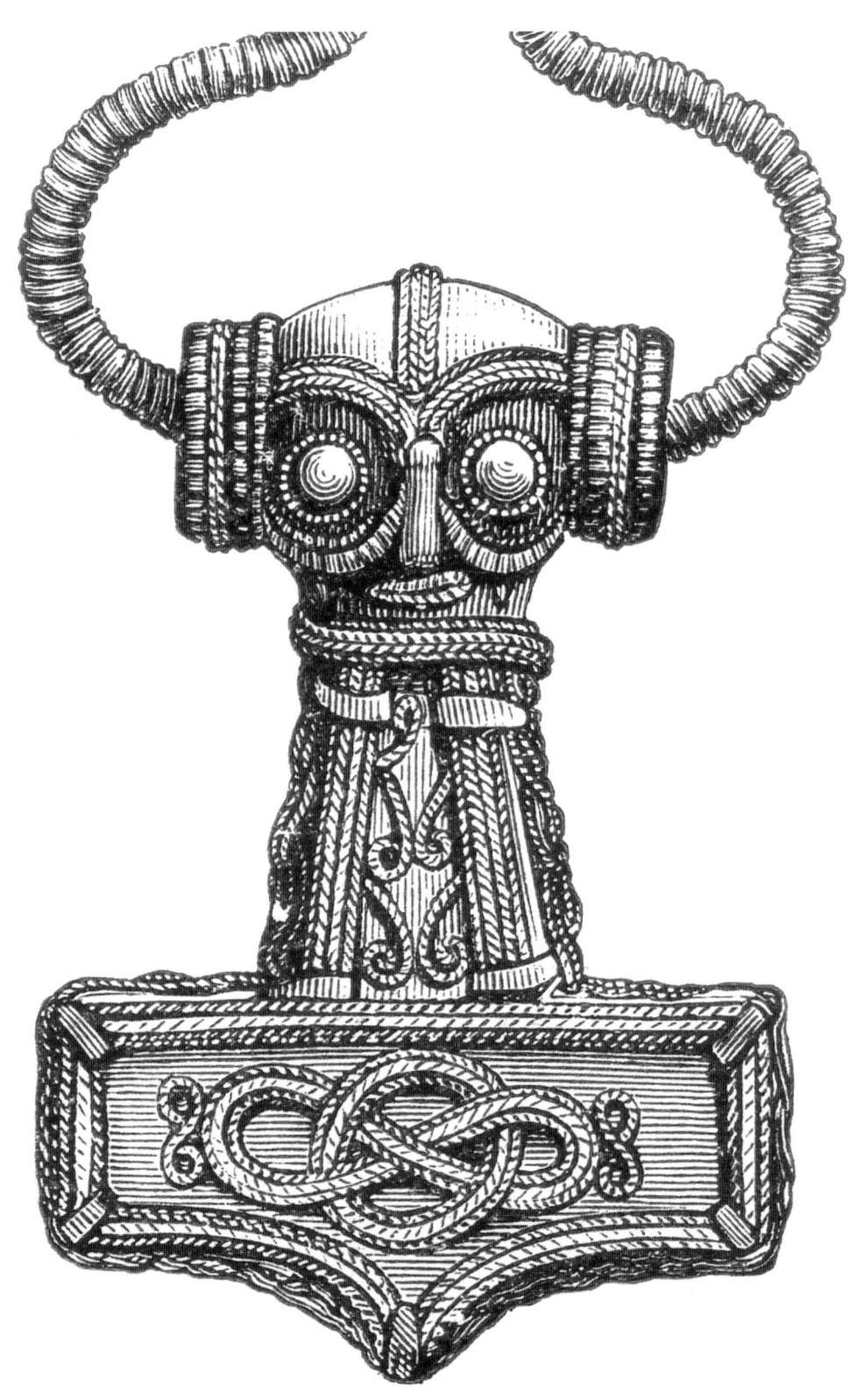

Mjolnir by Olof Sorling. (*Public domain via Wikimedia Commons*)

Loki. (*Public domain via Wikimedia Commons*)

THE PUNISHMENT OF LOKI.

The punishment of Loki by Louis Huard. (*Public domain via Wikimedia Commons*)

Freyja riding with her cats. (*Public domain via Wikimedia Commons*)

Aslaug/Kraka, a painting by Marten Eskil Winge. (*Public domain via Wikimedia Commons*)

Brynhild and Gudrun, an illustration from Fredrik Sander's 1893 Swedish edition of *The Poetic Edda*. (*Public domain via Wikimedia Commons*)

Sigurd killing the dragon Fafnir from the 32 colour plates illustrating Richard Wagner's *Siegfried*. (*Public domain via Wikimedia Commons*)

The death of Ragnar Lodbrok by Hugo Hamilton. (*Public domain via Wikimedia Commons*)

Cnut the Great. (*Public domain via Wikimedia Commons*)

Discovery of the New World by Leif Ericsson. (*Public domain via Wikimedia Commons*)

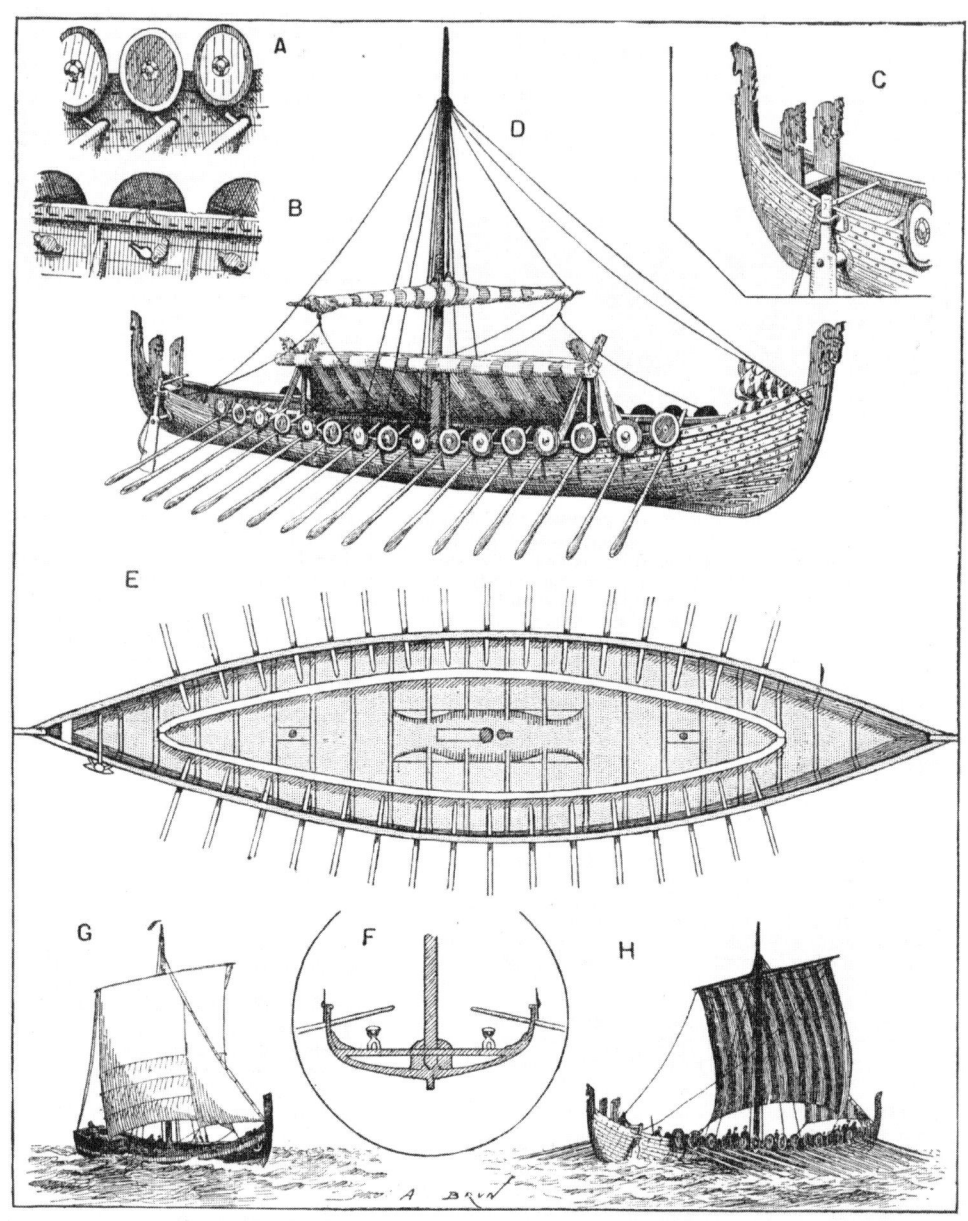

Drakkar : A, disposition des trous de nage ; B, disposition des tapons fermant les trous de nage ; C, arrière du drakkar montrant le gouvernail et le siège du pilote ; D, drakkar de 32 avirons (un des côtés de la tente est relevé) ; E, plan d'un drakkar de 32 avirons ; F, coupe au maître du drakkar ; G, caboteur norvégien moderne ; H, drakkar sous voiles.

Drakkar longship. (*Public domain via Wikimedia Commons*)

Berserker following Odin. (*Public domain via Wikimedia Commons*)

Leif discovers America, a painting by Hans Dahl. (*Public domain via Wikimedia Commons*)

Thorerus, vel Thoraldus taurinus. Thorer filium
habuit Ulf, ejus gnatus fuit Aswaldus, gignens Thorwal=
dum Erici Rauderi patrem;
Thorwaldus cum filio Erico ob perpetratum homicidium

*Effigies Erici Rauderi ad delineatio=
nem Einarsi Eiolfsonii adumbrata*

è Norvagiâ in Islandiam aufugit, ubi in promontorio ejus=
dem Insulæ caurum versus villam vocatam Drangar ad
Vitæ

Erik the Red. (*Public domain via Wikimedia Commons*)

Harald Hardrada coin. (*Public domain via Wikimedia Commons*)

Battle of Stamford Bridge from The Life of King Edward The Confessor by Matthew Paris. (*Public domain via Wikimedia Commons*)

The Norman Royal Court by Albert Kretschmer. (*Public domain via Wikimedia Commons*)

William the Conqueror. (*Public domain via Wikimedia Commons*)

Sigurd The Crusader by Edward Burne-Jones. (*Public domain via Wikimedia Commons*)

a coffin and gave it to the sea. At some point, the coffin floated ashore and was buried in Icelandic soil.

Skallagrim did make it to shore and when he was told of his father's death, he decided to build a farm not far from the burial site. An industrious man, he settled the land and called it Borg, where he lived in peace as a blacksmith and farmer. He had two sons, one of which would go on to become even more famous than Skallagrim or Kveldulf.

Egil's childhood

Skallagrim and his wife Bera had several children together, but many died. Two daughters and two sons survived. Sauenn and Thorrun were good girls, while their brothers would grow to carry the family's legacy. The first was Thorolf, named after his uncle who died and who embodied all the same positive traits. The other was Egil, dark-haired, swarthy and unattractive, who would grow to have the gift of words.

By the time Egil was 3, he was already as strong as a boy of 7 or 8. So restless and talkative was he that he defied his father's wishes to stay behind at the farm while he and Thorolf went to a feast at a neighbour's. Egil gate-crashed the feast in the middle of the party and composed his first poem to praise Yngvar the host. Egil spoke of a gold shedder who was generous with his gifts and how he would never find a greater poet than himself at three winters old. Yngvar was impressed with the boy's moxy and talent and he was rewarded for his efforts.

When he was 7 years old, Egil made his first kill. As an avid wrestler, Egil enjoyed playing games of strength and he took part in a ball game. Being paired with an older boy named Grim, Egil was outmatched in strength but not in temper. He swung his bat at Grim, who knocked him into the mud and told him to know his place. Leaving the game, Egil heard the jeers of the other players dogging him.

Egil went to a young man he admired called Thord Granison and told him what had happened. Thord handed him an axe and said they would take revenge together. Grim was in the middle of running with the ball and Egil buried the axe into his head, starting a battle between the people of Borg and those who'd come to see the game. Skallagrim was indifferent to the actions of his son, while Bera said he had the makings of a true Viking.

Egil's love of ball games and roughhousing didn't stop. When he was 12 years old, he and Thord were playing against Skallagrim. In the middle of the game, the wolfen fury of Kveldulf got the better of Skallagrim. He crushed Thord with his strength. In his frenzy, he seized Egil, but was stopped by a servant named Thorgerd, a foster mother to the boy. She stood up to Skallagrim and he chased after her all the way to a cliff. Jumping to safety and trying to swim away, Thorgerd didn't get far before she was hit by a boulder that Skallagrim tossed at her.

When he heard of his foster mother's death, Egil was angry. At the evening feast, he went up to his father's favourite servant and killed him with a single blow. Father and son didn't speak to each other until a year had passed and Thorolf had returned from raiding. Egil asked to go raiding with his brother and both his father and sibling refused. So, Egil took matters into his own hands. He slashed through the ropes that kept Thorolf's ship moored and let it drift out into the fjord. Egil claimed he would continue with such antics until his brother took him abroad and so he finally gave in.

Pissing off a king (and lots of other people)

Egil joined Thorolf on a trip to Norway and the latter renewed his good relationship with the son of Harald Finehair, King Eric Bloodaxe. The king had sent Skallagrim a precious gold-lined axe that the man had shattered out of spite and old wounds. To maintain a friendly relationship, Thorolf told Eric that his father had loved the gift. He even presented Eric with a longship sail that Thorolf claimed was from Skallagrim. Thorolf also took his bride-to-be, Asgerd, with him to see her father Bjorn and uncle Thorir in the hopes of accepting his marriage proposal. The marriage was granted and much joy was shared on the day.

For young Egil, his defining moment came when he met Thorir's son, Arinbjorn. A few years older, Arinbjorn already possessed a wise and noble character that captivated Egil and this would be the start of a lifelong friendship.

When the day came for his brother's wedding, Egil was unable to attend because of illness. On recovering, he joined Thorir on an errand to the island of Altoy, where they sheltered on the farm of King Eric's steward, Bard. The steward claimed he wished he had ale to serve them. But he only had milk curd for them to drink and a place to sleep as it was the same night he was preparing a feast for the king and his queen Gunnhild. When the royal couple arrived, Eric asked for Bard to bring his other guests to the feast and ale was served in abundance.

Drinking as much as every other man beside him, Egil prodded and needled Bard with scorn poetry, how he was a deceiver, a cheat and a cheapskate for holding the alcohol back from thirsty strangers. Egil drank and drank, irritating Bard and embarrassing him in front of the king and queen. So, Bard went to Gunnhild and told her of how this man was making a fool of them all. Together the steward and the queen mixed poison into the ale and had it served to Egil.

Recognising the treachery, Egil carved runes into the drinking horn. Then he cut himself and smeared his blood onto the horn, reciting magic poetry that caused it to shatter. Helping a drunken friend to the door, Egil gripped his sword tightly and waited for Bard to follow. Then he stabbed the steward through the belly and fled into the night.

When the king discovered that Bard had been killed, he ordered a manhunt for Egil but lost several men. Making it back home, Egil was convinced by Thorir to compensate Eric for the trouble he'd caused.

Eventually, Egil and Thorolf sailed to England because they'd heard the reigning king Athelstan was looking for soldiers to fight in his army. It was also an excuse for Egil to stay far away from Eric and his family. So, they ventured onto the battlefield in the name of the English lord to fight against Olaf the Red of Scotland.

The battles were fierce and though Athelstan's forces were victorious, Thorolf fell to the enemy. Egil chased and killed many of the men who were responsible for his brother's death. Then he buried Thorolf with full armour and weaponry. Filled with sorrow, the warrior-poet reflected on the victory that had come at a heavy cost. He resolved to keep his sadness to himself and keep moving forward. It's what his brother would have wanted. King Athelstan would not forget Thorolf's bravery. He gave Egil two chests overflowing with silver as compensation for the loss.

After leaving Athelstan's service, Egil found himself at a crossroads. He'd been warring and battling for so long that he felt that he ought to settle down and so he found himself thinking of his brother's widow, Asgerd. Even as a lad, Egil had felt a yearning for her that he couldn't hope to be fulfilled in the shadow of his more handsome brother. It filled him with melancholy and in the autumn, his friend Arinbjorn asked him why he was so depressed.

Egil muttered a poem: 'The goddess of the arm where hawks perch/ woman, must suffer my rudeness/when young I would easily dare/to lift the sheer cliffs of my brow./Now I must conceal in my cloak/the outcrop between my brows/when she enters the poet's mind/head-dress of the rock-giant's earth.'[6]

Arinbjorn deduced his friend was referring to Asgerd and Egil admitted as much. He asked Arinbjorn to help arrange the marriage, which he accepted. That winter, Egil and Asgerd were wed and for a time, Egil achieved some sense of peace in his life. It wouldn't last.

Curses and queens

A few years later, Egil was informed that his wife's father Bjorn had died and that his brother-in-law Bergonund had claimed the entire estate for himself. Asgerd had received no inheritance and Bergonund had taken it on account of being married to her half-sister Gunnhild.

Egil decided to claim rights on his wife's behalf. He flew in the face of his old enemies King Eric and Queen Gunnhild, who'd outlawed him and favoured Bergonund.

A *thing* assembly was formed where both parties would get to voice their perspectives. Egil came with twenty men, among them his wise counsellor Arinbjorn to debate in his favour.

Much posturing transpired. Bergonund claimed his wife had a superior claim to the inheritance, that Asgerd was little more than a slave-woman. Arinbjorn brought in several witnesses to assert that Asgerd was a rightful heiress.

As Eric considered his decision, his queen chipped in, 'Why do you let this fool Egil run circles around you? Would you even object if he tried to take the throne from you? You may choose not to rule in Bergonund's favour, but I won't stand for having the honour of our friends questioned.' With that, the queen ordered her henchmen to disrupt the assembly.

Egil held fast and demanded a duel with Bergonund for the right to the estate, though Arinbjorn cautioned against it. Heeding his friend, Egil stood down, but not before making the promise that any who dared lay a claim to the land of his father-in-law would incur the wrath of the gods. Then he left and Eric sent men after him. In the end, Egil managed to escape Norway.

When he heard about Egil running away, Bergonund dismissed his bodyguard, confident the poet wouldn't be able to strike at him. The son of Eric and Gunnhild, Prince Rognvald acted as his spy on the waters. Bergonund retired to the king's farm. By chance, the wind carried Egil and his men to the same destination. As soon as Egil discovered that Bergonund was nearby, he came up with a plan. He'd heard about a bear that was causing trouble for the farm and passed on a rumour that it was resting in the woods not far away. This got back to Bergonund, who took some friends to rid himself of the beast, only to find out it was Egil lurking in the woods, waiting for him. Egil massacred the entire farm. Prince Rognvald numbered among the dead, a boy of no more than ten or eleven winters.

But Egil wasn't finished. Butchering a horse and crafting a hazel pole, the son of Skallagrim thrust the pole into the ground and stuck the horse's head on top. He turned his scorn-pole towards the land and carved curse runes into the wood. Then Egil announced, 'With this Nithing pole I turn its wrath upon King Eric and Queen Gunnhild. I turn it upon the nature spirits that live in the land and that they will find no peace or respite, no relief from the pain of unfixed direction until they've driven the king and queen from Norway.' With his curse made, Egil returned to Iceland, waiting for it to take effect. During this waiting period, Skallagrim died and Egil buried his father with respect. A year later, Eric Bloodaxe and his wife were finally driven from Norway by Hakon the Good, fleeing to England.

Meanwhile, Egil had grown restless on his farm and felt the itch to return to England to claim more of what King Athelstan had promised him years ago. When his ship washed up on England's shores, Egil soon realised he was in the kingdom of Eric, who'd been granted rulership over the domain of Jorvik. Thinking through his options, Egil decided to go to Jorvik, as he'd heard Arinbjorn lived in the city and was on good terms with the king. Once again reunited with his friend, Egil listened to his wise counsel and agreed to see Eric. It was time to settle their dispute once and for all.

On recognising Egil, the king scoffed at how brazen the poet was for daring to come before him. He said death was a certainty, a fact echoed by Queen Gunnhild. She despised Egil more than any living being and had used her own magic to make the poet's life Hel through all the years of their strife.

Arinbjorn stepped in to say Egil could make amends with a poem of the highest praise, a proposal Eric agreed to. And so Egil spent that night trying to compose his poem but couldn't because of a swallow that constantly distracted him with its twittering. Arinbjorn went to the place where the bird sounded. The swallow turned out to be a shapeshifter that hastily left, perhaps a final act of spite from the queen herself.

In his friend's company, Egil finally found the inspiration and head space to write. He remembered the *drapa* that would save his head. In the morning, Egil came before the king and recited his verse, bringing the court into silence. In twenty stanzas, he hailed the grandeur of Eric Bloodaxe, the battles he'd fought and won, the depth of his generosity and the endurance of his legacy. The poem was well received and Egil was free to leave, free to live, so long as he never crossed paths with Eric again.

Vomiting, vikingr and victory

Putting his conflict with Eric and Gunnhild behind him, Egil reunited with King Athelstan. Over the next few years he was involved in many adventures and duels. One such duel involved the brother of Bergonund, Alti the Short, who staked his claim to the estate Egil had fought so passionately for.

Once again, an assembly was called and Egil and Alti went at each other with sword and shields. The duel ended with Egil ripping into his rival's throat with his teeth and leaving him to bleed out. And so Egil finally succeeded in claiming the estate for himself and his wife.

Egil also entered the service of King Hakon on behalf of Arinbjorn's kinsman, Thorstein. On one such occasion, Egil was staying in the home of a wealthy landowner called Armod Beard and during a feast, Egil drank more ale than anyone else. He drank when his companions couldn't finish their horns. He drank until he needed to do something about how he was feeling. So, he went over to Armod, dragged him out of his seat and threw up all over him, as Odin had vomited the mead of poetry into Asgard. His vomit went all over the man, clogging his beard and nostrils, making Armod vomit too. Armod's men were outraged by this display, to which Egil replied, 'I'm only following the master of the house's example. He's spewing his guts the same as I am.'

Then wiping his mouth and sitting back down, he reeled off a poem. 'With my cheeks' swell I repaid/the compliment you served./I had heavy cause to venture my steps across the floor./Many guests thank favours with sweeter-flavoured rewards./But we meet rarely./Armond's beard is awash with dregs of ale.'[7]

After more drinking, Egil and his men retired to their beds. In the morning, Egil broke into Armond's room and grabbed him by the beard, making it clear that he would accept no violent reprisal for his antics the night before. In front of the man's wife and daughter, Egil said he would spare Armond's life, but not before cutting his beard off and gouging out one of his eyes.

In his later years, Egil remained closer than ever to Arinbjorn and then went raiding together in Saxony and Frisia. So great was Egil's admiration for his blood brother that he composed a praise poem, lauding Arinbjorn's wisdom, patience and nobility.

Heartbreak and old age

The twilight years of the warrior-poet who'd made his name across England and Scandinavia weren't without loss and heartbreak. His most beloved son, Bodvar, died in a shipwreck. Grief-stricken, Egil locked himself in his bed-closet, intending to starve himself. On the third day, his wife called on the help of their daughter Thorgerd. Recognising that her father's melancholy could not be met with warm words, she tried a different approach. 'I've not eaten anything tonight and I will follow my father's example. I don't want to live after he and my brother are dead. Open the door, Father. I want to join you in your path.'

Egil unlocked the door and let his daughter lie down beside him. 'You're a wise girl, daughter and you honour me. How am I expected to go on living with such sorrow?'

Thorgerd started chewing on seaweed and Egil asked her what she was doing. 'I'm eating this seaweed because it'll make me feel worse. Otherwise, I'll go on living too long.'

'How bad is it?' Egil wondered.

'Very bad. Do you want some?'

'What difference does it make?' Egil ate some seaweed and later, Thorgerd called for water to be delivered. She started drinking and Egil felt how parched his throat was.

'Would you like a drink, Father?'

As Egil was about to drink, Thorgerd said, 'We've been tricked. This is milk.'

Egil drank the milk and his daughter sighed. 'What are we to do now? Our plan has failed and now it's important we live. At least long enough for you to write a poem about Bodvar and I'll be able to carve it into a rune-stick. Then we'll be free to die.'

Egil didn't think he could muster the energy to compose a poem, but his daughter's trickery helped him to process his emotions enough to make the attempt. Egil lamented the gift of poetry that Odin had gifted him. How the High One had favoured him, given with one hand and taken with another. He cursed the sea for taking his son from him, even though he knew to fight such a thing was foolish. He praised the courage and steadfastness of his boy, the love that existed between them. He reflected that he would see Bodvar again when his own death came.

In his old age, Egil became blind, frail and senile. He concocted a plan where he wished to take the silver from the chests that King Athelstan had given him long ago at the *thing*. There he would toss the silver to the crowds so they would push and shove each other to claim the riches. This plan was quickly shot down by his relatives and friends.

Unperturbed, Egil decided to carry his silver out into the wilderness with two slaves. When he returned, the treasure and slaves weren't with him and the mystery of where Egil buried his silver was never solved. Egil died not long after and he too was buried.

When Christianity was made the law in Iceland, Egil's bones were dug up and moved to a church. The priest of the church was shocked by how large the bones were. The skull was particularly big and heavy. Curious to know how thick it was, the priest struck it with an axe. The skull couldn't be penetrated. Only a white mark was left behind where the axe blade struck.

A skald's legacy

Egil Skallagrimsson was undoubtedly a complex figure. In one light, he could be seen as a juvenile delinquent turned psychotic murderer who rushed headlong into situations without thinking about them (although in the context of the time he was embodying the ideals of his society and a harsh environment). Yet this recklessness and bloodlust is tempered by limitless creativity and a gift for words.

Several times throughout the saga, Egil's head is referenced, such as when his head is saved by virtue of his poetry with Eric Bloodaxe and when his skull is being examined long after his death. This would suggest insight, intelligence and a massive ego. Because Egil was an egomaniac and his poems reflect that. This is interesting in the context of praise poetry where rulers and kings are the subject of the verses. But Egil always took the opportunity to make himself the centre of the poem, bragging about his deeds, virtues and accomplishments.

But in his poetry, we also see a man who cared deeply for his friends and family. His ode to Arinbjorn is a testament to that, who in many ways is the opposite of Egil. Another example is the poem *Sonatorrek* (loss of sons), where he laments the deaths of his sons Bodvar and Gunnar. The language is emotionally rich and complex, showing a grieving father stripped of all his tough-guy posturing and trying to process his pain.

Egil's life is certainly inspirational for writers and has inspired me to compose a poem of my own saga inspired by eddic and skaldic poetry:

> *Voyaging towards England*
> *came a voiceless man*
> *from volatile lands*
> *where he met a woman*
> *from the land of Caesars*
> *in the city of rain*
> *the string of their fate-threads*
> *bound together tightly*
>
> *From a culture cauldron*
> *came different daughters*
> *the number of the Norns*
> *whose paths were uncertain*
> *but had firm, guiding hands*
> *to protect and shelter*
> *against the blows of fate*
>
> *The youngest of the girls*
> *married a local man*
> *and she was like daylight*
> *bright and always rising*
> *while dusk ran through his veins*
> *making him mule-headed*
> *stable, steady, stone-faced*
> *faithful to each other*
>
> *In the changing seasons*
> *when leaves became blood-red*
> *a boy was born, healthy*
> *named after his father*

The Warrior Poet and The Wisdom of Verse

his names became reversed
From his earliest days
the boy was raised to think
upon a bed of books

A son without siblings
childhood was spent in care
during innocent days
at millennium's dawn
playing, running, learning
guided by family
to search for his own path
among a thousand roads

Along art's avenue
he strolled and discovered
new worlds filled with wonder
he drank from Odin's horn
scoured the forests and trees
leafed with precious language
spilling forth his pen-blood
to create his own worlds

One day, darkness crept in
sweeping over the boy
not as waves crash on shore
as the slow drip of rain
leaking into a house
until the young soul-seat
drowned in melancholy
of an older spirit

Sword-showers and spear-storms
were waged within himself
the lighthouse of the sky

seemed dull and far away
his sea-steed cast adrift
among jagged rocks and teeth
bulwark beyond repair
ravens circling above

The chanting of weapons
clashing steel and iron
the ferocious blade-wind
so loud and furious
it was too much to bear
in his thought-battlefield
so he gathered a rope
to hang high like Havi

But he cut himself down
at fourteen winters old
he realised there was
more living to be had
more fighting to be done
life-giver, Freyja-wise
tried to salve mental wounds
his healing would be slow

A couple years later
illness struck his uncle
who fell and hit his head
his father's sister died
breathless and bed-ridden
his father grew weakened
muscle wasting disease
spanning generations

At eighteen winters old
he escaped illness-talk
pursuing his studies

*roaming as he willed it
in the creative realms
making merry mistakes
weaving his fate-cotton
patchwork experience*

*The black cloud over him
thundering like Mjolnir
obscured his view sometimes
making it hard to see
the goodness of people
making it hard to see
a future for himself
with skies more blue than grey*

*Then he met a woman
from another world-view
different from others
he'd wiled away time with
while she carried no shield
she was a shield maiden
unafraid of combat
life's arena was hers*

*Her beauty was bone-deep
face star-mapped and shining
with eyes that told stories
look into them enough
to see a Cheshire smile
that would make Loki proud
look into them enough
and he would see his home*

*Did she come from a dream?
she was complicated
not a fairytale*

*he loved her for herself
how she went through the world
she healed his place of thought
calming the strife of shields
he grew into himself*

*The time finally came
to confront the disease
dogging his family
and so he was tested
'remember you will die'
he told himself that day
after the dust settled
he was a healthy man*

*Philosophy freed him
from the anxious fetters
plaguing stone of valour
'first learn the meaning of
what you say, then speak it'
determined he became
to share this true knowledge
from these seeds wisdom grows*

*Beneath the learning trees
of civilisations
he listened carefully
searching for the meaning
justice, wisdom, courage
self-control and patience
fated to keep searching
until his thread ran out*

*At the age of thirty
look back to look ahead*

*he sees how far he's come
with new lessons to learn
whatever obstacles
become the way forward
in the voyage of life
meaning is yours to find*

Chapter 9

The Deep-Minded Matriarch and the Uncertainty of Starting Again

There's a story in Norse mythology about Thor and Loki taking part in a competition with giants. Arranged by the giant Utgarda-Loki, the games began when Loki boasted there was no one who could best him in an eating contest. He lost the bet to a giant named Logi. Next, Thor took on a giant called Hugi in a swimming contest. The god of thunder was bested by Hugi's superior speed and stamina. Then Thor challenged anyone in the palace to a drinking contest and Utgarda-Loki gave him a drinking horn that one of his men usually drank from. Thor was unable to finish the mead in the horn and gave up.

Utgarda-Loki suggested that since the god of thunder was so strong, he should be able to lift his pet cat from the floor. Struggling and straining, Thor was unable to make the cat budge and this was the last straw. He bellowed that he would outwrestle anyone in the palace. So, Utgarda-Loki pointed out that one of his servants would be happy to take him up on the wager. When Thor saw his opponent, his blood boiled. She was a frail old woman and announced herself as Elli. He would not let this insult stand. Launching himself at the crone, Thor gripped her, but the more he struggled, the taller she seemed to stand. No matter what technique he used, the old woman slipped from his grasp or took him off balance. Eventually, Thor went down to one knee, spluttering, red-faced and beaten.

Through the contests, Utgarda-Loki had tricked the Asgardians with illusions. Logi had been pure fire, so no wonder he could consume more food. Hugi was thought personified and nothing was faster or more enduring than a memory. The giant's cat was Jormungandr the world serpent in disguise, whose grasp on the nine worlds wouldn't be relinquished. But Thor's toughest trial was Elli. Old age. The force that no being, mortal or immortal, could defeat in the end.

The presentation of old age as a woman hints at the importance of the elderly in Norse culture – and of the role that women played in their twilight years. According to Johanna Fridriksdottir, 'women's consistent characterisation as intelligent and wise takes on a new dimension when they are old – their lifetime of experience bestows respect, but their memory of things in the distant past and knowledge of the future often appears uncanny or sinister.'[1]

A figure associated with the wisdom and prudence of old age is Aud the Deep-Minded. One of the true Norse matriarchs of her time, her story involves deciding the fate of her family and securing the future for her descendants.

Daughter of a sea-king

Aud was the daughter of Ketill Flatnose, a Norwegian chieftain. Depending on the source, Ketill may have been in the service of Harald Finehair during a raid on the Orkney and Shetland islands. Or he may have led the raids himself to get away from the King of Norway's tyranny. Aud grew up in the Hebrides with her family, where she would be exposed to Christianity and embrace it for the rest of her life.

Given her father's status, Aud would have mingled with many high-ranking and ambitious Norsemen making a name for themselves across the British Isles. One such man was Olaf the White, who became the King of Dublin. He and Ketill were sea-kings, rulers who'd taken their power on the might of their maritime armies. They controlled territories that were directly linked to the oceans, securing passageways between Scandinavia and the lands they conquered. Neil Price describes how they operated within 'warrior manors – bases for the warlords of the sea, with hinterlands that kept them in food and drink, as well as raw materials to equip and maintain the ships. The farms of the surrounding districts could provide men for emergency defence and a ready supply of crew for the ships themselves'.[2]

Forming alliances with other powerful Norse rulers in foreign countries that could easily be accessed by the sea would have been to Ketill's advantage. So, we can imagine him offering his daughter to Olaf for political reasons.

After marrying the King of Dublin, Aud bore him a son called Thorstein the Red. For a time, Aud lived a relatively good life in Ireland with her husband and son. But that all changed when Olaf fell in battle and Aud saw which way the wind was blowing. With her son, she travelled back to the Hebrides under the protection and rule of her father.

Here, Thorstein flourished, growing to become a formidable warrior in his own right and forged an alliance with Sigurd Eysteinsson, jarl of Orkney. The two of them worked so well together that they conquered large parts of Scotland, including Caithness, Sutherland, Ross and Murray. Half of Scotland paid tribute to the son of Aud the Deep-Minded and he went on to have seven children.

Yet power can't protect against sheer hatred, willpower and strategy. The Scottish chieftains, pushed to the brink by Thorstein and Sigurd's demands, hatched a scheme to take back their country and Thorstein was killed in battle. This was terrible news for Aud, who'd lost her father not long before and now she'd lost her only child. Without her husband, son and father, Aud was left alone in a hostile country and the Norse were being driven out of Scotland. She was the head of her family and there were only two choices for her: death or survival.

Taking fate into her own hands

Choosing the latter, Aud took her grandchildren with her to Caithness and resolved to escape to safer lands. So, she devised the construction of a *knarr* ship that would take her family across the Atlantic to Iceland.

To pull back from our story for a moment, it's worth investigating the construction and capabilities of Viking ships, as they were a crucial part of how Scandinavian settlers became so successful. The dragon-headed longship is one of the most enduring motifs of the Viking image. But they were only one type of vessel involved in maritime travel and warfare, which could range from simple dugout long boats to larger transport ships for both people and cargo. Viking ships were traditionally clinker-built, meaning the edges of wooden planks were overlapped together and riveted. Through this method, a ship became strong, light and flexible.[3]

Then there were the sails, which could be made from either wool, flax or hemp. The sails would be greased with fish oil or tar to make it more weather- and water-resistant. The attire of the crew was also an important consideration, particularly for the long journeys that *knarr* ships made. The sea clothing would have to be insulated and coarse to be able to withstand cold weather.

As a *knarr* was a larger vessel with a greater expense, it would have needed to be a commissioned project that someone of Aud's social standing could afford. But to build it successfully, it would have required a team of skilled builders working together in what may have taken a year of constant work from around thirty men to fully equip the ship and crew.[4]

Fortunately for Aud, she commanded great respect among her people and the ship was built in secret in the forests of Caithness. Perhaps on the surface, Aud presented herself as calm and agreeable to the native Scots who were becoming increasingly restless around her. She may have asked her people to do the same so they could go about their business without suspicion and maintain the peace for the sake of her family. Inside, she would have surely felt great trepidation about the task at hand. To transport all her family, wealth and slaves without raising any alarms was one thing. To get them all to a land that they may not even reach only added to the pressure.

Nevertheless, the ship was completed and Aud personally captained the vessel to Orkney. This was no easy feat, as she acted in a role traditionally done by a man, a role that she excelled in, having the loyalty of at least twenty-five strong men to rely on.

On the voyage, Aud knew she couldn't let the fate of her family be left to chance. She needed to give her granddaughters the opportunity to wed into strong, reliable families and preserve the legacy of her father and husband. Breaking another tradition, Aud assumed the role of marriage maker. Stopping first in Orkney, she arranged the marriage of her granddaughter Groa to the most powerful family in the region and then moved on after resting. Her next destination was the Faroe Islands, where she brokered a union between another of Thorstein's daughters to an influential family. Both girls were said to have created an enduring dynasty in their new homes.

Aud then carried on to Iceland with her remaining grandchildren, Thorhild, Thorgerd, Osk and Olaf. The rest of the journey passed uneventfully. On arriving on Iceland's shores, the ship was wrecked, though her kin and belongings survived. Aud had come too far to let misfortune stop her now. She navigated over land towards the home of her brother, Helgi. He offered to let her stay on his land but would only host half of her party. This angered Aud and she left for the residence of her other brother, Bjorn, who was more generous and allowed everyone to stay.

In the spring, Aud carried on through Iceland, searching for a place to call home. She found it on a farm she called Hvamm and chose to make all her slaves free men. Sending those who'd travelled with her off to find their own way, Aud worked on improving the farm and giving the freedmen their own land to make a living. A man who benefitted greatly from his loyalty to Aud was the steward Dala-Kollur. Aud arranged the marriage between him and her granddaughter Thorgerd.

As a devout Christian, Aud had relied on her faith through the most trying of times and would bravely practise it in Iceland at a time when it wasn't popular. She erected crosses nearby her farm which became known as Krossholar. She continued to secure the future of her family, binding her remaining grandchildren to local families that would elevate them to powerful positions in Iceland's government.

Her final great act came with the marriage of her grandson, Olaf. At a party surrounded by all her family, she announced that he would be the heir to Hvamm and convinced him to marry a woman called Alfdis. It was said that she held Olaf dearer than all else. Her final male relative who carried all the strength and promise of his father Thorstein, grandfather Olaf and great-grandfather Ketill.

Aud planned the wedding feast for the end of summer and as the big day drew near, she sensed in her gut that this would be the last feast she would ever hold. The wedding of Olaf and Alfdis lasted for three days and Aud's feelings proved true. She died during the festivities, but her grandson and all her family would never forget her. A great cairn was built and Aud the Deep-Minded and her wealth were buried within. The story of her survival, of her shaping the direction of multiple dynasties would last through the ages.

* * *

Aud's life goes a long way to dispelling Viking stereotypes. First, the notion that they were exclusively raiders and that any woman who appears in the sagas must automatically be a warrior. Aud wasn't a shield-maiden or fighter. She was a survivor who used her intelligence, ingenuity and wealth to engineer a daring escape for her family. She came to Iceland to farm and settle, not to conquer and dominate.

The image of seafaring warriors going out to raid is just one aspect of the Scandinavians of the Viking Age. Many were farmers who stayed at home to till their land and work with sheep and textiles to carve out a living for themselves. That might not sound as glamorous or exciting as what pop culture would have us believe, but it's usually the case with a lot of what happens in history. Everyday people do everyday things to make their lives a little bit easier or at least more bearable. Aud was deep-minded because she understood that her situation had to change for the sake of her family, not just for herself. She was thoughtful in how she spoke to people, a consummate diplomat who moved her grandchildren into positions that were either the most pragmatic or political choices.

Even into old age, she remained a force to be reckoned with and it's instructive of how to look at the elderly in our society. These are people who've lived a wealth of experiences, who've probably forgotten more than we'll ever know. Yet it's sometimes easier to think of the old as a burden that should be kept out of sight. Instead, we should look to learn how we can, to hear their stories, to see what does and what doesn't align with our value systems and make an informed decision. That is how we can start to become as deep-minded as Aud.

Chapter 10

The Vikings of the East and the Founding of a New Kingdom

When looking at the start of Viking expansion, it's usually done from the Western perspective on the attack on the Lindisfarne monastery in England. This is because it was written down and recorded in texts like the *Anglo-Saxon Chronicle*. From an archaeological point of view, Viking expansion started in the East, with a raid that predated the Lindisfarne attack by forty years.

In 750 AD, a group of Swedes came to a violent end around Saaremaa, an island off the coast of Estonia. We know this because two ships were found in what is now the village of Salme in 2008 and 2012. The first ship contained the bodies of seven men alongside a few weapons, meat and tools. The second ship was larger and carried thirty-four corpses. They were buried with highly decorated swords, practical seafaring clothes and shields. Many of the bodies showed signs of a fight, with blade wounds, blunt force damage and arrow penetration.[1]

This indicates a Viking diaspora that wasn't focused in one part of the world. Or that their raiding was a sudden phenomenon that took the world by surprise. Indeed, it was in the East that many Scandinavians found unprecedented levels of success and gave rise to a culture that would become known as the Rus'. It would also lead to the founding of a legendary dynasty started by Prince Rurik that went all the way down to the tsars of Russia. But before we get to his story, let's look at how the Rus' culture developed.

Early history of the Rus'

The first time the word Rus' appears in written form was in the *Annals of St Bertin* in 839 AD. The text described an envoy from Byzantium arriving in the Frankish court of Louis the Pious and a group called *Rhos* accompanying them. Louis was suspicious of these men and asked about their backgrounds and the answer was they were Swedish.[2]

The men were trying to get home after a visit to Constantinople (Istanbul); they had experienced so much hostility from local tribes that it had been safer for them to travel via the Frankish route. Interestingly, this situation reveals how the Rus' were not yet powerful or established enough to feel secure enough to travel without help. It wouldn't be until the tenth century that they would start to gain influence and impact the Great City of Constantinople itself. Alex Woolf also backs up that many of the early Rus' were from Sweden: 'In terms of the Rus' and their relationship with Scandinavia, we need to think in terms of time slices. It's made clear in the eighth and ninth centuries that there were lots of Swedes and Gotlanders travelling down the Russian rivers and the people that the traveller Ahmad ibn Fadlan met when he visited the Bulgar capital were Rus' and probably of Swedish origin.'[3]

What we see over time is a change in the meaning of the word. What may have started from the Finnish word *ruotsi*, which means rower, indicates the mobility and industriousness of the people who came to be associated with the term. Some scholars have compared the development of the Rus' to the frontier lifestyle of the Wild West, with fur traders setting up shop to trade with the natives and then gradually assimilating into the local communities. The Scandinavians travelling East encountered, traded with and fought against various groups, including the Slavs, Pechenegs, Byzantines and Khazars. All were part of a sophisticated trading system that carried portable wealth, enriching those with the will to capitalise on opportunities.

As these fair-haired voyagers poured in from their northern lands and established a foothold through the decades and into the tenth century, another word for them developed: Varangian. Translating from the old Norse *var*, meaning vow, the word came to mean sworn companion. Eventually, the Varangian Guard came into existence, an elite unit of Scandinavian bodyguards that protected the Byzantine emperor. They fulfilled a similar purpose to the Praetorian Guard of the ancient Roman empire and stood tall for a hundred years until English exiles started to flood into the guard to escape the Norman Conquest of England.

Perhaps the most complicated written text about the Rus' is the *Primary Chronicle*. The book was written in the twelfth century by a Christian monk called Nestor, who detailed the eventual founding of Ukraine and Russia. It's in this text that the life of Rurik and his family are detailed. According to the source material, the realm of the Slavs was in chaos during the 860s; the local tribes were being harassed and dominated by foreign Varangians who forced them to pay tribute. Eventually, the Slavs rebelled and had a period of self-governance. But this wasn't to last, as the tribes started fighting among themselves and another group of Rus' were called on to come and bring order to the land. They were three brothers called Rurik, Sineus and Truvor, who all settled in different places. Before we go any further it's important to point out that the *Primary Chronicle* isn't without controversy.

There's something deeply problematic about the suggestion that people who rebelled against their oppressors were incapable of ruling themselves and then begged to be ruled over again. There's a 'history is written by the winners' argument to be made, motivating a debate between Normanist and anti-Normanist camps. The first faction wanted to emphasise that places like Russia couldn't have been created without the influence and guiding hand of Scandinavians. The other side rejected that notion entirely, arguing the Rus' were something else and Norsemen had no hand in shaping the early history of Russia. Stuck in the middle were Slavic scholars that had to either accept that their countries were crafted by an aggressive foreign power – or accept another version of events that wasn't exactly in their favour either.

Under Soviet rule, it seemed there was censorship of the idea of a Russia with Scandinavian origins. And while this identity crisis conversation may have been relaxed in recent years, this is still the backdrop that we must be aware of when looking at Vikings in the East.[4]

Laying the foundations of a dynasty

Going back to the legends of Rurik, let's assume that this story is being passed on from generation to generation, with it becoming grander with

The Vikings of the East and the Founding of a New Kingdom

each renewal. It would follow the narrative that Rurik set himself up in Novgorod, while his brothers established themselves in Beloozero and Izborsk. When his brothers died shortly after creating their territories, Rurik absorbed them into his own kingdom.

The circumstances surrounding Rurik's death are unknown, but it's thought that he passed away in the 870s and left his territories to his relative Oleg. A skilled commander, Oleg marshalled support from the Slavs, Balts and Finns and took the city of Kiev from the Khazars. The city became the foundation for the Kieven Rus' and by the early 910s, Oleg had brokered a treaty with the Byzantines to recognise the Kievan Rus' as equals.

For all his military might, Oleg died in unfortunate circumstances. As the story goes, he was at the height of his power when a seer told him that his favourite horse would be his downfall. Taking the prophecy to heart, he had the horse put down. Years later, Oleg wanted to find out where the remains of the horse were. He found them in a field and laughed at his own paranoia and the uselessness of folk magic. Kicking the horse's skull, Oleg was about to leave when a snake that had been living under the skull bit him. Days later, he died from the poison, though he'd left the state of Kievan Rus' in a strong position. He'd shepherded and guided Rurik's son Igor and prepared him to rule.

The upstart prince

Rurik and Oleg had taken Kievan Rus' from a handful of tribes to a thriving kingdom. Prince Igor looked to build on his predecessor's success, but it didn't go the way he planned. His rule would come to be defined as trying to topple the Byzantine Empire that had recognised the work of his relatives.

The seeds for this ambition were planted through Igor's association with the Pechenegs and Khazars. The former were nomadic tribes of the Eurasian Pontic Steppes. These hardy folk specialised in mounted archery and battle wagons that acted as moveable fortresses. The latter were Turkish traders who had a firm grip on the Silk Roads.

In 941, Igor started a campaign to attack Constantinople with armies filled by Scandinavians, Rus', Slavs and Pechenegs. Igor was confident in his plans to take the city, for he'd heard that the bulk of the Byzantine forces were away in the Mediterranean fighting Arabs. But Emperor Lecapenus wouldn't let the empire of his ancestors fall without a fight and so he came up with a ruse. Fifteen scrapped ships were set afloat to engage Igor's forces and his soldiers took the bait, eager to seize glory and riches.

As the Prince of Kiev's army descended on the ships, the Byzantine soldiers revealed their secret weapon: Greek Fire. The chemical weapon blazed across the surface of the water, burning through enemy vessels and sending many to a watery grave. Igor's army retreated and, in his rage, the prince unleashed his forces on the countryside, sacking towns and villages and slaughtering indiscriminately.

In 944, Igor made a second attempt to strike at Constantinople, but the Byzantines weren't interested in another war. They met him to discuss a truce and bought him off with gold and promises. This new treaty ensured the Rus' had access to a lasting trade and cultural exchange that would lead to the economic development of Ukraine, Russia and other nations into the future.

But ever grasping beyond his reach, Igor still wasn't satisfied. He wanted more for himself. In 945, he assaulted the Slavic Drevlians, who'd already paid tribute to the Rus' but demanded even more from them. After collecting his gold and silver, Igor had another thought on the road while he was travelling back to Kiev. He still deserved *more*. Only the year before, he'd brought the most powerful empire in the world to its knees, had made them recognise his power and glory. The peasants of these lands would learn to venerate him as well.

Dismissing his army and sending them back to Kiev, Igor turned around with his personal bodyguards and went back to the Drevlians. Again, he demanded tribute and the Drevlians answered by killing his men. Dragging the lord of the Rus' out into the forest, the Drevlians decided to make an example out of him, a warning to those who allowed their ambitions to go unchecked and pillage their land. Bending back and tying down two birch trees, the Drevlians tied Igor's limbs between them. Then they cut the ropes holding the trees, which sprang back to their original positions. Igor went with the trees, his body torn apart.

Through the stories of Rurik, Oleg and Igor, we see how nations can form upon the backs of entrepreneurial, risk-taking travellers that venture into the unknown. Regardless of the historical evidence of Vikings influencing the East, the stories that have been told about them repeat the tenaciousness and adaptability reported everywhere they set foot. And where the Kievan Rus' are concerned, their influence would only grow in the days, months and years following Igor's death.

Chapter 11

The Saintly Sinner and The Brave Pagan

In the aftermath of Prince Igor's death, his wife Olga took command of the Kievan Rus'. A Varangian princess who'd married into the Rurik dynasty at a young age, Olga might have seemed out of her depth in the rapidly changing power vacuum created by her husband's death. She certainly seemed like easy prey for Mal, a Slavic prince and the ruler of the people who'd killed Igor.

The princess was in a vulnerable position because her son Sviatoslav was still a boy and far too young to take over from his father. Mal also didn't expect the Rus' to fall in line behind a woman and so it was to his advantage to come to her aid as protector and future husband. Mal sent a delegation to inform Olga that her husband had been killed and with a marriage proposal.

On hearing the delegation's news, Olga said, 'Your prince speaks wisely. As my husband cannot rise from the dead it's only prudent that I accept a protector for my son and people. I wish to honour you all with a celebration worthy of such an event. Return to your boat and come back tomorrow so I can make the city ready for your prince's glorious arrival. Know this: there's no need for you to enter the city by foot or horse. You will be carried by your boat on the backs of my retinue as the heroes you are.'

Pleased with this arrangement, the Drevlian envoys went back to their boats. When they returned in the morning, the Drevlians awoke to find their boats surrounded by hundreds of Rus.' Olga's people were true to their word and dragged the boats out of the water and onto their shoulders, carrying the Drevlians towards Kiev. In the near distance, the envoys could see the city ready to open before them. Suddenly, the boats lurched away from the main road and towards a deep trench dug by the wayside.

The Rus' hefted the boats into the ditch that had been dug on Olga's orders the night before. The princess herself appeared among the crowd, standing over the Drevlians in their hole. As her men buried them alive and their mouths were filled with dirt and gravel, Olga called out to them. 'How does this great honour taste? I do hope it's to your liking.'

Leaving the delegation to their fate, Olga returned to Kiev, where she had a message dispatched to Mal that if he really planned to marry her then he should send more than common warriors. He should send the most noble of the Drevlians to attend her, all the most important governors and chieftains. Mal complied with her request and when the new delegation arrived, the princess invited the nobles to rest and relax in the royal bathhouse. After they entered, Olga ordered the doors to be locked and poured fire into the room, burning the delegates alive.

Next, Olga sent another message to Prince Mal that she would agree to marry him on one condition: that he would meet her at the place where Igor had been killed and a great funeral would be held in his memory. She couldn't expect to marry again until she'd mourned properly. Accompanied by a small retinue, Olga and her son met with Mal and his men in the forest where Prince Igor had been torn apart.

When Mal finally met the princess he'd been courting so aggressively, he wasn't disappointed. She was beautiful, polite and virtuous. While Olga's servants built the funeral mound, Mal inquired where his delegates were. She told him that they weren't far behind and that he would see them soon. With the mound completed, a great feast was held and Olga encouraged the Drevlians to toast her late husband. They knocked back mead after mead, growing merry in the face of death.

Mal most of all. He was finally going to get his wish and win a princess and a kingdom that had oppressed his people for far too long. His eyes, heavy with drunkenness, fell upon her. Olga was smiling and Mal smiled back at her, raising his drink. If there was any part of him that felt her smile was sinister, he was too slow and sluggish to give it much thought.

The next thing Mal heard was the sound of swords clashing and the pained cries of his men being butchered. Olga ordered her soldiers to give no quarter or mercy to the Drevlians and Mal was killed along with his people.

As she did with everything, Olga moved quickly and ruthlessly. No sooner had Mal been slaughtered, she went back to Kiev and raised an army to meet the surviving Drevlians on the battlefield. At the head of the Rus' she stood beside her son Sviatoslav and even though he was only a few years old, he clutched a spear in his hand. Olga felt pride to see her boy on the field, to know that he was following in the footsteps of his ancestors who'd called to the wisdom god Odin to bless them in battle with his spear Gungnir. Sviatoslav tossed his weapon to mark the occasion, and even if it didn't go very far, the boy's tutor Asmund bellowed to the warriors that their lord had entered combat and they should fight with all their hearts to prove themselves worthy of his valour. This was all the encouragement the Rus' needed and they overwhelmed the Drevlians. The few survivors fled to the city of Iskorosten and barred the gates.

Olga laid siege to the city for a full year and when the Drevlians were weak and starving, they begged for peace. The princess of Kiev admitted that she was tired of the bloodshed too. 'Thrice I have avenged my husband's death. Thrice I have had my fill of violence and all I ask for now is one final tribute. Give me three pigeons and three sparrows from every house.'

For the Drevlians this was an easy price to pay. The city was full of birds and they gave Olga what she wanted. When all the birds had been gathered, Olga instructed her troops to tie a piece of sulphur to every animal. When night came, the princess's men set the sulphur alight and let the birds fly back to their nests. Iskorosten erupted into infernos and those who weren't burned in the conflagration were driven into the waiting jaws of the Rus' at the gates, cut down or sold into slavery. With the fall of Iskorosten and the conquering of the Drevlians, Olga had finally satiated her revenge-lust, but there was still so much to do.[1]

Ruling as regent

In the years after her war with the Drevlians, Olga led Kiev competently, making legal reforms and establishing herself as the most powerful monarch within the Rus' territory. She avoided all marriage proposals, even turning down the emperor of Constantinople. Olga's devotion was to her people and son. But in the 950s, Olga did agree with the Byzantines on one thing: Christianity.

She met with the emperor, who was enchanted by her beauty and intellect. He told her she would be worthy to reign beside him. Olga admitted that she was still pagan and that he should baptise her himself, otherwise she wasn't interested in converting. Accordingly, the princess of the Rus' was baptised by the ruler of the Byzantine Empire.

While it's been suggested that Olga genuinely wanted to be a Christian, there may have also been some political savviness at work. Having been baptised by the emperor, she had become a kind of spiritual goddaughter to him. To marry him would have been seen as religious incest and this allowed her to maintain her independence and control over Kiev.

Although Olga felt secure in her Christianity, all attempts to convert her son fell on deaf ears. By this time, Sviatoslav the Brave had grown into a strong and respected warrior, a man who firmly believed in the old ways and was far more Slavic in his presentation than Scandinavian. While he looked like his father with blond hair and blue eyes, Sviatoslav worshipped the Slavic gods Perun and Veles, sported a bushy moustache and dressed like the fighting men of his *druzhina*, his company of hardened warriors. He also shaved his head, styled his Northern hair into a long sidelock and refused to be branded a Christian, believing he would be laughed at by his followers. But Sviatoslav did agree not to persecute Christians in his kingdom, which was a small victory for his mother.[2]

Hail to the conqueror

As Olga ran the kingdom for her son and built churches, Sviatoslav pursued his favourite pastime and way of life: war. He expanded Rus' territory across the Volga Valley and Pontic Steppes, subjugating Slavic tribes and fighting the Pechenegs. But his real prize came with the conquering of Khazaria, the domain of the Khazars.

Sviatoslav's battle prowess was enough to catch the attention of the Byzantines who commissioned him to strike against their enemies, the Bulgarians. With an army that numbered 60,000, the Grand Prince of the

Rus' ran roughshod through the Balkans until at one point he controlled the largest domain in Europe. Only in his late twenties at this point and already with three sons to secure his legacy, Sviatoslav was on his way to surpassing the greatness of his grandfather Rurik.

Yet the Bulgarians weren't ready to roll over to this brash invader. The Bulgarian emperor, Boris II, bribed the Pechenegs to betray the Rus' and attack Kiev. Sviatoslav had a problem on another front. The Byzantines expected him to give up his new Bulgarian turf to them but he had no intention of surrendering any of his hard-fought gains. To answer the Pecheneg threat, Sviatoslav sent a general called Pretich with 10,000 men to Kiev.

Meanwhile, the jewel in the crown of the Rus' lands had been surrounded by the battlewagons of the Pechenegs. Inside the capital, Olga did all she could to help her people and keep morale going. But it was a losing battle and even as Pretich's forces arrived, she realised that they would be overwhelmed if the enemy attacked. With starvation creeping in, Olga managed to get a message out to the general that it was now or never: either the Pechenegs or the Rus' would fall that day.

Through guile and bravery, the Rus' eventually pushed back the enemy and within hours of Kiev starting to lick its wounds, Olga sent a letter to her son, damning him for not coming to her aid or his sons. It was enough for Sviatoslav to direct his troops back towards Kiev and take revenge against the Pechenegs until he was satisfied. Then, he prepared to return to the Balkans and his new capital of Pereyaslavets (modern Nufaru in Romania). For a final time, mother and son would have an exchange.

'I return to the Danube, mother. That is the centre of my realm where all wealth will flow. The centre of gold, silver, silk and fur. Where wax, honey and slaves are in abundance.'

But Olga would have none of her son's preening. 'You behold me in my weakness and are so quick to depart from me and your sons. If you are to leave, then grant me this final request. Bury me and then go wherever you must.'

Three days later, Olga died and her family and people mourned the loss of a great woman. Sviatoslav honoured her wishes by having his mother buried in one of the churches she'd built. And as per her request, the funeral was a modest, quiet affair. There was no grand feast for her memory. Only the voice of the priest who performed the last rites for a good Christian woman.[3]

Sviatoslav's final days

Rather than consolidate or stabilise his position after his mother's death, Sviatoslav rushed back to his new capital and found that it had been reconquered by the Bulgarians. In a frenzy of violence with heavy losses on both sides, Sviatoslav was ultimately successful in retaking Pereyaslavetes.

Next on his hit list was the Byzantines. He announced that he was coming to conquer Constantinople and at first, the empire pretended they were interested in making peace. But really, they were assessing the Rus' prince's strength and when they were confident they could overwhelm him, they met his army in the field.

Despite the Rus' being terrified, Sviatoslav is said to have given a rousing speech. 'Let us not be dishonoured. Let us not disgrace the Rus'. Let us meet the enemy head-on and sacrifice for our people. I will march beside you and if you see my head fall, look to your own. For wherever you see heads fall, we will lay down our own.'

Emboldened by their Grand Prince's words, the Rus' cut through the Byzantines, winning victory after victory on their road to Constantinople. But not every fight could be won and Sviatoslav suffered a crippling defeat at the Battle of Arcadiopolis in 970. Retreating to the Bulgarian town of Dorostolon, Sviatoslav held out in a siege of sixty-five days until he was forced to come to terms with the Byzantine emperor John Tzimiskes. Sviatoslav relinquished his power over the Balkans as his army haemorrhaged men from famine and weakness.

Determined to return to Kiev, Sviatoslav and his *druzhina* attempted to cross the Dnieper River, only to be hounded by Pechenegs led by a chieftain called Kurja. Sviatoslav fought his pursuers through the winter and into the spring of 972, but his company was exhausted in a final ambush. The Grand Prince of the Rus' died in battle and according to legend, Kurja had Sviatoslav's body decapitated. His skull was inlaid with gold and turned into a drinking cup, a trophy Kurja would often bring out when he was telling his stories.[4]

*   *   *

Centuries after their deaths, Olga and her son continued to have a lasting impact on history. In 1549, she was canonised by the Eastern Orthodox Church because of her efforts to spread Christianity throughout Russia (even though it was her grandson Vladimir who converted all the Rus' into the faith).

Sviatoslav changed the direction of his people forever. The Rus' had become something more than traders and raiders in their journey to the East, but the Norse who had held all the power in these societies were gone. This may have been because all the Scandinavian elite had been killed during Sviatoslav's wars and in the power vacuum, Slavic nobility filled the space. The Rus' took on their own identity while still maintaining the warrior spirit that had brought them to the dance.

If a woman as bloodthirsty and vengeful as Olga can be made a saint and if someone as war-hungry as Sviatoslav the Brave can shape a people, then what does that say about us? It says that we're all saints and sinners. That we're capable of doing one thing and then being judged for something else. We're also bound within the boxes of our times but can choose to push against those walls to chart our own destinies. The Rus' certainly did and entire nations were forged by their actions.

Chapter 12

The Well-Travelled Voyager and The Mystery of Runes

In the south of Sweden, there are some structures that are truly a sight to behold. Large stones with detailed inscriptions and symbols carved into the surface piece together a story and the emotional handiwork of the scenes they depict. Depending on scholarly research, these mysterious runestones number between twenty-one to thirty[1] and all commemorate the life of a Viking called Ingvar the Far-Travelled.

Collectively called the Ingvar Runestones, the tableaus offer a fascinating insight into eleventh-century Swedish expansion across the Caspian Sea and into territory that is now modern Georgia. The nature and purpose of the runestones, alongside the historical accuracy of Ingvar's life, are open to debate and this chapter will explore those connections. Everything known about Ingvar's experiences is recorded in a few legendary sources. The first is the *Yngvars saga vidforla*, which may have been written by the Christian monk Oddr Snorrason in the twelfth century that was probably translated from oral traditions he'd encountered.

According to the saga, Ingvar was the son of a Swedish king and great-grandson of the tenth-century monarch Eric Segersall. He set off on an expedition with a large gathering of ships (perhaps thirty with around 700 men) towards Serkland, between the Black Sea and the Caspian Sea. Along the way, Ingvar and his men encountered several fantastical misfortunes. They had to fight their way through cyclops and dragons, the latter being a popular motif for Norse sagas that's explored in detail in chapters 1 and 3. The expedition was disastrous and Ingvar died through unknown circumstances at the age of twenty-five. Of all the ships, only one came back to Sweden.

Naturally, this story should be taken as fictitious, but what's interesting about this saga is that it gives a realistic date of when the expedition occurred, in the 1030s and ending in 1041 (the year of Ingvar's death). This differs from other legendary sagas like the Volsung family that are set in an ancient Scandinavian past, with it framed as being a part of real history.[2]

Other theories about Ingvar claim that he was the son of Swedish prince called Eymund, who was the son of Eric the Victorious and there's another source that shows his activities in the East. In the *Gregorian Chronicles*, texts that show the history of Georgia, the 1046 AD Battle of Sasireti points to a group of Varangians (Vikings) being involved in the fight. The *Russian Primary Chronicle* also records Scandinavian mercenaries being active during this time. The Battle of Sasireti was fought between the Georgian king Bagrat IV and his former general, Duke Liparit IV. One version of the story is that Ingvar and 1,000 men were in the service of Bagrat and they fought valiantly, but the king's forces were overwhelmed by an alliance between Liparit and the Byzantine Empire. Again, there are contradictions, as the battle took place five years after Ingvar's supposed death and the *Gregorian Chronicles* claims that Ingvar fought for Liparit.[3]

Returning to the Ingvar runestones, each one follows a similar style of mentioning the name of the people who created the monument, who the memorial is for and where they travelled. Some examples include an inscription that reads, 'Tola had this stone raised in memory of her son Haraldr, Ingvarr's brother. They travelled valiantly/far for gold,/and in the east/gave food to the eagle./They died in the south in Serkland.' Another is, 'Hrodleifr raised this stone in memory of her father Skarfr. He travelled with Ingvarr.'[4]

Despite it being unclear if the runestones are referring to more than one Ingvar, we can feel the emotion that seeped into the rock from those who were left behind, those who wished to preserve the memories of their loved ones. Viking runes have a long history of being otherworldly, mysterious and beautiful.

The magic of runes

In Norse mythology, runes originate with Odin when he hung himself for nine days and nine nights on the World Tree in sacrifice to himself. In the *Havamal*, the Aesir king described the power of the runes: 'I took up the runes, screaming I took them,/And fell from the tree./. ... I began to thrive, and much wisdom got,/I grew and all was well./Each word led to a word,/Each deed led to another deed./You will find runes and signs to read,/That the Dread Speaker has stained,/And the mighty gods made,/And the most famed of gods has carved.'[5]

Odin goes on to describe all the perks and benefits that rune magic provides, which ranges from healing and protecting against the sting of swords to defending against countermagic and raising the dead. Odin being Odin never tells the reader how to use rune magic, only that he knows it.

We also see specific types of runes used throughout the sagas e.g. Chapter 8's Egil Skallagrimsson is adept at speech-runes that contribute to his gift with words and protection-runes that aid him in his battles against sworn enemies Eric Bloodaxe and his wife Gunnhild.

Taken out of a magical context and put into reality, runes weren't created exclusively by the Norse. They have their origin as an alphabet of sounds from earlier Germanic tribes and the Latin of the Romans. Generally speaking, there are two versions of the runic alphabet. The first is the older *futhark*, which reads as f-u-þ-a-r-k and is pronounced with the 'th' sound. This has twenty-four signs, while the second version is the younger *futhark*, which has sixteen signs. The development of the shorter alphabet was likely a practical need that helped rune writers and carvers spell phrases out.[6]

There are also specific symbols that have been associated with Norse runes. Their origins are more dubious, perhaps a combination of medieval and New Age melding. For instance, the *Vegvisir*, which is framed as a kind of runic compass for lost travellers to find their way home, was recorded centuries after the Viking Age in the Icelandic *Huld* manuscript. There's no guarantee that it's an authentic Norse symbol.[7]

Another interesting sigil is the Helm of Awe, which appears as a circle with eight spiked tridents shooting out from the centre. Associated with might and dark protection, the Helm of Awe is mentioned in the saga of the Volsungs and was used by the dragon Fafnir to explain his invincibility. The arms of the Helm may also feature letters from the runic alphabet, reflecting a powerful symbol favoured in Germanic Iron Age communities and Viking Age Scandinavia.[8]

Now, given the diversity of runes, it's useful to ask the question as to how much they were understood by people across different rungs of Norse society. For a period, in the study of runes, there was the assumption that they were the province of the elite, that only the wealthy could afford to erect the monuments and have highly detailed markings carved into stone. But this myth was debunked by the discovery of hundreds of wooden blocks carved with runes in Bergen and Trondheim. The runes show a window into the day-to-day life of average people, featuring love notes, dirty jokes, shopping lists and drunken regrets.[9] This act of inscribing and carving runes probably served a deeper purpose than books could fulfil for the people who left them behind.

We may never know what happened to Ingvar the Far-Travelled on his expedition, but he travelled farther than many others of his age through the carvings that celebrate his life. He traversed the swan-roads of time and space to our modern era, just like every other Viking memory and thought immortalised in the runes.

Chapter 13

The Wanderluster and The Mediterranean Sojourn

The day was hot and humid. Two armies glared at each other from across the field. On one side, the hard-bitten warriors of Ragnar Lodbrok, king of Denmark; on the other, the implacable warwolves of Sorle, ruler of the Swedes. The Danish king, having wanted to avoid a bloodbath, agreed to a duel between a small band from both sides. Accompanying him were his three sons Fridleif, Radbard and Bjorn.

Bjorn stayed close to his siblings and father, watching the expressions on their faces. He turned his head to study their foes. Sorle had chosen the champion Starkad and Starkard had chosen his seven sons to fight at his side. The prospect of fighting against a larger force got Bjorn's blood up and he looked back to his father and brothers for a final time, recognising the battle-speak between them. Enough words had been spent. To Bjorn, only one thing mattered: to protect his family at any cost and prove himself worthy of Ragnar.

As he raised his axe, Bjorn felt something in the air. Perhaps it was the valkyries screaming past him. Perhaps it was the *disir*, the female spirits that watched over his clan and guided each swing and strike that he made. Whatever it was, Bjorn lost himself to the rhythm and flow of battle until he was left standing with his father and brothers, Starkad and his sons lying dead at their feet. With the fighting frenzy slipping away, Bjorn became conscious of injury. He checked his armour and body. He remained unbloodied, unpierced, unbroken. So impressed was Ragnar with his son's bravery that he left Sweden in his hands to govern.

From that day forward Bjorn would also carry a new name, a name that spoke of his strength and imperviousness: Bjorn Ironside.[1] The life of Bjorn Ironside is as legendary as those of his father Ragnar and brother

Ivar the Boneless. It's also an interesting case study for looking at Viking raids in the Mediterranean.

Raiding in new waters

While the exact date of the first raid of the Iberian Peninsula and Al-Andalus (Muslim Spain) is hard to determine, some ideas can be seen in the story of Don Teudo Rico and his defeat of the Norsemen in 842. According to the story, the Norse first landed in the fishing port of Luarca, close to the city of Gijon. Don Rico and his soldiers drove them off and killed a Norse chieftain with his mace. A plaque was even created to commemorate the victory.

In Arabic texts, there's a strong indication of the fear these Northern raiders inspired. According to the historian Ibn Idhari, who may have been referring to a similar stretch of time when the Norse moved on to Al-Andalus, they 'arrived in about 80 ships. One might say they had, as it were, filled the ocean with dark red birds, in the same way as they had filled the hearts of men with fear and trembling. After landing at Lisbon, they sailed to Cadiz, then to Sidonia, then to Seville. They besieged this city and took it by storm.'[2]

So, while Bjorn Ironside wasn't the first Norseman to reach the Mediterranean and even though his expeditions are filled with fantastic elements befitting a legendary saga, the stories of his raids show the ingenuity and tenacity of the Scandinavians who journeyed south.

In the 850s, Bjorn set out to raid Francia with either his brother Hvitserk or another accomplished leader called Hastein and kept going along the Frankish coast, voyaging beyond the waters that Ragnar Lodbrok had raided. An early attack on the city of Santiago de Compostela didn't go to plan for Bjorn and his co-captain, but it didn't deter them from moving forward. At some point, the raiders came into conflict with Muhammad I, the Emir of Cordoba, whose forces burned longships with the perennial repeller of Norse ferocity and grit: Greek Fire. Bjorn made the decision to try his luck elsewhere and pushed further south, passing through the Gibraltar Straits. In these warm, Mediterranean waters, Bjorn finally found success, being responsible for plundering some of the cities that Ibn Idhari mentioned in his damning prose.

Bjorn's next target was the coast of North Africa, where he led raids against the Emirate of Nikor, going so far as to hold it for a week. The Norse took Moorish slaves, whom they called *blamenn* and sold on in Irish slave markets.

The man named Ironside carried on plundering into the south of Francia in the area that would become the French Riviera and settling down into a strategic position for the winter. In the spring, Bjorn guided his ships deep up the River Rhône, sacking as he went. But on reaching the city of Valence, they were pushed back.

Changing course again, Bjorn directed his battle-tested warriors towards Italy and into the shadow of a city that had birthed one of history's greatest empires. Bjorn caught wind that he was near Rome and wanted to plunder the Holy City. In one of the most famous legendary examples of Viking guile, messages were sent to Rome to inform the clergy that the Norse leader had died. But his last wishes had been to convert to Christianity, and he wanted to be buried on holy ground.

The Christian leaders swallowed the lie and opened the gates to let in a coffin carried by a small gathering of Norse pallbearers. On reaching the main cathedral, Ironside (or Hastein depending on the sources) pounced from his coffin and he and his men revealed their weapons. They cut through the crowd and flung open the gates so the Norse horde could rush into the city. Bjorn believed he made Rome submit to his will. Only later did he discover that the actual place he'd plundered was the town of Luna. Still, he revelled in his success. Moving on to Pisa, Ironside took more plunder and decided to circle back to the Straits of Gibraltar. It was finally time to go home.

Securing a legacy

Bjorn Ironside carved his name across the Mediterranean, though his violence and ambition had put a target on his back. Muhammad I and his fleet were waiting for him in the Gibraltar Straits and blocked his path. Like the blaze of some dragon from a Norse tale, fire rained down on Bjorn's ships until only a third of his ships remained. He and his most loyal followers were still able to escape and as they headed towards the

Loire River and back home, Bjorn and Hastein couldn't resist leading one final raid. So, they turned their attention towards Navarre and attacked the city of Pamplona, where they captured King Garcia and ransomed him back to his people for a large sum of money.[3]

After this final score, sources differ on the fate of Bjorn Ironside. One theory is that he never made it home, that he was shipwrecked in Frisia and died losing everything. A more optimistic theory is he was able to avenge the death of his father Ragnar with his brothers in England and returned to Sweden, heavy with riches and stories. In this version of his lifepath, Bjorn went on to found the Munso Dynasty of Sweden. In time, this great house would also become the ruling family of Denmark with generations of brave kings and explorers following the trail blazed by their legendary forebear. Bjorn was buried on the island of Munso, beneath a mound marked by a potent runestone. As to whether this is his true gravesite, there is little evidence to back up the claim, though valuable grave goods have been found in the area surrounding the mound, indicating the presence of a wealthy and respected Norse warrior.[4]

In Bjorn Ironside, we see the wanderlust of the Norse personified and there is something timeless we can take away from this attitude to life. Travelling to new places and expanding our horizons is a healthy and worthwhile exercise, both physically and mentally. Expanding the shores of our knowledge and voyaging through mental planes helps us grow, just as it can erode our sense of self if we go too far the wrong way. Travelling can be a means of escape, but it should never be to escape ourselves. For to find a fixed position within ourselves, a place to come back to means we'll carry our homes with us wherever we go. And as J. R. R. Tolkien, an admirer of Norse mythology and who found his own inspiration in the sagas, wrote so eloquently, 'All that is gold does not glitter, Not all those who wander are lost; The old that is strong does not wither, deep roots are not reached by the frost.'[5]

Chapter 14

The Exile and The Discovery of a Lifetime

The Norse who first settled in Iceland were entrepreneurial and risk-taking, even by Viking standards. This was because they originally wanted to escape the tyranny of kings and rulers and set up a democratic system that's still in effect to this day. Through the generations, many Icelanders kept the explorative spirit of their ancestors alive by discovering and settling in new lands. One of those people was Erik the Red, the discoverer of Greenland, who inspired his children Leif and Freydis to journey even further.

The main sources that chart the voyages of Erik and his family are the *Saga of Erik the Red* and the *Greenlander's Saga*, yet before we get into his story it should be noted that the landscape that would be called Greenland was not some uninhibited wilderness before the Norse came along.

The first people to arrive in Greenland were Inuit, setting foot there in roughly 2500 BC, with various communities arriving from North America via Canada.[1] The first Norse interaction with Greenland came before Erik arrived and is credited to Gunnbjorn Ulfsson, an Icelander who spotted the landmass when he was blown off course from Norway to Iceland. Later, another Icelander called Galti would attempt to be the first to set up a colony there on the eastern coast. Allegedly there was a saga of Galti that has been lost to time and the details of the first colonisation attempt are sparse. All we know is that it ended in disaster and Galti was killed by his own comrades.[2]

By the time Erik's family moved from Norway to Iceland roughly a hundred years later, stories of this mysterious land and the adventurers who'd disappeared trying to tame it would've possibly been a well-established story passed around drinking halls and the communities. By the time he was grown, Erik would be called the Red for his fiery temper, red beard and hot-blooded tendencies. Erik the Exile would have been another fitting name, as he carried a lineage of outlawry with him. His father Thorvald Asvaldson had been exiled from Norway for killing a man and had taken his family out to new pastures in Iceland. Years later, Erik would be undone by the same temperamental streak that would force him outwards into the world once more. After Thorvald died, Erik married Thorhild, a woman from a wealthy family and inherited land and property. On this land, he built a farm in honour of himself called Erikstad.

Around 982, Erik got into a dispute with his neighbour Eyjolf the Foul. Erik's thralls had accidentally caused a landslide, which the neighbour didn't take kindly to. Seeking compensation, Erik confronted Eyjolf and, having lived near each other, the latter was probably aware of how belligerent Erik could be. So Eyjolf brought some backup with him in the form of a man known as Hfran the Dueller. Swords were drawn and Eyjolf and his dueller fell to Erik. A *thing* was called and Eyjolf's family brought charges against the man who'd killed their kin. Erik was found guilty by the jury and exiled from his homestead.

Moving to another part of Iceland, Erik tried to rebuild his life. But his temper got the better of him again and he got caught up in another feud, this time with a neighbour called Thorgest, who wouldn't return property he'd borrowed. In the fight, Thorgest lost two of his sons. Neither man went anywhere without a personal guard, ready to do whatever they had to for survival. But the community soon tired of all the violence and another *thing* was called. Erik was outlawed again; perhaps when he was several cups deep in mead, he recalled the stories he'd heard about Gunnbjorn Ulfsson, Galti and the new land that seemed so inviting. It was time to make his fortune elsewhere.

Settling in Greenland

In 982, Erik the Red set off through rough waters and weather as temperamental as his own moods. After a week at sea, he arrived on an island that was larger than all of Scandinavia put together, the largest island in the world. He and his explorers found a harsh and rugged landscape where fjords froze in winter and rich bounty appeared in the summer months. The plains and surrounding waters were rich in game – reindeers, walruses, narwhals – while the land itself could be tamed with farms and livestock.

Erik and his people wandered far but that first winter they stayed on the eastern coast. Then they moved further inland throughout the spring and summer, Erik naming many places after himself as they went. Erik and his people stayed for three years until his exile in Iceland was over. Through those years, the explorers came to see just how tough it was to live on the land, that adaptation was the only way to survive out in this wilderness. Tally sticks were made to keep track of every item, counting each object needed to get by. Runes were carved on belongings to make it clear what belonged to whom. Food was preserved rigidly. Homes were built and adapted to anticipate the changing seasons.[3]

Even through the harshest of times, all Erik saw was an opportunity to be rich, to be truly free from the laws of a society too soft to contain a man of his bearing. He needed more settlers to believe in what he saw, in what he felt. All he needed was a name. Greenland. That was what he would call the place that had given him a new lease on life, for more would follow if they knew they were coming to a land with a good name.

As soon as he returned to Iceland, Erik wasted no time in telling anyone who'd listen about his Greenland, about all the opportunities that were waiting to be seized. His message struck a chord with many and in the summer of 985, thirty-five ships left with him, carrying cattle, clothing and goods to forge new lives. But only fourteen ships made it to Greenland. Nevertheless, Erik and the settlers pushed on, creating the Eastern and Western Colonies.

Having finally carved his own little piece of the world, it would've been easy for Erik the Red to play king like the old rulers of Norway. But he was still an Icelander at heart and so Greenland was set up democratically, where men would be judged for their deeds by their peers. He settled with his wife Thorhild at Brattahlid in the east. For his wife he built a Christian church nearby, though he never relinquished the old ways of Odin, Thor and Freyja. Here they would raise and guide their three children, Leif, Freydis and Thorstein, all who set off on their own adventures.

Soon, Erik felt the calling for another voyage, perhaps even more important than his settlement of Greenland. The colonies were in desperate need of wood and he'd heard of a ship that had travelled too far south on its initial voyage to Greenland. When the ship finally arrived, the captain claimed he'd seen a world filled with wood. The old itch to explore returned and Erik started discussing plans with his sons to venture to this mysterious place. Not long before they were due to sail, Erik took a tumble from his horse and landed roughly. This was an ill omen, a sign that he should stay at home. Erik would spend the rest of his life in Greenland while his sons and daughter struck out on their own. He would live long enough to hear that the voyage to the world of wood and vines had been successful. And with that news, Erik the Red could pass away in peace or plague, having spent his whole life struggling and scraping for an opportunity to find a place of his own.[4]

The disappearance of a people

The Norse who started afresh in Greenland did need to adapt to the harsh environment quickly; their means of survival was trading in various goods with other communities, including their prestige item – walrus tusks. The inhabitants clung on to their way of life into the 1300s, still carrying out voyages and hunting expeditions across Arctic Canada. But this way of life was a slow decay, as changing temperatures and circumstances robbed the Greenlanders of agriculture and food they needed to get by. Their trade routes became harder to manage and their communities became increasingly isolated, forcing the Greenlanders to the edge of self-sufficiency.

No one is entirely sure how Erik the Red's people disappeared. The final message from Greenland came on 16 September 1408, a message that a wedding had happened at a place called Hvalsey Church between a man and woman known as Thorstein Olafsson and Sigrid Bjornsdottir. On the ship brought back to Iceland from Greenland, rumours of witch trials and a culture that had cannibalised itself came with it.[5] Whatever happened to the rest of the Norse Greenlanders has been thrown into the realm of conjecture. We can imagine that many left for better lands before it was too late. For those who remained, their hardiness would be tested until it could be tested no longer.

Chapter 15

The Siblings of Luck and Savagery

The settling of Greenland was a major accomplishment for Erik the Red and all the Norse who followed him into the unknown. Yet for all the lore surrounding that expedition, it would not be the last adventure for Northmen travelling in the North Atlantic. Within a few years, Vinland would be discovered, a large coastal area that covered Newfoundland, Nova Scotia and the Gulf of St Lawrence. The discovery of this place, named for the grapes in the region, is popularly credited to Leif Erikson. Taking inspiration from his father's roving ways, Leif played an essential role in navigating ships to Vinland; there are varying accounts of his story with parallels in the *Saga of Erik the Red* and the *Saga of the Greenlanders*.

According to the mythos, Leif had established himself in the service of King Olaf Tryggvason of Norway. The king desired to make all of Norway Christian and in his young bodyguard, he found a capable man who could help spread his message into Greenland. In response, Leif told his king that Christianity wasn't going to be the easiest thing to sell. Olaf told him he thought he'd have luck with the venture and Leif said that would only be if he could carry the king's good fortune with him.

Sailing back to Greenland with a group of hardy men, Leif and his company ran into a storm that blew them off course. Moving through uncertain waters, Leif had only his maritime skills and luck to rely on, the luck he'd taken with him from King Olaf (who was slain in battle not long after his bodyguard had left).[1]

Days later, they washed up on land that was unlike anything the Greenlanders had experienced. Sprawling maple trees, wild grapes, golden wheat and countless other curiosities. Leif and his company moved inland and with winter approaching, they decided to stay. After building a longhouse for shelter, the Greenlanders settled in; a man in the company knew how to make wine from the grapes. Leif and his men got drunk and were content throughout the warmest winter they'd ever experienced.

When spring came, the Greenlanders packed their ships with all the new materials they'd discovered and set off for home. Along the way, Leif came across a shipwreck with some of his countrymen and took them with him back to Greenland. On his return, Leif was hailed as a hero. With his new fame, he was able to open the door for King Olaf's message and many Greenlanders converted to Christianity. He also earned the name Leif the Lucky, for his *hamingja* was strong and potent. It had been imbued with the strength of the King of Norway and although his luck had left him, it'd found a good home in the son of Erik the Red.

Eager to prove himself, Leif's older brother Thorstein mounted his own expedition to Vinland. But luck wasn't with him, as Thorstein blew around in ill winds all year until he came back to Greenland without a thing to show for his efforts. Around this time, Erik the Red died and Leif became the de facto leader of Greenland.

Another notable expedition came from the couple Thorfinn Karlsefni and Gudrid Thorbjarnardottir. Following in Leif's success Thorfinn wished to establish a permanent settlement in Vinland. A crew of 160 Norse sailed over and soon came face to face with natives whom they called *skraelingar* (savages).

Initially, trade between the two peoples was peaceful. The Norse were cautious, but fascinated by the indigenous tribes who travelled in small armadas of skin boats, brandished bows and arrows and slept in skin bags. They couldn't believe that the natives were willing to trade high-quality furs for something as simple as milk.[2] For a time, the relationship worked, but as history has shown from a colonial force trying to 'civilise' a savage world, there would inevitably be conflict.

Hero or villain?

Eventually, communication between the Norse and First Nations people descended into violence. Thorfinn's colony was attacked and even with the strength of shield walls and iron weapons, they were no match for the great host that intended to kill or drive back the foreigners to their strange ships. But in the centre of this discord, one lone woman decided to take a stand.

She'd been running for some time, following her compatriots back to the longships. Even though she was heavily pregnant, she knew that it afforded her no special treatment among the men. They would not stop to wait for her, and it wasn't long before she couldn't keep up. Behind her, she heard the relentless footfall of the warriors, the whistle of flying arrows dropping men who had fallen behind as well.

As the *skraelingar* closed in, she knew she had to act – for herself, for her unborn child. Picking up a sword from a fallen Viking, she faced her pursuers and ripped open her tunic to expose her breast. With a fierce cry, she slapped her breast repeatedly with the flat of the blade, facing down the host, and berating her own people, the men who'd run away like cowards. This act of defiance stopped the natives in their tracks. It startled them so much that they fled back to their skin boats. Panting heavily, the woman clutched the sword with one hand, belly with the other and turned around, heading back to the longships. She found her companions and they left Vinland. The woman was Freydis, sister of Leif the Lucky, daughter of Erik the Red – a woman who wasn't finished with Vinland yet.[3]

As a side note, it's interesting that this anecdote from the sagas focuses on Freydis as a pregnant woman. It wasn't her fighting prowess that repelled the First Nations people but the fact that her pregnant belly was exposed. It reflects the power of motherhood in the Norse mind, while also carrying on the tradition of women being seen as complex figures that show them having any influence or notable characteristics. Freydis is portrayed as courageous in her stand. Just as Chapter 2's Brynhild and Gudrun are noted for their feminine beauty and womanly virtues, who spurred their men to prove their honour. Freydis is no different in this regard.

When she returned to Greenland, Freydis wanted the prestige of leading a Vinland expedition for herself. Making a deal with two brothers Helgi and Finnbogi, Freydis convinced them to split the profits equally between them. She also asked her brother Leif for permission to use the house and stables he'd built in Vinland at Leifsbudir. With everything set for the voyage, the brothers expected an equal number of men to be brought with them. But Freydis smuggled five additional men onto her ship, which could have been for her own protection or because she'd always planned to betray the brothers. As it happened, Helgi and Finnbogi got to Leifsbudir first and when Freydis arrived, she ordered them to move because the houses had been intended for her group. This was the first of several disagreements that sprang up between the two camps.

Tensions started to rise, leading to the brothers creating their own settlement. Freydis went to them to see how they were doing and Helgi and Finnbogi expressed a desire for peace. To their face, she agreed, shaking with one hand while keeping a knife concealed with the other. On the voyage, Freydis's husband Thorvard had accompanied her and she went to him claiming that the brothers had beaten her. She demanded he protect her honour and that of his family, otherwise she'd divorce him.

Spurred into action, Thorvard took his men to the other camp and killed Helgi and Finnbogi in their sleep. But they weren't alone: there were five women too, women who weren't warriors, who'd come to Vinland seeking only a better life, who'd surrendered. Thorvard and his men didn't want to kill them and so Freydis took up an axe and slaughtered the women herself. She was truly her father's daughter. To make sure that no one would know of her betrayal, Freydis threatened to kill anyone who spoke of the massacre.

By this time, Thorvard and the men likely realised that Freydis had lied to them, but they were in too deep to go against her wishes. This lack of trust, paranoia and in-fighting led to the colony failing and within a year, Freydis had sailed back to Greenland empty-handed. When her brother asked her about the fate of Helgi and Finnbogi, Freydis told him they'd decided to stay in Vinland.

But nothing remains hidden forever and Leif found out about the killings. He tortured three men from the expedition to hear the truth of it. Even with this knowledge, Leif refused to harm his sister and so cast a curse on her descendants. He also exiled Freydis and her husband, repeating the cycle that had dogged their father Erik for so many years.[4]

Freydis's portrayal as either a heroic woman warrior or deranged villain follows the pattern of different authors having varying opinions on how to treat the Norse. Freydis's stand against the natives comes from the *Saga of Erik the Red*, which was written either before or after the psychotic episodes depicted in the *Saga of the Greenlanders*.[5] As the former deals with the exploits of a dynasty, it makes sense that the members of the bloodline would be shown in a favourable light. The latter showcases a broader range of experiences and adventures in Vinland. While embellishment from the writer is likely, there is less of a reason to be positively biased towards specific characters. Together, Leif and Freydis show the opposing extremes of what being in a new place can do to people, even if you're starting with the best of intentions. But when examining the migration and settlement of different communities, stories can only take us so far. The real evidence comes from archaeology.

Historical evidence of the Norse in Vinland

One of the most important finds of Scandinavians crossing over into Canada was found at L'Anse aux Meadows in the 1960s. Located in Newfoundland, the site was excavated by archaeologist Anne Stine Ingstad. Eight buildings were found, including a hall built in the Icelandic style of the tenth and eleventh centuries. Objects in the site covered ship repair and iron smelting. Plus, the buildings appeared to have been burnt, perhaps by the local natives or from fleeing Norse in a godly sacrifice.[6]

The L'Anse aux Meadows site made scholars reassess the exact location of Vinland, as the evidence suggested that it was too far north to produce the wine grapes that gave Vinland its name. So, perhaps Newfoundland was a waystation that gave Norse explorers the chance to resupply before moving further south into the coastal region of the Gulf of St Lawrence and the Miramichi–Chaleur Bay area of New Brunswick.[7]

Another site for Norse activity is Nanook on Baffin Island. What was previously thought to be a Dorset Paleo-Eskimo site contains anomalies in the remains. For example, a crucible used to melt bronze, an artefact that has been commonly found throughout the Viking world, was discovered. This suggests that we might have only scratched the surface as to just how far Vikings travelled in North America, with the North Atlantic region being one of the last great frontiers of Viking Age archaeological discovery.

As a final point, it's worth asking why the Norse chose not to establish a permanent foothold in the area. Several theories have been advanced, which include there not being enough settlers to create lasting colonies, pushback from the natives and changing climate. While the Norse were some of the hardiest people of their time, they weren't going to mistake unsustainable living for strategic adaptation. But their presence in America and Canada remains nonetheless, as it does across all the lands they travelled to and made a go at changing their circumstances for the better.

Chapter 16

The Hard Ruler and The Path to Greatness

The year was 1030 and a great army moved across the lowlands of Stiklestad in Norway, lands steeped in the legacy of Norse heroes. For the land had been named after Stikla, a brave shield-maiden who'd raided with the indomitable Rusla the Red Maiden in her attacks on the Irish. Stikla had fought by her shield sister's side until she could no longer when she put down her weapons once and for all. She settled in the area and the memory of her exploits lived on in the soil.

The army that trampled the earth beneath their feet was a patchwork of beliefs: exiled Norsemen, Christianised warriors, mercenaries and sellswords who placed their faith solely in their own strength and the coin it brought them. All of them served the same cause – fighting in the name of the exiled King Olaf of Norway, who'd returned to reclaim the country from King Cnut the Great of England.

Olaf moved at the head of his army and as they crested onto the high ground, the king saw the foe that awaited him: an army of thralls, bondsmen, *thegns*, landowners and peasants, his former subjects, ready to resist him. This army that outnumbered his own was led by a Cnut's general, Kalf Arnason.

Beside Olaf, his younger half-brother Harald Sigurdsson observed the throng of enemy humanity that was four times the size of Olaf's army. Then he looked to Olaf and what a sight his kin was to behold: dressed in a thick hauberk of chainmail and helmet encrusted with gold, his hands were full with a spear and a white shield decorated with a golden cross. At his hip, Olaf wore his gold-hilted sword Striker and he seemed to shimmer with the grace of God as he addressed everyone: 'The farmers may outnumber us, but it is fate that decides the victor. I will not flee from this fight and either we will triumph or die. In victory, you shall have land and wealth. In death, you will have the greater award of Heaven above. We must attack first and take them off guard and then push our advantage. If we fight too long, they will overwhelm us and so we must force their front line to retreat. Then they will run into the soldiers behind them and we will be able to kill more of them.'

At only 15 years of age, Harald was already an accomplished fighter who commanded the respect of men who would die for him and had accompanied him to the front line. But he was in awe of his brother, the way he could inspire action in his men and who had once brought all of Norway under his rule. He followed Olaf as they took shelter behind the shields and standard, and as the king arranged his army into strategic positions, Harald remarked that he and his men would cover the right flank until reinforcements arrived.

Olaf saw further than the point of a sword. Unwilling to risk his kin and knowing that their mother Asta had no more heirs to gamble with, announced, 'Harald should not be in this battle. He is but a boy.'

Harald took this response as a challenge. 'You will see me in battle. I'm not too weak to handle a sword and if needed I'll have my hand strapped to the hilt. No one more than I desires to give these peasants and farmers a beating and where men go, I will always follow.' Puffing out his chest, Harald composed a poem on the spot: 'I will dare to defend/My place in battle,/according to my mother's wish./Let us redden our shield-rims in rage./This young skald will stand,/battle-maddened before spears/and the swing of swords./Men harden themselves in war.'[1]

Harald was permitted into battle, though the fighting didn't start until midday. This was because Kalf's army of farmers was so big that it took them a while to arrive. When at last the battle commenced, Olaf and his people raced against the shield wall that had been erected against them, their weapons held to the heavens.

At some point, amongst the blood spilling, flesh rending and the grunts and yells of men giving no quarter or mercy to one another, Olaf faced down fighters that he'd been eager to meet in combat. Yet for all his valour, the king took an axe to his left leg above the knee.

Dropping his sword, Olaf fell against a large rock and called out to God, though exactly what he said was lost to the roar of clashing iron and shields. A spear struck Olaf through his mail, piercing his belly. The final blow came from Kalf Arnason himself. A quick, surgical strike to the neck with his blade. As Olaf died, so did the ambitions of his army.

It was as if Olaf's death had caused something in the air, something that couldn't be explained by anything other than the divine. For the sky slowly blackened and the sun, bathed in darkness, cast shadows across the land. Wounded, but alive, Harald had been close enough to see his brother fall. Now, he gawped at the omen that darkened the battlefield. Was it the promise of Odin One-Eye or the wrath of God? He couldn't move. He couldn't go anywhere. All he could do was let the Fates spin their threads. But as it happened, they were far from done with him.

The 'Last' Viking

The Battle of Stikelstad was a turning point in the history of Norway and with such a momentous event it's natural for there to be debate about the exact sequence of events that took place on the day. The solar eclipse that darkened the sky is a prime example. From a storytelling perspective, it's fitting to include the trope of a divine act that makes the battle sound more thrilling and godlier, given Olaf's status as a Christian king. Academics have found that there was indeed an eclipse in Norway in the year that the battle happened, though the dates don't line up with the sources. In the sagas, the date of the eclipse is the 29th July but based on historical calculations, the eclipse likely happened a month later, on 31st August 1030.[2]

However, the narrative holds that Olaf the Saint died, setting off a chain of events that would lead to his younger brother Harald Sigurdsson becoming the King of Norway sixteen years later. Also known by his nickname Hardrada (Hard Ruler), Harald in the popular imagination is known as the last Viking after his death at the Battle of Stamford Bridge in 1066. As we've already seen in previous chapters, the designation of anything final with the Viking Age isn't nearly so black and white. There have been multiple beginnings and endings across the Viking diaspora from West to East and this didn't stop after Harald's death.

In his case, it's more fitting to say that he was the progenitor of a dying breed. A breed that didn't die with him. A hard, ruthless conqueror that extolled all the traditional ideals of a Norse hero who fought with the power of Thor and the cleverness of Odin. These traits carried on through Harald's bloodline. As a ruler, he mostly turned his fighting spirit inward instead of outwards. He waged war within Denmark and Norway, fighting his own people, which is where the shift came in terms of the next phase in Norse history. There were civil wars across Scandinavia. Squabbling over countries and their crowns. Overseas expeditions that were about fulfilling divine or political missions instead of mercenary ambitions, well into the Middle Ages.

That said, Harald's life is certainly extraordinary and worth learning more about, starting with the events of Stikelstad and it was Snorri Sturluson who recorded his saga with all the panache, death-defying feats and machismo that one would expect from the life of the Last Viking.

Life in exile

Unable to move because of his wound, Harald was in luck: the future jarl of Orkney, Rognvald Brusason, rescued him and led him away from the advancing forces of Cnut. Going off the beaten path into the forests, Rognvald guided the young prince into Eastern Norway, where Harald recuperated on a remote farm. Rognvald carried on with his men into Sweden and a promise that he and Harald would see each other again. To blend into his surroundings, Harald would have had to live like the peasants whom he'd been so eager to kill at Stikelstad. He slept in humble lodgings, ate simple food and may have needed to till the fields and farm to keep up appearances.

When he was fully recovered and fit to travel, Harald was led out of the wilderness by the son of the man whose farm he'd been staying on. An arduous journey through the mountains brought the prince into Sweden, through wild lands that had yet to adopt Christianity, until Harald was reunited with Rognvald. Passing through the pagan realm of King Onund, Harald bided his time through winter, perhaps finally having the breathing room to reflect on his lot in life: a royal prince on the run; a dead brother; a dead mother (Asta passed away in 1030 too); an exile with nothing to his name except the will to survive. It was time to seek his fortunes elsewhere and so when spring came, he and Rognvald acquired ships and sailed east towards the land of the Rus.'[3]

A year later, Harald arrived in Kievan Rus', the domain of Grand Prince Yaroslav the Wise. Stopping off in the former capital Ladoga to recharge, Harald met Yaroslav's son Eilif and continued to their main destination: Novgorod, the New City.

A sprawling megapolis, Novgorod had been built in the shadow of the Byzantium Empire's glory. Yaroslav intended his city to be the gateway to an empire of the North. To that end, he'd built the Golden Gate of Novgorod in the same image as the Golden Gate of Constantinople. It was through this gate that Harald crossed into the inner city and inner sanctum of the Grand Prince at his palace.[4]

The sources say that he was greeted warmly by Yaroslav and his queen Ingigerd, who had been Olaf's sister-in-law. The former king of Norway had also spent his time in Novgorod during his own exile. Olaf's bastard son and Harald's nephew Magnus was also being raised in the Rus' court. Among these powerful relatives, Harald finally had the opportunity to turn his luck around. Yaroslav saw great potential in the young prince, putting him to work in his army.

Over the next three years, Harald fought against the Slavs, Pechenegs and Chudes, building his reputation as not only a fierce warrior but a leader who commanded and demanded respect. At 18, he stood as a young man on the rise in the service of the Grand Prince. Yet if Harald had intended to reclaim the Norwegian throne, then his hopes would be dashed.

In death, Olaf had become a martyr, canonised and hailed as the icon of a new independence movement. Cnut's bloodline had been ousted from power and in this power vacuum, a saint was a worthy message to build support around. A passionate advocate of Olaf's sainthood was none other than Kalf Arnason, the man who'd struck the killing blow against his former friend.

Seeking to restore Olaf's lineage to the throne, Kalf came to Novgorod to retrieve Magnus. In the boy, he would find an easy candidate to mould and shape, rather than the hot-blooded Harald that had seen his older brother cut down and betrayed. Any thirst for vengeance Harald had would likely have been quelled by Yaroslav and so the exiled prince's hands were tied. As he had in those early days of his escape from Norway, Harald felt there was more for him to see, more for him to do in the world. His desire to marry Yaraslov's daughter Elisaveta could never come to fruition because he didn't have the clout. If he stayed in Kievan Rus' he would never rise any higher than he had and for a man of his ambition, that would never be enough. It was time to move on and truly establish himself as a name to be remembered.

Varangian Guard

In 1034, Harald and a force of 500 men took their ships across the Dnieper River, sailed over the Black Sea and into the narrow straits of the Bosporus towards the place where all Norse in the East made something of themselves. To Harald and his countrymen, it was *Miklagard*, The Great City, the metropolis that was thought to have inspired the stories of Asgard, the home of the Aesir. To the Rus' it was *Tsargard*, City of Caesar. To the ruling Byzantine emperor and the world at large it was Constantinople, the power base of the Eastern Roman Empire that remained unconquered for nearly a millennium.

Its impregnable walls were known throughout the Norse, Rus' and Christian worlds and the architecture within was breathtaking for travellers and residents alike. From the imperial Palatium Magnum with its gardens, courtyards, throne rooms and baths extending between the hippodrome and the magnificent Hagia Sophia Church, to the bustling horse track that served as the beating social heart of the people,[5] this supercity where West met East was the ideal proving ground for Harald and his men.

His arena was to be the Varangian Guard, the personal bodyguard of the emperor that went back to the days of early Rus' and Byzantine interaction. Constant raiding and defeat had taught them to sell their services to the empire. In 988 the emperor Basil II was dealing with chaotic rebellions against his rule on multiple fronts. He reached out to Prince of the Rus' Vladimir I (the son of Chapter 11's Sviatoslav the Brave) for aid. In exchange for help, Basil brokered the marriage between Vladimir and his sister Anna. Vladimir sent 6,000 Rus' warriors to accompany the

Byzantine emperor and quell the revolts. After squashing the rebellions, Basil saw an opportunity to keep the burly, axe-wielding Norsemen around and the Varangian Guard became a focal point of defence for all the emperors that came after him. In time, they would be recognised by their two-handed Dane axes which made them an intimidating presence even when not in combat.[6]

The rules within the Guard were that they governed themselves, punishing their own for various crimes and swearing loyalty to the throne, not the person who sat upon it. A famous case of this happened in 969 when Emperor Nikephoros II was stabbed to death in his sleep by his nephew John Tzimiskes. By the time the Varangians got to the imperial bedroom, Nikephoros was already dead. Instead of killing his assassin, they bowed before him. Their duty was to protect a living emperor only. Another curious detail of the way the Guard operated was that on an emperor's death they had the temporary power to ransack the palace for 24 hours[7] (though this might have been hyperbole).

Regardless, the Norsemen in service to the emperor were able to become extremely wealthy. And this was a means in which Harald could increase his fortune and renown. Buying a position within the Guard, sources claim that Harald was hesitant to reveal his identity and went by the name of Nordbrikt. In reality, this is unlikely because a man bringing 500 well-armed warriors into Constantinople wasn't going to go unnoticed and as a prince of Norway and the brother of Olaf the Saint, Harald would probably have been seen as an even more favourable addition to the Guard given his royal pedigree.

Entering the world of Byzantine royals was unlike anything Harald had experienced before. The power struggles and court intrigues between the main players would give the most power-hungry characters in George R. R. Martin's *A Song of Ice and Fire/Game of Thrones* series a run for their money.

The emperor Romanos III had a reputation for being a poor leader and had been unable to produce an heir. Meanwhile, his wife Empress Zoe, vain and vengeful, exiled her younger sister Theodora to a nunnery to make sure her position would never be threatened. Both were the daughters of the previous emperor Constantine VIII and born in the purple, meaning their status as heirs to the throne was special indeed. There was the *Orphanotrophos* (chamberlain) John, always on the lookout to advance his position and those of his brothers Constantine, Nikitas, George and Michael.

John introduced Michael to the empress, who was besotted with the young bureaucrat. They made no attempt to hide their affair and it wasn't long before Romanos' health started to decline. In April of that year, the emperor suddenly died in his bath. His death, according to Byzantine sources, was at the hands of Michael and Zoe. The couple wasted no time in moving forward, as they were married that same day and Michael was crowned emperor. But if Zoe had been hoping for a better marriage than her first, she was sorely disappointed. Michael and John set out their own agenda for the court, cutting the ageing empress out of the equation.

Harald came before the new emperor and empress, careful in how he manoeuvred between them. Aware of the power of life and death that Michael wielded, Harald was content to be directed wherever he needed to go to fight, kill and prove his worth to the Byzantines. The prince's relationship with Zoe has been sensationalised in the sources. Snorri and the Byzantine historians seem to paint her as a lascivious woman forever grasping for power and the attention of younger men. But it's possible that she would take note of the tall, blond Northman who was sworn to defend her husband and that his own royal status would at least have some passing interest to her. For an idea of the complex relationship that the sources wanted to portray we can look to an exchange between Varangian guardsman and the empress early in Harald's career.

One day Zoe had been let out of her chambers to roam the palace grounds and saw Harald conversing with his men. Approaching him, she said, 'Give me a lock of your hair, Norseman.' This was no idle request as to own a piece of hair in the ancient world implied a sense of ownership over that person. Shrugging his broad shoulders and speaking with a smile, Harald said, 'Let's make a fair trade, Your Grace. I'll give you my hair in exchange for one of your nether hairs.'

Such a ribald joke could have rubbed Zoe the wrong way, given her spiteful reputation. She was well within her rights to imprison and do worse to the Northern barbarian who'd treated her as casually as he would some courtesan. But she went on her way with no punishment forthcoming.[8]

Harald was put to good use across the empire frontiers, fighting and taking cities across Arab and Christian territories from Sicily to North Africa, serving under the influential Byzantine general George Maniakes. He and Maniakes developed the kind of rivalry that stems from two aggressive personalities clashing with each other in an environment where the worth of a man was measured by how many bodies he left in his wake.

Between 20 and 23 years old at the time, Harald had won the support of his fellow Varangians and they hailed him as their leader. The Norse looked to their own to lead, operating as a separate unit within the Guard. A seasoned general and supreme commander of the Guard, Maniakes wasn't intimidated by the young upstart's posturing and they constantly butted heads until Harald left with his Varangians to pursue their own campaigns in the name of the empire.

In his telling of Harald's saga, Snorri naturally presented a biased view of Harald's accomplishments during these campaigns and being responsible for a lion's share of success. One siege had him take a leaf out of Chapter 11's Saint Olga's book by sending flaming birds into a city to burn it down and conquer it. Another feat came through taking an impenetrable city by cleverly digging under the walls and Harald and his men springing out to catch the people unawares. It's possible that Harald had been acting on the orders of Maniakes and wanted to spin events as best he could. Yet another off-the-wall tactic came when Harald told the general that he and his men should play sports outside the walls of a town to distract the sentries. Harald set up the games outside bow range. After a few days, the sentries were lulled into a false sense of security and left their posts. Harald capitalised on their complacency by having his soldiers rush the gates and despite losing men, he was able to take the town by nightfall.[9] With all these victories, Harald achieved his ambitions of becoming a wealthy man and sent his fortune back to Kiev for safekeeping under Grand Prince Yaroslav's watch. Overall, Harald did well for himself during the campaigns he participated in and any losses the Byzantines suffered were blamed on Maniakes, who was imprisoned for his rough handling of the emperor's brother-in-law but released again to wage a sadistic campaign in the Mediterranean.

During Maniakes' imprisonment, Harald returned to Constantinople, where he was promoted by Emperor Michael and elevated into the personal bodyguard. But Michael had always been living on borrowed time. Over the years, dropsy and epilepsy had affected his health and his death came as an inevitable blow to the people of Constantinople. Michael's death set off a reaction of shuffling allegiances. His nephew, Michael V, became emperor and dismissed the Varangians in favour of Scythian bodyguards. Not wanting to concede any power to his adoptive mother Empress Zoe, he banished her to a nunnery.

Even through all the changing leadership and political machinations, Harald continued to do his duty as a Varangian guardsman. The sagas claim that he even personally carried out the blinding of Michael V and his uncle Constantine when they fell from power and Zoe was restored to power to reign alongside her sister Theodora. Whether Harald was still in Byzantine at all by this time is doubtful as he'd likely returned to Norway to reclaim his throne. The *Heimskringla* makes the mistake of combining Michael V and Constantine, whereas academic research only ever showed that Michael V was blinded in an uprising, along with potentially fictionalising a love interest for Harald called Maria that led to his imprisonment by Zoe.[10]

But as Snorri tells his aggrandising version of events, Harald could see which way the wind was blowing. After Michael V was ousted, the tension between the co-empresses was suffocating and Harald had fallen in love with Zoe's niece, Maria. Tempestuous as ever, Zoe accused Harald of stealing from the royal treasury to mask her jealousy of him wanting to marry a younger woman. Thrown into jail, Harald had a vision of his brother Saint Olaf, promising to help him escape (which positioned Harald as the rightful heir to the Norwegian throne in the minds of Snorri's Icelandic audience). In the vision, Olaf is every bit the saintly martyr that he was turned into and told his brother that there would be a follower of his coming to free him. Miraculously, Harald and his right-hand men Ulf and Halldor were indeed freed by a distinguished lady. The mysterious woman isn't named in the sagas and is presented as only highborn. She came to the prisoners to inform them that Saint Olaf had appeared to her too and when Harald asked her what his brother said, the woman replied, 'The saint came to me in my sleep and told me I would be cured of my illness. He also said that he didn't want his brother to suffer far from home, even though he didn't always agree with his plans. After I woke up, I came here.' Out of prison, Harald raced to escape Byzantium and finally fulfil his destiny.

Prodigal son

Once freed, Harald reunited with his loyal Varangians and before heading for the harbour, he kidnapped Maria. Fighting through the city, Harald clambered into whatever ships he and his crew could find. But before they could escape there was one final obstacle to overcome: a massive iron chain blocking the Bosporus that could only be opened through gatehouses.

Harald hadn't come this far to fail. As the ships approached the chain, he ordered the rowers to put in twice the effort. At the right time, Harald bellowed for everyone to run to the back of the vessels, shifting the weight so the ships could rise over the chain. Screeching over the keels, those bold, crazy and desperate few who'd survived and followed the exiled prince of Norway could have been wrenched overboard at any second. Then Harald's booming voice compelled them to run to the front, tipping the prows down and over the chain completely. But one ship wasn't so fortunate. It cracked under the strain and pressure of the iron barrier, splitting in two and carrying the unfortunate souls down to the depths.

Yet Harald was a free man and clear skies were before him. He'd escaped Constantinople with his head intact and his fortune secured. There was one last thing to do before he could head home. Stopping upon the shore, Harald let Maria go and gave her an escort back to Constantinople. Whatever feelings had been between them, good or bad, Harald's path lay elsewhere. His final request was for Maria to deliver a message to Zoe. 'I had the power to take her if I wanted to and you couldn't stop me. Who has the power over who?' This girl whom he'd taken and let go would continue to be in his memory for years to come and he would give his daughter the same name in another time and place.

From Constantinople, Harald returned to Kiev as a man both rich in coin and world experience. The boy that had departed from the home of the Rus' ten years ago had grown into a battle-tested leader with renown to his name. Claiming the loot he'd left with Yaroslav, Harald claimed an even greater prize: the hand of Princess Elisaveta that he'd wanted a decade past. Harald and Elisaveta were wed in a ceremony that blended the ritual of Christianity with the revelry of pagan celebrations. Like Norse rulers before him, Harald had accepted Christianity into his life. Whether he was a true believer is another matter. Life in the East had seen him steeped in those traditions and when he was able to do so, he brought Eastern bishops and monks to Norway and built various Orthodox Christian churches. This would earn him the ire and condemnation of the Roman papacy, though Harald had never cared for whose feathers he ruffled. Kings, popes, jarls, emperors and empresses were all fair game in the pursuit of his ambitions.

With his family connections and wealth, Harald was ready to return to Norway, yet his home was in a precarious position. Harald's nephew Magnus had ruled Norway for the past few years and was in dispute over the rulership of Denmark with King Sweyn II (the grandson of Sweyn Forkbeard, Cnut's father). Harald could be the deciding factor in the war between both and he needed to pick his side carefully. To side with Magnus would make him subordinate to his nephew, while Sweyn seemed more pliable as the outsider trying to reclaim land. Harald was older than both and pitting them against each other could prove to be a worthy strategy on his way to claiming a throne.

Harald sailed to Denmark to meet with Sweyn first and decided to keep his options open. He then sailed to meet his kin and Harald was received warmly by his nephew. Magnus personally greeted his uncle and though Harald towered over him, the young king showed no intimidation. To his people, he was called Magnus the Good, but that didn't mean he was battle-shy or blood averse. He'd led the charge against Sweyn's armies, taking territory after territory in Denmark and had a way with words that made him quick-witted.

Harald boasted to the crowds of his adventures in Kievan Rus' and Constantinople. Magnus informed his uncle of everything that had happened while he was away: how his stepmother Queen Astrid of Sweden had rallied behind him to legitimatise his rule, how he'd shown clemency to the Norse who'd fought against Olaf, even the treacherous Kalf Arnason who had been named a jarl.

If the news of his brother's killer still being alive angered Harald, he didn't show it. He pushed on and asked how Magnus would prefer to divide Norway between them. Magnus answered that he would rely on the counsel of his subjects and chieftains, the loudest voice belonging to Einar Thambarskelfir, a friend and collaborator of Kalf. The man had gone with Kalf to Kievan Rus' and sworn an oath before Prince Yaroslav that he would act as the boy's foster father and protector.

'You weren't here when we took this land back from Cnut, Harald.' Einar puffed up. 'It's the people's way that we serve only one king at a time and it's King Magnus we serve. Know that I will oppose your rulership with every breath I take.' The rest of the chieftains fell in line behind Einar and Harald saw the decision he had to make as clear as day. He and Magnus parted ways without any violence, though his honour was damaged and he would never accept such a slap in the face without retaliation. Harald returned to Sweyn and the two made plans to seize Norway from Magnus.

In 1045, the new allies ransacked Zealand and other Danish settlements. Those displaced souls Harald and Sweyn spared were made to carry messages back to Norway and with the threat of a full-scale invasion of his kingdom looming, Magnus felt the pressure mounting. His previous skirmishes with Sweyn had bled his treasury dry and there wasn't enough money in his coffers to finance another war. Conferring with his council, Magnus decided it was better to have Harald on his side than against him.

Agreeable to his nephew's terms, Harald saw the benefits before him. He was still without land and could not take any tax. Far better to save funding a war out of his own pocket and protect and grow his fortune further with minimal effort. Now, all that remained was for him to sever his association with the wayward king of Denmark without being accused of betrayal. One night, he and Sweyn were drinking together, and Harald was asked what the most precious possession was. Harald claimed it was his raven banner Land-Waster, the banner he carried with him into every battle.

'Why is your banner so valuable?' Sweyn inquired.

'Whoever holds it in battle will forever be victorious. I've always found it so.' Harald spoke with pride, toasting himself and the standard imbued with the luck of Odin himself.

'I'll trust in the power of your flag when you've defeated your nephew three times in battle.' Sweyn prodded, perhaps light-heartedly.

Harald bristled and put down his cup. 'I know my situation with Magnus and I don't need you to remind me of it. That doesn't mean we can't come to terms.'

Now Sweyn put his hackles up. 'Is that so? It must be true what they say about you then. That you only keep your word when it suits you.'

Getting more belligerent Harald snarled, 'I've broken my word less often than my nephew would claim you've broken yours.'

Cooler heads prevailed and Harald and Sweyn walked away from each other. But Harald couldn't shake the feeling that something underhanded was going to happen. He told his servant, 'I'm going to sleep elsewhere tonight. Sweyn took offence to my honest words and I believe he'll make an attempt on my life. Keep a lookout.' Putting a log in his bed and throwing the covers over it, Harald left his bed chamber.

Indeed, Sweyn did try to murder Harald while he slept. A lone man snuck into the chambers and buried an axe into what he thought was the prince of Norway's skull, only his weapon got stuck in the log. In the morning, Harald called a *thing* so a resolution could be reached. Before the assembly, he said the alliance had been broken because of Sweyn. Oathbreaking was as natural as breathing for him, considering how he'd also broken his oaths to King Magnus.

Sweyn defended himself by saying he'd broken faith with Magnus out of a right to take his Danish lands back. He hadn't done it lightly and it was the only way he could claim what what his. He laid the blame for the assassination attempt at Harald's feet, stating the would-be king had planned it all from the start.

Aware he didn't have the manpower to fight Sweyn, Harald snuck away with his troops in the night. He reunited with Magnus at a ceremony to claim the title that had eluded him for all these years. Over three days, Magnus sent gifts to his uncle, sending shields, gold and clothing to each man, working his way up through the pecking order. When Magnus came to Harald he presented his uncle with a pair of reeds.

'Which reed do you accept as my gift, Uncle?' Magnus asked.

Perplexed, Harald decided to humour the boy. 'The one nearest to me.'

Magnus handed him the reed. 'With this gift, I give you half the kingdom of Norway with all its riches. You will be my equal as king of Norway on one condition. When we're together and when another ruler visits, I will take precedence in everything. You will support all my decisions and elevate me as I've elevated you in this moment.'

Harald thanked Magnus for the honour and reciprocated by having his gold brought before his co-king. 'It will be as you say, nephew. Let this gold be a symbol of our pact. It's taken me many years of great risk and danger to attain this wealth and I would share it with you. I know you don't have nearly as much, though each of us can do what we like with our share.'

Measuring devices were brought out and both kings balanced the scales with their power and money. After much drinking and carousing, Harald drew Magnus's attention to a large golden nugget as big as a man's head. 'What gold have you compared to this, Magnus?'

The young king didn't shy away from the truth. 'Most of my wealth has been spent on war. The only gold I have is my arm ring.' He took off his armlet and gave it to his uncle.

Harald turned over the ring, studying it, the familiar craftsmanship. 'Hmm. Not much for a king of two kingdoms. Some would say that this isn't even rightfully yours.'

'If that bracelet isn't mine then I don't know what is. It was given to me by my father the last time I saw him.'

At this, Harald slapped his knee and laughed. 'Yes, that does sound like something my brother would do. He took this from my father without good reason. Back then, it wasn't easy being a petty king in Norway when Olaf ruled over them all.'

The tension in the air dissipated and the festivities went on, yet this exchange was the first of many cracks in the dynamic between the kings of Norway.

Hard ruling

Throughout 1046, Harald and Magnus ruled side by side, sailing together as much as tending to their own affairs. It was only a matter of time before disagreements between co-rulers became the norm. Once, Harald arrived at a destination before Magnus and moored his longship in the royal dock. When Magnus saw this, he directed his men into a fighting stance and as his own ship bore down on his uncle's, Harald had the good sense to move out of the dock. He circled back to find that Magnus had docked his own ship and called out to him. 'Here was I thinking us all friends but then you showed violent intent towards me and my men. They say youth is impulsive and I'm going to wager your actions were down to youth.'

Magnus replied. 'It was because of my heritage, not my youth, that I carried out this act. If I'd have accepted this overstep of yours it would have tarnished my honour and invited you to continue overstepping. I will hold to the agreement we made and I expect you to hold to yours as well, Uncle.'

Other times, they clashed over the amount of respect they garnered among their people. At a feast, Harald and Magnus were visited by the famed skald Arnor Thordarson. Known as the Jarl's Poet, Arnor served the jarls of Orkney, including Harald's old friend Rognvald Brusason. He'd been invited to write two praise poems for the kings of Norway. As a lover and practitioner of poetry, Harald was curious to hear what the skald had to say about him. 'Which king will hear their poem first?'

'The younger one.' Arnor said.

'How so?' Harald demanded.

'King, everyone knows youth is impatient.'

The Jarl's Poet started off with the jarls of Orkney and his adventurers among them.

'Why must we listen to this fool drone on about nothing but his own glory and the jarls of the west?' Harald complained, likely still stung by the poet's rebuttal.

'Patience, Uncle.' Magnus interjected. 'By the time he finishes I suspect you'll have heard more than enough praise about me.'

Arnor transitioned into the next verse. 'Magnus, hear my potent poem./I know one surpassing you./Prince of Jutes, I aim to praise/your prowess in this flowing poem./Lord of Hordaland, you're heroic./Other leads fall short of you./May all your success surpass theirs/until the heavens are sundered.'[11]

Harald continued to grumble through all the poet's embellishments and presentation of Magnus's accomplishments. When it finally came time for his poem, Harald perked up somewhat and listened to the skald's poem called *The Black Goose (Raven)*. When asked his opinion on which poem was better, Harald said, 'The difference is clear. My poem will soon be forgotten, while the poem of Magnus will be remembered and recited for as long as there are men in the North.' Nevertheless, he rewarded Arnor with a gold-embossed spear and sent him on his way. Taking another drink, Harald muttered. 'I thought he'd never shut up.'

Outside of his pissing contests with Magnus, Harald had his hands full with matters both personal and stately. His wife Elisaveta gave birth to two girls. The first, Harald named Ingigerd, after his mother-in-law. The second he named Maria, a name that spoke of the warm Mediterranean and not the frozen lands of Scandinavia. He battled at his nephew's side against Sweyn and his ongoing reclamation of Denmark, beating him back once more into the wilds of Sweden.

By all accounts, the co-rulership of Norway lasted for two years and in 1047, Magnus the Good died in murky circumstances. Some stories say he fell ill from disease, others from poison. On his deathbed, he announced that he was handing over rulership of Denmark to Sweyn and control of Norway to Harald. But Harald had no intention of handing Denmark over to a man as slippery as Sweyn. The country was his by right. But before dealing with his rival, he needed to secure his own position back home. Magnus's right-hand man, Einar Thambarskelfir, continued to oppose his rule, as did other Norwegian aristocrats in the north of the country. Harald also needed to legitimise his sole rule with a Norse wife and so took a second wife, Thora Thorbergsdottir. Although Thora would never be recognised as Queen of Norway, she could prop up her husband and give him the dynasty he craved with a Norse son. In 1049, she gave birth to a boy called Magnus.

Travelling throughout Norway, Harald whipped up hatred against the Danes, trying to stoke his subjects' ire against Sweyn, who continued to escape the jaws of death despite Harald's best efforts to put him in the ground. By 1050, Harald was ready to launch a new campaign and on a no-show rendezvous with Sweyn's armies at the Gautelf River, he pillaged Denmark, travelling all the way to Hedeby.

At the time, Hedeby was the cultural hub of Scandinavia, a crossroads where the trading of Eastern and Western goods changed hands. When Harald and his people arrived, he razed it to the ground, taking everything not nailed down, killing and raping indiscriminately. After Harald was finished with the richest town in Denmark, it was little more than scorched earth, a husk that never recovered. When Harald sailed home with his loot, Sweyn finally met him with an overwhelming Danish force that forced the King of Norway to flee, throwing gold, captives and ale overboard to distract the Danes and buy time to escape.

Back in Norway, Harald imposed his will on his own people, none more harshly than the descendants of Hakon Sigurdsson, the rulers of the North and the family to which Einar Thambarskelfir belonged. It was these conflicts that gave Harald the name of Hard Ruler as he sought to dominate his land and silence any opposition to his rule.

His rivalry with Einar is case in point, which ultimately led to Harald ordering the death of the jarl who had put his nephew Magnus on the throne. With Einar accompanied by no less than 500 men everywhere he went, Harald knew he needed to strike where he held the advantage. When one of Einar's men was accused of thievery and dragged into court, Einar and his men freed him before Harald passed judgement. To smooth things over, the King of Norway allowed the jarl to come to his court and parley. Walking into the royal hall alone, Einar was set upon by Harald and his *thegns*. Einar's son got involved too and he and his father were killed. Einar's people, surrounded by enemies, could do nothing except let Harald have his victory.

The Hard Ruler's ruthlessness was so excessive that it made men who'd followed him for years question their loyalty. One such man was Halldor Snorrason, who'd served with Harald in the Varangian Guard. Harald had repeatedly stiffed and alienated him, e.g. by claiming to give him silver for his service when he'd debased it with copper. Arguments became more frequent between the former friends, with Halldor demanding a ship of his own when the king's poor orders led to his own longship being damaged. To placate Halldor, Harald took a ship from one of his chieftains, which was then stolen back. Harald set up a fleet to recover the ship but had to return it to the original owner to end the feud. He also paid Halldor off but not the full amount, leaving out half a mark of gold.

Halldor had had enough. He made ready to return home to Iceland and broke into the royal hall with sword in hand. Shocking Harald and either Elisaveta or Thora from sleep (Harald remained married to the Rus' princess despite marrying Thora), Halldor threatened the king. 'It's time you repay your debt to me.'

'I can't do this in the spur of the moment. I promise I'll pay you tomorrow.' Harald insisted.

'You'll pay me now and I'm never coming back to Norway when this business is done. I know your temper too well and what you do to those who get the better of you. Nothing you'll say will make me trust you and I'd rather be gone as soon as possible. Your queen is wearing an armlet that will pay for the debt you owe. Give it to me.'

Harald's wife convinced him to give Halldor what he wanted, and he left for Iceland, where he lived out the rest of his life in peace as a farmer. Even though his old friend called him back with the promise of wealth and glory, Halldor never fell for it. Still, Halldor took pleasure in recounting to his family the daring battles of his youth alongside Harald. These stories were passed down through the family. It was said that when a family member ventured back to Norway to inform the Hard Ruler of Halldor's stories, he happily approved of them as the truth. Years later, the same stories reached the ears of Halldor's descendent Snorri and he recorded them for posterity.[12]

Harald also finally settled his old grudge with Kalf Arnason. Acting through Kalf's brother, Finn, Harald convinced the slayer of his brother to return from Orkney to Norway on the promise that all was well. The king restored all Kalf's previous properties and income. In 1051, Harald had Kalf come with him to Denmark, where there was a large army waiting for them on the shore. Harald ordered Kalf to engage the

Danes first until the rest of the Norwegian army showed up. By the time Harald and his troops came ashore, Kalf and his men were dead and the Norwegians came inland for plenty of looting and killing as the Danes fled before them. Freed of one of his most hated enemies, Harald continued to ravage and take from the Norwegians of the south, along with demonstrating his Christian piety.

In 1054, the Great Schism between the Western and Eastern churches happened because an agreement couldn't be reached about whether the Pope in Rome or the Patriarch of Constantinople was the head of the faith. While Norway was part of the Western church, as previously mentioned, Harald preferred to bring in Eastern influences. He built churches at Nidaros for St Gregory and St Mary, also completing the church dedicated to Saint Olaf.

Well into the 1060s, Sweyn of Denmark continued to be a thorn in the side of Hardrada. In 1062, Harald wanted to settle their rivalry once and for all with a show of absolute domination. At the Battle of Nisa, he sent 300 ships to a prearranged rendezvous at a prearranged time. Sweyn used the same tactic he had in the past of not showing up at the appointed time, causing Harald to send home his non-professional soldiers who made up half his army. When the immovable object that was Harald met the irresistible force that Sweyn represented, the Battle of Nisa was a bloody affair.

On longships tied together, warriors from both sides poured onto floating islands of combat. Harald led his men onto Sweyn's boat, smashing the Danes with sheer force and ferocity. Although the Norwegians were victorious, Sweyn slipped away once again and Harald couldn't get his decisive victory. For all his dominance, Harald still couldn't occupy Denmark permanently. This wasn't a sustainable way to run a kingdom for either Harald or Sweyn.

By 1065, fatigue and the immense costs of financing a war forced Harald into making unconditional peace with his long-time enemy. At this point, Harald had well and truly established himself as an autocratic tyrant who brutally struck anyone who opposed him, Norwegian, Dane or Swede. He busied himself by continuing to make war in the south of Norway, collecting payments where he could and building churches.

While Harald was indeed a hard ruler, the sagas don't really pay much attention to his domestic policies. This had led some historians to emphasise the stability and prosperity that he brought to Norway with his military mindset. Harald was the first king to introduce a monetary system to his homeland,[13] which soon replaced foreign coins. This opened Norway to international trade and Harald established networks with Constantinople, the Rus', Ireland and Scotland.

When Harald made peace with Sweyn, he must have had some thought about the course of his life. He'd been warring on his own people and the Danes for fifteen years and had little to show for his efforts. But he wouldn't be denied one final chance at glory in an old stomping ground of the Norse conquerors who'd come before him – a land that had been settled by the likes of Ivar the Boneless and Cnut the Great.

Seven feet of English ground

In the summer of 1066, a man named Tostig Godwinson washed ashore in the King of Norway's domain. Brother to the current king of England, Harold II, and the former Earl of Northumbria, Tostig had an axe to grind with his brother and sought to unseat him. Through a complex web of oathbreaking and duplicity among the English nobility, Tostig had lost his lands and title, while his brother had seized the English throne and succeeded the previous ruler, Edward the Confessor. In his mind, Tostig was one of the most aggrieved victims of his brother's actions and he wanted revenge. He'd been back and forth across the English Channel, looking to strike up alliances with his brother-in-law Baldwin IV the Count of Flanders, Duke William of Normandy and Sweyn of Denmark. Rejected at every turn, Tostig finally came to Harald for help. Harald was sceptical of the man's intent, though he had a strong claim to the English throne having taken up the previous claim from his nephew Magnus. This was the opportunity he'd been looking for to truly secure his legacy and revive the old North Sea Empire that had died with Cnut. At this point he was 51, an old man by the standards of the time. He would do all in his power to make the invasion of England happen and prove why he was called the Thunderbolt of The North.

Tostig swore an oath of fealty to Harald and so the King of Norway got to work on financing the operation. He had men fetch coin that had been with Elisaveta, while he made plans on how to divide and protect his heirs. To England, he would take his first wife, their daughters and his youngest son Olaf, while he left his second wife in Norway. Harald also appointed his eldest boy Magnus as king and regent in his absence.

On setting out for England, Harald stopped off at the Orkney and Shetland islands to pick up additional support. Sources vary on where exactly Harald landed in England to meet Tostig's troops, though it's likely it was Tynemouth. From there they travelled and established a stronger position around the River Tees and the Cleveland area of Yorkshire. The sagas mention a prophetic detail that is unlikely to be true in terms of location. But it does offer insight into Harald's thoughts of the expedition and was used for dramatic effect to signal the outcome of his invasion. The Hard Ruler became fixated on a mountain and asked Tostig what it was called.

'Not every hill has a name, lord,' Tostig said.

'I'm sure this one has a name. Tell me what it is.' Harald demanded.

'It's said to be the burial mound of Ivar the Boneless.'

Harald's brow furrowed and he muttered. 'Few who've seen Ivar's grave have been able to conquer England.'[14]

Despite the omen, Harald and Tostig ploughed on along the coast, pillaging places like Scarborough. The town had refused to surrender, so Harald had his warriors climb to higher ground and toss firebrands onto homes. The thatched roofs caught fire and the town was burned down. The burning of Scarborough struck fear into neighbouring towns, which surrendered to the Norse as Harald pushed towards the Humber, navigating raging waters to travel upriver towards Jorvik.

The invading force was met by Edwin of Mercia and Morcar of Northumbria. One might have thought it foolish to engage Harald head-on when the Northern earls could have stayed behind the sturdy walls of Jorvik and waited him out. But the English nobility didn't have the luxury of time. All summer the threat of an invasion by Duke William and the Normans had been hanging over their heads and King Harold II was down south waiting for the invasion. Edwin and Morcar couldn't wait around for the royal army to come to their aid and so they clashed with Harald on the outskirts of the village of Fulford. While the Norse were outnumbered to begin with and pushed back, Hardrada counterattacked until the English were forced to give ground. More Norse arrived until Jorvik was forced to surrender, on the promise that there wouldn't be a forced entry into the city. Tostig may have convinced Harald to stay his hand as the former earl didn't want his capital to be plundered.

The Battle of Fulford and the taking of Jorvik on 20th September was a major accomplishment for Harald, but there would be little time for celebration. Harold II had heard about the Northern invasion and moved his army from London to Jorvik – travelling 200 miles in four to five days – to reclaim the city. King Harold arrived near Jorvik on the eve of 24th September, well away from the Viking encampment at Riccall. Hardrada and Tostig had returned to the encampment and expected to negotiate for hostages and English surrender in the morning. For his part, the King of England was likely aware of the Thunderbolt of the North's tactical abilities. The Norse couldn't know about the surprise attack, so Harold II sent soldiers into Jorvik to kill any spies. As Hardrada had only left a small garrison in Jorvik, this made it much easier for Harold II's people.

So, when Harald and Tostig came to Stanford Bridge, they didn't find Englishmen ready to surrender. They found an army of Englishmen ready to fight. Caught off guard, Harald found himself in a tough spot. He'd been outplayed and outnumbered and he was without his legendary mail shirt Emma, which had been with him since his days in Constantinople, a mail so strong that it'd never been pierced. However, he was still a Norseman, a king who would not go quietly and so he laughed off Tostig's suggestion to retreat. Ever the warrior-poet, Harald is said to have composed a poem. 'Advance, advance!/No helmets glance,/But blue swords play/In our array./Advance! Advance!/Now mail-coats glance,/But hearts are here/That ne'er knew fear.' Even Harald knew these words weren't inspiring and so he tried again. 'That wasn't a good verse. I'll compose a better one. In battle storm we seek no lee/With skulking head, and bended knee,/Behind the hollow shield./With eye and hand we fend the head;/Courage and skill stand in the stead,/Of panzer, helm and shield,/In hild's bloody field.'[15]

With that, Harald dispatched three riders back to Riccall to bring the rest of his army to Stamford Bridge. Amid this, a lone rider from the English side rode over to meet Tostig and his retinue in the middle of the bridge. The rider addressed Tostig. 'The king, your brother, would offer you all Northumbria if you agree to peace.'

Tostig stood firm. 'If this offer had come last year, then many men who now lie dead would still be here and England would be a better place. What will the king offer my friend?'

The rider, appraising the King of Norway, replied. 'He will give your friend six feet of English ground. Or perhaps seven, given he's such a tall man.'

'The king can prepare for battle then,' Tostig declared. 'I won't let it be said among the Norsemen that Earl Tostig abandoned them in their time of need. We will fight and die together with honour or win England with our strength.'

Returning to Hardrada, the king asked Tostig who the rider was.

'That was my brother King Harold.'

'You should have told me. For if I'd known he'd have never escaped. Hmm. A small man indeed. But he stood well in his stirrups.'

The posturing over, the battle for Stamford Bridge commenced with the Norse at a major disadvantage. It was about surviving the onslaught of the English until backup arrived. The advantage they had was that they held both sides of the River Derwent and the English would have to cross the bridge to stop the Scandinavians before their reinforcements arrived. Harald stationed trusted, hardy fighters to block the bridge and shield walls came up to fend off the deadly arrows of the English archers. Depending on the accounts, a single, giant Norwegian or the garrison of Norse *drengr* were able to keep the English at bay long enough to have Harald coordinate another portion of his fighters into a shield wall that surrounded him and Tostig. English cavalry hurled themselves at the wall, but the circular defence could be penetrated by neither spear nor arrow.

Seeing that this living fortress of men was impregnable, Harold ordered his soldiers to feign retreat. In their battle fury, many of the Norse broke ranks to chase after the English. The ruse worked and the housecarls of the King of England, who were claimed to be worth two Norsemen, wheeled back on their horses and broke the Norse ranks completely.

Even though he saw his men dying in droves, Harald Hardrada refused to meet a quiet death. The way of the Viking was a glorious death and so he rushed ahead, lost in the frenzy of a berserker. He swung his sword with both hands, cleaving left and right, moving beyond even the certainty of his banner Land Waster. In that great cacophony of battle hymns and blood fury, Harald didn't see the barbed arrow that came sailing over the shield wall and embedded itself into his mouth. Tearing the arrow out and spitting blood, the Hard Ruler went on fighting until another arrow pierced his throat and he died. The mighty Thunderbolt of the North had fallen, yet the battle waged on. Tostig lifted Land Waster, rallying English and Norse to his side. Harold II again tried to make peace with his brother, but it would not be so. The reinforcements from Riccall, led by Eystein Orri, arrived and they waded into the corpse-strewn fray. The Norse battled on and on, but even stubborn valour broke against the walls of superior numbers. By nightfall, Land Waster fell for the last time. The English had saved their country.

The next day, Harald's son, Olaf, surrendered to Harold II. Still determined to show mercy, the king spared Olaf and the Norse who yet lived. He allowed them to go home in exchange for never again returning to England.

Only the Battle of Stamford Bridge was a reprieve for England and its king. William the Bastard had finally made his move and had landed in the south with his army of Normans, Franks and Bretons.

Harold dragged his army back onto the 200-mile journey that had almost brought his soldiers to the brink of exhaustion on the way north. When Harold engaged Duke William at the Battle of Hastings three weeks later, an arrow through the eye stopped him cold. A lance running him through finished him off. One could imagine a raven flying overhead when the arrow pierced Harold's head, Odin and the Fates working in their mysterious ways as always.

With Harold II's death, the Norman Conquest of England changed the landscape of the country forever. But arguably it wouldn't have happened without the iron fist of Harald Hardrada and his own boundless ambitions.

He followed the pattern of Norsemen changing the status quo wherever they went, whether it was in the far-ranging cityscapes of Constantinople and Novgorod, or the political landscapes of their own countries, Norway and Denmark. The Viking Age didn't die with Harald Hardrada. It veered off in different directions as it had for hundreds of years. But for a time, all its qualities seemed to converge and burn brightest in the *hamr* and *hugr* of Harald Sigurdsson. Prince. Exile. Varangian Guardsman. King of Norway. Warrior. Tyrant. Tactician. Poet. A Hard Ruler.

Chapter 17

The Norman Conqueror and the Conquest of England

The 14th of October 1066. The day that England changed forever at the Battle of Hastings. The English king Harold Godwinson had lost his life after trying to stop two simultaneous invasions of his country from north and south. He had done what he could, but in the end, it hadn't been enough to defeat all his enemies, enemies that had once been his allies.

Duke William of Normandy had counted Harold as an ally in another life. Or, if not allies, at least worthy rivals that respected one another's strength and position. Two years before, Harold had been left stranded in Normandy, captured by a bandit. When William heard about Harold's plight, he'd had him freed and treated as an honoured guest. They had fought and bled together against William's enemy Conan II in the Breton-Norman war and after William had won, he rewarded Harold for his service with gifts.

While stories vary, Harold seemed to have sworn an oath to William that positioned the duke as his lord, that he'd made a promise to support his claim to the English throne without him fully realising what he'd agreed to.[1] But once Harold had declared himself king of England, any sense of civility between the men went out the window and put them on a collision course. Once William defeated Harold, he was no longer the bastard son of Duke Robert the Magnificent. He was a conqueror who extolled all the qualities that the Normans had inherited from their Norse ancestors. And before we investigate his story, we'll see how a band of motley Vikings founded a culture that would become one of the most warlike and successful European societies the world has ever seen.

The founding of Normandy

The beginnings of the Duchy of Normandy started with a Norseman called Rollo the Walker. By the 880s, he was raiding in Francia and had launched an assault on Paris in 886, governed by Charles the Fat. Rollo had gathered one of the largest Viking hoards Europe had seen at that time and brought with them ballista and catapults to aid them in siege warfare.

A brutal siege of Paris that lasted months, Rollo's forces finally breached the walls in the summer, looting quickly and then retreating to their camp, as Charles the Fat's reinforcements were on the way. Charles eventually gave in to diplomacy, paying off Rollo and his warriors to leave Paris alone and turn their attention to the Burgundians. Rollo went on pillaging and fighting across Francia and when he returned to Paris in 911, the city was different than when he'd left it. For one, there was a new king in charge. Charles the Simple must have remembered the Norseman's last visit and had no intention of letting history repeat itself. He offered a deal to Rollo by granting him lands in Francia in exchange for his fealty. The Northman also had the privilege of marrying Charles's daughter Gisele but would have to be baptised. Rollo accepted, becoming the Count of Rouen and the first Duke of Normandy. The name 'Normandy' comes from the Scandinavian word *noromenn*, meaning men from the North.[2] It would come to define Rollo's heritage and the Norse settlers who joined him.

True to his word, Rollo defended Francia against his own people and all incoming threats to the region. He and his wife Gisele were childless, yet he'd already sired children with other women in his pagan days. Rollo's son and heir, William Longsword, and his grandson, Richard the Fearless, would consolidate Normandy into its own distinctive region and forge the Norman identity to come. Over a few generations, the Norse married local women, adapting to Frankish culture just as the Rus' Vikings had in the East. This adaption also extended to customs, traditions and perspectives.

The Norman lords styled themselves as aristocrats, dukes and counts, distancing themselves from the pagan savagery of their ancestors. Christianity was their religion of choice and the democratic concept of the Scandinavian *thing* morphed into feudalism. Serfs and peasants became tied to their lords who held the power of life and death over the lower class.[3]

In other ways, the Normans remained true to their Norse roots. They had a lust for adventure and conquest that sent them out across the world, giving them a reputation as hated enemies and fickle allies, West and East. They were also looked down upon by the Frankish nobility, who whispered of the second-class citizenry and heathen blood that could never be washed clean from their family trees.

Perhaps this snobbery only made the Norman dukes more focused on proving themselves and combat was the best way to show their strength. The classic Norse longship gave way to a pure land-based fighting style made up of cavalrymen. Norman knights were arguably the most skilled cavalry fighting force in Europe, as they rode horses called destriers that were specifically bred to carry a man in full armour. The archetype that would become the classic knight in shining armour had never been seen before; they carried lances, swords and spears while attacking on horseback.[4]

Another unique element of Norman warfare involved the use of castles. They weren't the first culture to utilise them but the Normans may have built more than any other society in the time that they were at the height of their power. The first Norman castles built in England were of a motte and bailey style and although they weren't very durable, they were key to subjugating the country. Later, the castles evolved to become long-lasting and defensible. For example, doors were made from oak and held together with iron nails and set in stone arches. This meant entrances were reinforced and could blunt attacks from sharp weapons and arrows. Crenelated towers, another distinguishing feature, gave Norman archers spaces to fire and to duck in cover too.[5]

Normandy's green and lush environment also differed compared to the cold and hard-wearing landscape of Scandinavia. There was food and trade in abundance, though this gave rise to a kind of second-son syndrome among the Norman nobility.[6] What this meant is that a landowner with more than one son had his land divided up among his heirs and with each generation the size of the land inherited gradually shrank. The eldest son would always inherit the lion's share of the wealth and property. So, the last son would have to make do with a lot less or go and seek his fortune. There we see the Viking spirit come to the fore, just as with William the Conqueror.

Bastard born

William was born into a world where the odds were stacked against him and he would have to fight for everything he achieved. His father, Robert I, had remained unmarried throughout his life but one day he saw a humble-looking woman called Herleva from the roof of his castle tower. She was trampling barefoot on garments covered in liquid dye. Herleva felt eyes on her. Looking up, she saw the Duke of Normandy noticing her. So, she lifted her skirts up casually, enough to signal clear intent to the duke, who wanted her to be brought into his castle through the back entrance.

But Herleva refused to be snuck through the back like some commoner or whore. She would only enter through the front gate on horseback. Robert agreed and a couple of days later, Herleva, dressed in the finest clothes her father could provide, showed up on a white horse and entered through the main gate. From that day on, Herleva became the Duke of Normandy's mistress and bore him a son in 1027.[7] Herleva's background is obscured by history, with some stories depicting her as the daughter of a tanner and servant. Or, she could have been a daughter of a senior minister.

Robert and Herleva never married, meaning that when William was born he wasn't recognised as a legitimate heir to his father's titles and lands. Thus, he was William the Bastard, a name used as a mark of shame and justification by his enemies for taking power for themselves. Even so, it seemed Robert had always intended for William to become his heir. In 1034, the duke went on a pilgrimage to Jerusalem, though on the trip he became ill and died before he could return home.

At 8 years old, William was declared Duke of Normandy; the young lord would have to grow up quickly in the dog-eat-dog world of nobles doing whatever they could to become the dominant power in Normandy. William's youth and illegitimacy made him an easy target for strongmen, and he needed to be protected at all costs.

Throughout the 1030s and early 1040s, William had a revolving door of guardians who moved him across the region. There was Alan of Brittany, who had custody of William from 1039 to 1040. Then Gilbert of Brionne took over but was killed within a few months. More of his guardians were killed and it's suggested that William found the most stability being raised among his cousins William FitzOsbern, Roger de Beaumont and Roger of Montgomery, three men who would become valued members of the duke's circle of trust in the years to come. Throughout these challenges, William also had the support of his uncle Archbishop Robert and King Henry I of France; these connections would be pivotal in a decisive moment in William's rule. In 1047, he faced a rebellion from his cousin Guy of Brionne and several other disgruntled nobles. At the Battle of Val-ès-Dunes, William and King Henry defeated Guy, which was the turning point for the duke wrestling back full control of his duchy.

Becoming a stable ruler

William's next move was to disarm the other rebellious nobles not through sheer force of will but through strategy and religious piety. He enacted the Truce of God, a compact that made Christian lords reach peace with each other. That didn't mean peace was a given and William still faced opposition on multiple fronts. One of the most pressing concerns was the souring of his relationship with King Henry, who supported William's rivals throughout the 1050s. There were a few reasons for this. William was becoming increasingly powerful within his duchy and in Henry's mind the Normans were upstarts who owed complete fealty to him as their overlord – especially William as it was becoming harder to put a leash on him. When William started pushing into the county of Maine, finally securing it for Norman interests in 1063, this was one such affront to Henry's sovereignty and he fought against his former ally every step of the way. The king may have also felt threatened by William's marriage to Matilda, the daughter of Count Baldwin V of Flanders. A powerful man in his own right, Baldwin controlled a region that was a strategic stepping stone between England and the rest of Europe. As William had a connection to the English throne, having sway in this area certainly helped his chances of staking his claim by gathering manpower and support. But the marriage didn't come easily.

An independently-minded woman, Matilda wasn't impressed with the proposal of a low-born bastard. Through her own lineage, she was higher born than William and the law of consanguinity seemed to stand in the way as they were distant cousins once removed. This didn't deter William and according to one story, on hearing her refusal, he rode from Normandy to Bruges. Finding Matilda on her way to church, he yanked her from her horse and beat her badly before riding away.[8] Her father took exception to this brutality, but before he and William drew swords, Matilda stopped the bloodshed by agreeing to marry the Duke of Normandy. In 1052, they were wed and the couple had nine children: Robert, Richard, William, Henry, Adelida, Cecilia, Constance, Matilda and Adela. In the coming years, William would have strained, complex relationships with his sons.

Between 1053 and 1057, William defended Normandy against King Henry's invasions until he scored the ultimate win at the Battle of Varaville. Here the duke showed his penchant for catching his opponents off guard with unexpected moves. As the invading army was crossing a ford and the tide came in, it split them in half. William attacked the half that had yet to cross, leading to a retreat by the French. From that point on the tide turned and William expanded his influence across Northern France, which brought him plenty of resources for future conquests.

With his duchy finally secured and stabilised, William pushed west into Brittany, fighting against Conan II and kicking off the Breton-Norman War. During this time, William and Harold Godwinson crossed paths and the latter could have been in the area to reaffirm the offer that the King of England, Edward the Confessor, had made to William to succeed him. Edward and his family had been supported by the dukes of Normandy for decades and many sources back up that his promise for William to succeed him was legitimate.[9] The relationship between William and Harold would remain contentious and the rival claimants to the English throne would finally do battle in 1066 after William had finished warring with the Bretons.

Conquering England

In the summer of 1066, William mobilised his forces on the continent for his invasion of England. According to one of his main biographers, William of Jumièges, the Duke of Normandy amassed 3,000 ships to transport his troops. This is likely an exaggeration and we need to take the events that were recorded by Norman sources with a pinch of salt. Both William of Jumièges and the duke's other principal biographer, William of Poitiers, had reason to paint the Conqueror in a heroic light and be critical of English defences and tactics. The Norman Conquest is also depicted in the Bayeux Tapestry, which captures the events leading up to the confrontation between William and Harold at the Battle of Hastings. Although it's a stunning piece of art, the tapestry is told from the perspective of the Normans and can't be taken as an objective piece of historical evidence.[10] Because, as the saying goes, history is written by the victors, yet William's victory wouldn't come easily.

Bad winds delayed William's invasion by a couple of months; perhaps he was also biding his time for the right moment to strike. Harold had been alert to the Norman threat all summer and had sentries posted along the southern coast. With the northern invasion of Harald Hardrada and Harold's brother Tostig, William had an opening that may or may not have fallen into his lap. The Normans finally arrived in England at Pevensey Bay on the 28th September. William was soon ready to defeat Harold near Hastings, to the north at Senlac Hill.

On the day of the battle, both sides were evenly matched. On the Norman side were the famous cavalrymen and infantry backed up by archers. On the English side were the housecarls that carried intimidating long, two-handed axes. Like the Normans, they were also descended from Norsemen who'd imposed their will on foreign lands centuries before and assimilated into the culture. The housecarls had already soaked their axes in the blood of their countrymen against Harald Hardrada's warriors and their training and discipline helped bolster Harold's *fyrd* militia of freemen. The Englishmen were tired from travelling from one half of the country to the next in days, but they weren't ready to go down without a fight.

Harold had his soldiers put up a shield wall, which seemed so unbreakable that it forced William's men to retreat. Throughout the chaos, a rumour went around that Duke William had fallen. But as the Normans were pulling back, the duke removed his helmet to reveal he was alive and rallied his troops into harrying the English until the shield wall broke and they chased after the English. In the end, the English were worn down and William emerged victorious. He was no longer a bastard, the illicit result of a lusty duke and a lowly tanner's daughter: he was a conqueror who'd fended off allcomers to his crown; he was on the cusp of transforming the Western world forever.

The first Norman King of England

The day after the Battle of Hastings, Harold's body was identified and presented to the duke. When word of this got back to the former king of England's mother, Gytha Thorkelsdottir, she pleaded with William to give the body to her. She was willing to pay Harold's weight in gold, but William refused. Instead, he had Harold's body thrown into the sea, or so one story goes. The duke's victory had come at great cost, though if he thought that would make him king, he was sorely mistaken. The nobles and clergy of England had gathered to name Edgar Atheling the new king. The grandson of Edmund Ironside, Edgar had a familial connection to the English throne, but he was young and untested in battle. The men who'd raised him saw him as a figurehead, a name to unite all England and assemble a second army to turn back the Normans.

William was having none of it. He marched on London, capturing Dover, Kent and Winchester. By November he'd reached the capital and smashed his way through any defences both physical and political. At the end of 1066, Edgar Atheling and his supporters swore fealty to William I of England, with the coronation at Westminster Abbey on Christmas Day. The Norman rule of England involved several political and societal changes that happened as a slow burn. It was the steady taking of power from English nobles by Norman leaders, a war of attrition that William threw himself into as soon as he was crowned king. He started the journey towards centralising the English government and merging it with a Norman mentality. Here are some of the main changes that happened under his rule:

- The concept of feudalism took over as William handed out lands in exchange for military service.
- Norman French became the main language of the elite, while most of the population continued to speak Old English.
- The church was restructured to feature Norman bishops, a move that led to a centralised Anglican church that distanced itself from the Roman papacy.
- Although slavery wasn't banned by the Normans, it was gradually phased out in the context of it being wrong to enslave fellow Christians in England.[11]

William took great steps to separate his roles as the King of England and the Duke of Normandy. In England he left many of the old governing tools in place such as sheriffs who ruled in his name across the local shires. This meant that new Norman landowners would be kept in check and would never grow so powerful that they could oppose William. In Normandy, he positioned his role as duke as being subservient to the King of France. He was compelled to travel back and forth across England and Normandy, further consolidating his power against uprisings and revolts, particularly from the North of England.

A non-sympathetic chronicler called Orderic Vitalis reported that William brought 'famine and the sword'[12] to the North throughout the late 1060s. The people of Northumbria rose against the Conqueror and he devasted their homes. There is evidence of how much destruction William caused in the Domesday Book. This tome was created for him in 1086 and recorded all the lands and holdings that he and his vassals owned. In the book, the value of northern towns plummeted from the 1060s to 1080s, showcasing William's path of destruction up the Great North Road through Yorkshire.

It took six years for William to fully bring England under Norman control, even at the expense of war with his own people. In 1075, a conflict broke out called the Revolt of the Earls that started when Ralph de

Guader, the Earl of East Anglia, had wanted to marry Emma FitzOsbern, the daughter of William's great companion, William FitzOsbern. William refused to sanction the marriage but Ralph and Emma went ahead with it.

This act of disobedience was encouraged by Emma's brother, Roger, the real power behind the rebellion. He had succeeded their father as the Earl of Hereford and was looking to carve out his own principality. The revolt was joined by Waltheof, Earl of Northumberland, creating a triumvirate of powerful lords who could pose a severe threat to William, especially since he was away in Normandy at the time. However, several events undid the revolt before it could really get going. Waltheof soon changed his mind and left his allies in the lurch. Meanwhile, the clergy raised an army to keep Roger's forces in check at the River Severn, while Ralph was overwhelmed by the superior might of William's brother Odo of Bayeux and advisor Geoffrey de Montbray. He fled to Denmark, leaving Emma behind to negotiate terms of surrender. She and Ralph were exiled to Brittany, a sentence that was better than the Earl of Hereford's. William had him imprisoned. The Revolt of the Earls was one of the last serious threats William would face to his rule in England.

Troubles at home and in the family

In between fending off rebellions in his English kingdom, William had to deal with instability back in Normandy, much of which came from within his own family. Throughout the 1070s, tensions had been rising between William and his eldest son Robert Curthose. Early signs of a fractious relationship came from William giving his son the derisive name Curthose, meaning short stocking for how short and stocky Robert was. Further humiliation came from an incident where Robert's brothers Henry and William Rufus dumped a full chamber pot over his head and William did nothing to punish his younger sons.

Most likely, the main cause of tension between Robert and William was about inheritance. In 1063, William had made Robert the Count of Maine and left him in charge of Normandy in 1066 when he invaded England. Perhaps he'd thought his father would be content to stay in England while he presided over the Duchy of Normandy, but the Conqueror had no such plans. After being rebuffed by his father, Robert attacked the castle of Rouen with a band of equally frustrated young men who went raiding through Normandy and Flanders, with William on their heels.

Robert's rebellion against his father culminated in a battle in 1079 at Gerberoy where he knocked William from a horse and would have killed him were it not for recognising the sound of his father's voice from beneath his helmet. Humiliated, William left the field and the following year peace was restored between father and son at the behest of Queen Matilda. Once again, Robert became the heir apparent to Normandy, though the relationship between father and son would never be fully healed.[13]

William's strife with his son signalled to others potential weakness and it wasn't long before the lords of Northern England were gearing up for another rebellion. In 1079, King Malcolm of the Scots raided south across the River Tweed, killing Walcher, the Bishop of Durham and Earl of Northumbria. Over the next year, William sent his brother Odo and his son Robert to deal with the bothersome Northerners who continued to be a thorn in his side. The rebellions were stopped when Robert forced Malcolm to submit.

Final years

There was no peace for the Conqueror in the last years of his reign as cracks within the royal family continued to show. In 1082, William had Odo arrested. The sources aren't clear on why there was a falling out between the brothers, but it's assumed that Odo wanted to make himself Pope and his grasping for power had become too much for the king.[14]

Adding to this pressure, Robert once again rebelled against his father and was exiled from Normandy. Queen Matilda died in 1083 and there was no longer a neutral party to stem the tide of resentment and ambition between the Conqueror and his eldest son. Robert aligned with the French king against his father, stirring up trouble while William focused on shoring up alliances. He married off his daughter Constance to Duke Alan of Brittany and during a campaign to seize the commune of Mantes, it's reported William was injured or became ill.

Taken back to Normandy, William was eventually moved to the Abbey of St Gervais outside Rouen. The king's health didn't improve and in preparation for the end he made his last will. To his eldest Robert he reaffirmed that the Duchy of Normandy would go to him, while his second son William Rufus was to be given England. William's youngest son Henry received money to buy his own land. William also ordered many of those he'd imprisoned to be released, including Odo.

Then, on the 9th September 1087, William the Conqueror died at the age of sixty. His death threw the European world into chaos, with all those who'd been at his deathbed scrambling to get ahead of the destabilising political systems across Normandy and England. Days later, the clergy of Rouen had the body transported to Caen to be buried in a tomb in the Abbey of St Etienne.

As a harbinger of warfare and bloodshed, it seems appropriate that William's body couldn't be buried without conflict erupting. The immediate aftermath of his death had already been marked by his supporters grabbing everything that wasn't nailed down and the newly appointed King of England, William II, departing with very little thought for his father's corpse, either as soon as William died or after the funeral.

On the day of the funeral, those in attendance were asked to forgive all William's sins. But a Caen peasant piped up and said that William had robbed his father of the land that the abbey was built on. The allegations proved to be true and the man was compensated for his trouble. If that wasn't bad enough, William's body had become bloated, to the point where the corpse couldn't fit into the small sarcophagus. When it was forced into place, the bowels burst open and a horrible stench swept through the abbey. The smell was so bad that even the strongest incense couldn't get rid of it and the mourners powered through the ceremony as quickly as possible.[15] The truth of this version of events must be considered against the sources that recorded William's death. Most of the chroniclers of the period were clerics and from their perspective, it would have been seen as divine that God had intervened and probably would have satisfied readers who'd had to survive the Norman tyranny for years.

The state of William's territories was left in disarray. By dividing up his lands between his sons, he'd put them all on a collision course to wrest power from each other. Robert Curthose warred with William Rufus over the English crown, the conflict then repeating itself when their younger brother Henry became king in 1100. The antagonism between the brothers plunged Normandy into civil war, which continued with new generations trying to one-up each other, to do it bigger and better than those before them.

Robert, William II and Henry all learned their brutal behaviour from their father, a man who favoured survival and power by any means necessary. William the Conqueror had been involved in constant warfare for nigh on fifty years. He was ruthless, cruel and tactical and had a relentless drive to achieve his goals. He may have carried on conquering well into old age if death hadn't stopped him. His impact on England was certainly profound and opinion on whether he changed it for the better or worse is still debated today. Was he the catalyst that put England on the path to greatness or was he the destroyer that remade everything in his image and wiped the slate clean? Perhaps he was all these things; we can't forget that it was the blood of the not-so-distance Norse that pumped through his veins. You can take a Norseman and a Norman out of the fight. But you can't take the fight out of a Norseman or a Norman. All who underestimated that fact paid for it dearly.

Chapter 18

The Crusader and The Holy Calling

We've traced the history of the Vikings across several cultures and continents. From the shores of northern England into Ireland and Scotland, across the sun-kissed Mediterranean, over the wintry fjords of Norway, Denmark and Sweden, to the Eastern frontiers of the Rus' and Byzantine Empire in the heart of Constantinople. Along the way, they carried their gods into conflict against Christianity, accepted them side by side and split apart again. And it's here at the crossroads between paganism and Christianity that the act of *vikingr* ultimately morphed into a similar activity: crusading.

The First Crusade of 1096–1099 was a call to arms for Western Christians to help the Eastern Christians of Byzantium against the rise of the Islamic Seljuk Empire of Asia. Once the call was made, Western Christians of all social classes marched to the Holy Lands that had been under Islamic control for 400 years. What followed was a storm of conflicting interests where princes, nobles, soldiers, dukes and commoners all set out to either fulfil a holy calling or win fame and fortune by any means necessary.

The First Crusade ended in success for the Western powers with the taking of Jerusalem. The Crusader States came into being, covering the Principality of Antioch, the County of Edessa, the County of Tripoli and the Kingdom of Jerusalem. The founding of the States was largely the work of Frankish and Norman lords who had the money and manpower to carve out their own territories. Decades earlier, William the Conqueror had proven the power of the Normans through his conquest of England and there were many, including his son Robert, wanting to make their own name in a foreign place. But it was a son of William's compatriot Eustice II that really etched his name into the history books by becoming the King of Jerusalem. His name was Baldwin I and he was an inspiration to the hero of this chapter, Sigurd the Crusader.

The Crusader and The Holy Calling

The life of Sigurd the Crusader is fascinating for several reasons. He was the first European king to personally lead a crusade. He was the great-grandson of Harald Hardrada, continuing the dynasty of Norse rulers who arguably held the last embers of the Viking spirit within them. Paradoxically, Sigurd would also be one to stomp those embers out in the name of God.

Growing up in the House of Hardrada

Born in 1089, Sigurd Magnusson came from a dying breed of lineage. His grandfather Olaf the Peaceful had been at the Battle of Stamford Bridge and had watched his legendary father Harald Hardrada die in England. Sigurd's father, Magnus Strife Lover, was the opposite of Olaf. Where Olaf sought peace with the likes of William the Conqueror and Christian leaders, Magnus was far more like his hard-ruling ancestor. He raided and warred across Norway and into Ireland and Scotland, bringing Sigurd with him and teaching him what it meant to come from the House of Hardrada.

Strife Lover's youth had been spent trying to claim the Norwegian throne. After Olaf the Peaceful died, the kingship was split between Magnus and his cousin Hakon. Magnus ruled over southern Norway, while his cousin reigned over the north. While the two kings governed together, there was tension about who had the definitive right to rule. When Hakon gave gifts to Magnus to try and ease the tension, it irritated him because he felt he was being given property that was already his. Compared to the wealth his father and grandfather had gathered over their lifetimes, Magnus had only a fraction of that and it weighed on his mind.

If he thought of slaying his cousin, Magnus would only have to wait for nature to take its course. Hakon died in a hunting accident, leaving him as the sole king of Norway. But there were hungry wolves waiting to strike from the shadows. Many chieftains didn't recognise Magnus's sovereignty and usurpers came out of the woodwork. One such rival was a man called Sweyn, an alleged son of Hardrada. Magnus met this supposed family member in battle, overcoming his forces and meting out death sentences to the chieftains who had opposed him.

Once he'd secured his kingdom, Magnus may have felt like he wanted to channel the spirit of his warmongering grandfather and complete unfinished business abroad. He sailed out to the British Isles, raiding in Wales, capturing the Isle of Man and extending his rule into Scotland. By the time he returned to Scandinavia, Strife Lover turned his attention to Sweden, fighting against King Inge the Elder. These skirmishes threatened the Danish monarch Eric Evergood, who encouraged peace talks between Magnus and Inge. The three kings reached an agreement, with Magnus marrying Inge's daughter Margaret.

But a man like Strife Lover would never be content with peace and quiet. In 1102, he went raiding in Irish waters, sparking conflict with the High King of Ireland. By the time of the Irish raids, Sigurd had accompanied his father in battle, experiencing the spoils and costs of war first-hand. The young prince would be instrumental in helping his father broker a peace between Norway and Ireland. At 14 years old his marriage was arranged to the High King's daughter. On the wedding day, Magnus named his son the co-king of Norway and put him in charge of Orkney and the Isle of Man. Norse and Irish sources depict Magnus as fighting in the service of the High King against a rival called Domnall. Magnus had intended to return to Norway and he'd agreed with the king that he'd be provided with cattle provisions for the journey home. As the cattle didn't arrive at the appointed time, Magnus sent his army inland to look for supplies, only for them to be ambushed by a large Irish force. Some say Magnus was betrayed by the High King, while another scenario is that the Irish mistook the Norse for Hebridean raiders.

Either way, Magnus prepared himself for battle and when his men expressed hesitation at attacking the bigger army, their king grunted, 'Kings are made for honour. Not for a long life.' Gripping his famed sword Legbit, the Strife Lover attacked with all the ferocity of his namesake. Two spears to the legs brought him down and an axe-wielding Irishman saw an opportunity. The man lunged forward and swung his axe into the neck of the King of Norway. This was his death blow. Magnus died on foreign soil. He was the last Norwegian king to die abroad, also giving him the title of the 'last' Viking.[1]

Three kings and the Norwegian crusade

With the death of his father, Sigurd went home to Norway without his Irish wife. He was made co-king with his half-brothers Eystein and Olaf. It hadn't been that long ago that Norway had been plunged into chaos by the battles between Magnus and the usurpers who wanted power for themselves. Would the brothers descend into the same quarrels and petty grievances? By all accounts, the three kings of Norway ruled peacefully together and it's possible they followed their father's example that he had set by living in peace with King Inge of Sweden and King Eric of Denmark. The reign of the brothers would be seen as a Golden Age for Norway and the country thrived with strong domestic policies and international recognition that Sigurd would bring through his own efforts.

By 1107, tales of the Crusades had swept across Scandinavia and the three kings of Norway all wanted to make a pilgrimage that had never been attempted before. After much debate, it was decided Sigurd would be the one to lead the expedition, as he had the most travel experience. The Norwegian Crusade was declared, and Sigurd set out in the autumn with sixty ships and 5,000 men. In years past, the Crusades had been made across land and though the First Crusade had been successful, all other attempts were met with disaster.

Sigurd didn't intend to travel by land. He had the blood of the seafaring marauders who could travel any waterway. He took a similar route that Chapter 13's Bjorn Ironside had hundreds of years before. That didn't mean the journey was easy or simple.

First, Sigurd sailed to England, overwintering with the blessing of King Henry I. Next, they headed south and after several months at sea, they stopped at Santiago de Compostela in Spain. Initially, a local lord gave the Norse permission to stay for the winter. But following a food shortage, the lord refused to give any provisions to Sigurd and his men. Sigurd had set out with divine intent. His mission was pure and good. How dare this tight-fisted miser refuse to shelter and provide for warriors of Christianity! Taking a leaf from his ancestors' blood-soaked book, he attacked and looted the city.

Then, he moved on to Portugal, where he became locked in another battle, besieging the castle at Sintra. Sigurd cut down any heathen who refused to be baptised, an action he would repeat more than once. Sailing into the Balearic Islands, Sigurd captured pirate ships and crushed Islamic resistance at Formentera, Ibiza and Menorca. In one instance, he and his men cornered a crew of Saracen pirates in a cave. The pirates had blocked the cave entrance with a stone wall, so Sigurd had his soldiers burn piles of wood, setting the cave on fire and choking the Saracens with the smoke. The Saracens had been sitting on a treasure hoard, which Sigurd happily claimed for himself.

Arriving in the Holy Land

In 1110, three years after leaving Norway, Sigurd and his longboats arrived at the port of Acre. From there he went the rest of the way to Jerusalem, coming face to face with King Baldwin I. Sigurd may have wanted to model himself after the crusader king and for his part, Baldwin took a liking to the Northman who'd completed a feat that had never been achieved before. Received warmly, Sigurd and his Norsemen spent time soaking up the courtly processes in the holiest of cities. Both kings also rode together to the River Jordon and back to Jerusalem, perhaps trading stories of their life experiences in the service of God.

Baldwin must have seen a spark of himself in the young Norse king and gave the Scandinavians many precious relics to take home with them, on the condition the gifts would be used to promote Christianity back in the North. Baldwin asked for Sigurd's help in dealing with several Muslim towns. So, Sigurd accompanied him to the town of Sidon. In a two-pronged attack, Baldwin attacked by land, while Sigurd struck from the sea. A forty-seven-day siege led to Sidon falling, with Sigurd's participation being crucial to the victory. For his heroism, Baldwin rewarded the Norse ruler with a splinter of the True Cross, the ultimate symbol of the Christian faith.

Going home

With this gift, Sigurd felt his pilgrimage in the Middle East had ended. Undefeated in every battle and with God's work now done, it was time to go home so he could continue his mission of spreading the faith in Scandinavia. On the way, Sigurd stopped in Constantinople, where he and his men were treated as heroes by the Byzantines and Emperor Alexios Komnenos. Staying in Constantinople for some time, Sigurd gave the emperor all his ships and much of the wealth he'd gained through his crusade. But before he could leave, there was another gift he needed to make to the emperor. The Varangian Guard had been a proving ground for his great-grandfather Harald Hardrada and Sigurd knew that he must carry on the tradition. He left behind several men for the guard and set off for Norway on the horses that the emperor provided him with.

On the journey home, Sigurd passed through Bulgaria, Hungary, Serbia and Bavaria, even stopping off to meet with the Holy Roman Emperor Lothar II. After three years of travel, Sigurd came to Denmark, where he was given a ship by King Niels to ferry him back to Norway. And what did Sigurd find in his absence? A country that had flourished under the guidance of his brothers Eystein and Olaf. At 21, Sigurd had acquired the life experience of a man thrice his age and he settled back into ruling. He built himself a castle and made his capital at Konghelle. True to the promise he'd made to King Baldwin, Sigurd increased the strength of Christianity in his country by introducing a tithe in Norway that went directly to the church.[2]

Yet Sigurd's crusading days weren't over. In 1123, he journeyed to Smaland in Sweden. The inhabitants clung to the old ways, the worship of Thor, Odin and Frejya. To him, the pagans were a relic of a darker, primitive time when the light of the Lord was obscured. True to his name, Sigurd the Crusader unleashed a violent campaign on the people of Smaland, forcibly converting them to Christianity and killing all who wouldn't submit. In many ways, Sigurd's Swedish campaign was a precursor to the devasting Northern Crusades of the late twelfth century that swept across the Baltic Sea to Slavic, Finnish and Prussian communities.

Sigurd died in 1130, though he left no legitimate sons to take his place on the throne. The Golden Age of peace that he and his brothers had ushered into Norway descended into feuds and civil wars between illegitimate heirs and pretenders. Sigurd had left big shoes to fill and no one quite measured up to filling them. In a way, he's the ideal example of a Viking mentality blending into true Christian purpose, changing the act of raiding and pillaging into the supposedly divine calling of crusading. He had the ruthless aggression of Harald Hardrada and Magnus Strife Lover and the desire to pacify his lands like Olaf the Peaceful. He was the amalgamation of his ancestors and a symbol of the endpoint of the Viking Age.

Epilogue

The craft of writing is an interesting experience. There's the romantic notion of being creative all the time, having work validated and read by people who you hope will take something useful away from the content. Then there's the reality of all the hours researching and sitting down to write, often in isolation. To me, the world in between the romance and the drudgery is what really counts.

It's stepping away from the desk to go outside and walk. It's the little moments where you're talking to people and see details that are the same as they were hundreds of years ago. It's the downtime of exploring other hobbies and curiosities that you can take back with you to the page and look for how subject matter informs your environment. The symbols and signs that show up. Because over the course of writing this book, I've seen the Vikings make their presence known. When walking, there have been several occasions where I've seen two ravens nearby, carrying Odin's endless quest for knowledge with them. I've found myself coming back to a specific tree that reminds me of Yggdrasil, with its huge, imposing branches and roots that seem to go down to the ends of the earth. I've examined the symbols of my own body, the Norse tattoos of my skin. I see a Viking warrior on my right arm, his head shielded by a dragon helm, eyes ready for war. Beside him, Thor's hammer Mjolnir wraps through the World Tree. Above the sigil of the Thunder God, a wolf perches, benign looking, yet mischievous, personifying the trickery of Loki and the finality of his son Fenrir. Across my chest, the Helm of Awe rune appears, a reminder to be fearless even when I'm scared or uncertain.

Writing about the Norse has changed me, just as they changed the societies and spaces of wherever they went. The act of writing about them has pushed me to be more adventurous with my choices and less anxious about taking risks. As the Norse pushed on with their longboats to new horizons, not knowing what the outcome would be on unpredictable tides, relying on balls, bravery and the convictions of their skills, so too have I wanted to push my own boat further into the world to explore more perspectives and understand life.

The Vikings were a product of their time and as with studying any culture, you can choose what resonates with you and what doesn't. What resonates with me is that the communities of Scandinavia chose to throw caution to the wind and venture out into the world in the hope of achieving their goals.

Every moment you encounter a new culture is an opportunity to learn. To grow. To discard old ideas and form new ones. To have your perceptions challenged and see more than one perspective. I'd appreciate having your perspective on *Norse Fighting Heroes* and if it resonated with you in any way, do leave a review online. It all helps with continuing to push me forward and grow.

Notes

Introduction
1. Seth Schein, *The Mortal Hero: An Introduction to Homer's Iliad*, University of California Press, 1984, p. 58.
2. Paul Begadon, *The Layman's Havamal*, 2021, p. 235.
3. David Rodgers & Kurt Noer, *Sons of Vikings: History of Legendary Vikings*, 2018, p. 10.
4. Johanna Katrin Fridriksdottir, *Valkyrie: The Women of The Viking World*, Bloomsbury Academic, 2021, p. 12.
5. Eldar Heide, *Viking – 'rower shifting'? An entymological contribution*, https://web.archive.org/web/20140714233409/http://eldar-heide.net/Publikasjonar%20til%20heimesida/viking%20rowshift.pdf, published 2005.
6. Neil Price, *The Children of Ash & Elm: A History of The Vikings*, Penguin History, 2021, pp. 11–12.
7. John C. Sharpe, *The Viking Expansion: climate, population, plunder*, https://scholarworks.umt.edu/cgi/viewcontent.cgi?article=4881&context=etd, published 2002.
8. Rodgers & Noer, pp. 44–46.
9. *Holmgang and Einvigi: Scandinavian Forms of The Duel*, www.vikinganswerlady.com/holmgang.shtml
10. Dan McCoy, *Outlawry in The Viking Age*, https://norse-mythology.org/outlawry-viking-age/
11. Rodgers & Noer, p. 49.
12. McCoy, *The Aesir-Vanir War*, https://norse-mythology.org/tales/the-aesir-vanir-war/
13. Price, p. 51.
14. *The Legendary Adventures Of Thor In Norse Mythology*, www.history.co.uk/articles/the-legendary-adventures-of-thor-in-norse-mythology
15. *The Death of Baldr*.
16. *The Tale of Thor's Wedding*, https://asgard.scot/blogs/news/the-tale-of-thors-wedding
17. Fridriksdottir, pp. 10–11.
18. Price, pp. 59–62.

Chapter 1
1. Jackson Crawford (translation), *The Saga of The Volsungs with The Saga of Ragnar Lothbrok*, Hackett Classics, 2017.

2. Crawford, 'Introduction', pp. xxi–xxii.
3. Robert Browning, *Andrea del Sarto*, www.poetryfoundation.org/poems/43745/andrea-del-sarto

Chapter 2
1. Crawford, pp. 31–44.
2. Price, p. 53.
3. Fridriksdottir, p. 2.
4. Price, p. 54.
5. Fridriksdottir, p. 57.
6. Ibid., pp. 66–67.
7. Price, p. 179.
8. Fridriksdottir, p. 21.
9. Carol J. Clover, 'The Politics of Scarcity: Notes on The Sex Ratio in Early Scandinavia' in *Norse Values and Society* (Scandinavian Studies) (Spring), University of Illinois Press, 1988.

Chapter 3
1. Crawford, pp. 89–98.
2. Rodgers & Noer, pp. 110–11.
3. *Risala: Ibn Fadlan's Account of the Rus*, www.vikinganswerlady.com/ibn_fdln.shtml
4. Price, p. 134.
5. Ibid., p. 125.
6. Rodgers & Noer, pp. 119–120.
7. Crawford, pp. 117–19.

Chapter 4
1. Crawford, pp. 112–14.
2. Rodgers & Noer, pp. 164–66.
3. Crawford, pp. 122–27.
4. Luke John Murphy, Heidi R. Fuller, Peter L.T Willan & Monte A. Gates, *An Anatomy of The Blood Eagle, The Practicalities of Viking Torture*, www.journals.uchicago.edu/doi/10.1086/717332
5. Roberta Frank, *Viking atrocity and Skaldic verse: The rite of the Blood-Eagle*, https://academic.oup.com/ehr/article/XCIX/CCCXCI/332/389819

Chapter 5
1. *Hakon The Good's Saga*, www.sacred-texts.com/neu/heim/05hakon.htm
2. Price, pp. 447–51.
3. Jackson Crawford, *Drengr: The Ultimate Viking Compliment*, www.youtube.com/watch?v=z0xSbY1lQLY

Chapter 6
1. Fridriksdottir, pp. 132–34.
2. Ibid., p. 41.
3. Ibid., p. 133.
4. Ibid., p. 133–34

Chapter 7
1. Price, p. 457
2. *Who were the dreaded Jomsvikings?*, https://thevikingherald.com/article/who-were-the-dreaded-jomsvikings/20?utm_content=cmp-true
3. Adam Farley, *The Viking Berserkers Were Norse Warriors Who Entered a Trance-Like Rage During Battle*, https://allthatsinteresting.com/berserker
4. *The Danish Conquest Part 11: The Battle of Sherston*, https://aclerkofoxford.blogspot.com/2016/06/the-danish-conquest-part-11-battle-of.html
5. History Profiles, *The True Story of Emma of Normandy |Vikings Valhalla|*, www.youtube.com/watch?v=PaNQ7_aGFJo
6. C*anute The Great (r. 1016–1035)*, www.royal.uk/canute-great-r-1016-1035
7. Dr Alex Woolf, in-person interview.
8. History Profiles, *The Greatest Viking King |Canute the Great | Vikings Valhalla*, www.youtube.com/watch?v=Z_ocWb5nO1A

Chapter 8
1. Jackson Crawford, *How Odin Got the Mead of Poetry*, www.wondriumdaily.com/how-odin-got-the-mead-of-poetry/
2. Debbie Potts, *Skaldic Poetry: A Short Introduction*, www.asnc.cam.ac.uk/resources/mpvp/wp-content/uploads/2013/02/Introduction-to-Skaldic-Poetry_Debbie-Potts.pdf
3. Leifur Eiriksson, Bernard Scudder et al., *Egil's Saga*, Penguin Classics, 2004. p. 100.
4. Ibid., p.100.
5. Ibid., p. 47.
6. Ibid., p. 103.
7. Ibid., p. 156.

Chapter 9
1. Fridriksdottir, p. 171.
2. Price, p. 301.
3. Making a Viking Ship, https://regia.org/research/ships/Ships1.htm
4. Price, pp. 386–87.

Chapter 10
1. Price, pp. 275–77.
2. Cat Jarman, *River Kings: The Vikings from Scandinavia to The Silk Roads*, William Collins, 2021, pp. 196–97.

3. Woolf, in-person interview.
4. Jarman, pp. 224–27.

Chapter 11
1. Rodgers & Noer, pp. 234–39.
2. History Time, *Sviatoslav 'the brave': Grand Prince of Kiev 945–972*, www.youtube.com/watch?v=KlAFetvDH1E
3. Alex Johnson, *Olga of Kiev: The One Saint You Don't Want to Mess With*, https://museumhack.com/olga-of-kiev/
4. Rodgers & Noer, p. 247.

Chapter 12
1. Jim Gritton, *Ynvgars saga vidforla and the Ingvar Runestones: A Question of Evidence*, file:///Users/jamieryder/Downloads/Yngvars_saga_vidforla_and_the_Ingvar_Run.pdf
2. Ibid.
3. Ibid.
4. Jonas Lau Markussen, *The Ingvar Expedition*, https://jonaslaumarkussen.com/article/the-ingvar-expedition/
5. Begadon, pp. 2, 65–77.
6. Price, p. 189.
7. McCoy, *Vegvisir*, https://norse-mythology.org/vegvisir/
8. McCoy, *Helm of Awe*, https://norse-mythology.org/symbols/helm-of-awe/
9. Price, p. 192.

Chapter 13
1. Saxo Grammaticus, *Gesta Danorum of Saxo Grammaticus*.
2. Anne Christys, *Vikings in the South: Voyages to Iberia and the Mediterranean*, www.bloomsburycollections.com/book/vikings-in-the-south-voyages-to-iberia-and-the-mediterranean/ch1-introduction-don-teudo-rico-defeats-a-viking-raid
3. History Time, *The Real Bjorn Ironside // Vikings in Spain & the Mediterranean*, www.youtube.com/watch?v=UgKQJ3WGJBk&t=2293s
4. *Burial Mound of Bjorn Ironside*, https://paganplaces.com/places/burial-mound-of-bjorn-ironside/
5. J.R.R. Tolkien, *Fellowship of The Ring*, Kindle, 2009.

Chapter 14
1. Tim Lambert, *A Brief History of Greenland*, https://localhistories.org/a-brief-history-of-greenland/,
2. Victor Rouă,, *The Norse Settlement Of Greenland and The Mystery Behind Its Demise*, www.thedockyards.com/the-norse-settlement-of-greenland-and-the-mystery-behind-its-demise/
3. Price, pp. 484–85.
4. *The Saga of Erik the Red*, https://sagadb.org/eiriks_saga_rauda.en
5. Price, p. 501.

Chapter 15
1. Rodgers & Noer, p. 256.
2. Price, p. 490.
3. Fridriksdottir, p. 117.
4. Rodgers & Noer, p. 261.
5. *Erik the Red*, https://visitgreenland.com/about-greenland/erik-the-red/
6. *L'Anse aux Meadows*, http://viking.archeurope.com/settlement/vinland/lanse-aux-meadows/
7. *Where Was Vinland?*, http://viking.archeurope.com/settlement/vinland/where-was-vinland/

Chapter 16
1. Don Hollway, *The Last Viking: The True Story Of King Harald Hardrada*, Osprey Publishing, 2021, pp. 42–44.
2. C. Keith Hansley, *The Dramatic Celestial Dating Debate Over The Battle of Stiklestad*, https://thehistorianshut.com/2023/04/19/the-dramatic-celestial-dating-debate-over-the-battle-of-stiklestad/
3. Snorri Sturluson, *Heimskringla, or the Chronicle of the Kings of Norway*, Kindle, 2011.
4. Hollway, p .60.
5. Jarman, pp. 266–67.
6. Charles J. Lockett, *The Varangian Guard: Who Were the Vikings of Byzantium?*, www.thecollector.com/varangian-guard-byzantine-empire/
7. Jackson Crawford, *The Varangian Guard*, www.youtube.com/watch?v=J0iTl-eEqVI
8. Hollway, pp. 99–94.
9. Rodgers & Noer, p. 299.
10. James Turner, *Harald Hardarda: Overthrowing of an Emperor*, www.medievalists.net/2022/08/harald-hardrada-overthrowing-emperor/
11. Elena Gurevich, *Skaldic Praise Poetry and Macrologia: some observations on Olafr Thordarson's use of his sources*, www.sagaconference.org/SC11/SC11_Gurevich.pdf
12. Hollway, pp. 270–72.
13. *The coin that established Norway's monetary system*, www.historiskmuseum.no/english/exhibitions/good-as-gold/the-coin-that-established-norways-monetary-system/
14. Hollway, p. 313.
15. Sturluson.

Chapter 17
1. *When Harold Met William in 1064: A Tale of Quicksand And Cunning*, www.normandythenandnow.com/when-harold-met-william-in-1064/
2. *Normandy History, Family Crest & Coats of Arms*, www.houseofnames.com/normandy-family-crest

3. *Norman People*, www.medievalchronicles.com/medieval-history/medieval-history-periods/the-normans/norman-people/
4. *The Weapons of 1066*, www.english-heritage.org.uk/learn/histories/1066-and-the-norman-conquest/the-weaponry-of-1066/
5. *Build A Norman Castle*, www.english-heritage.org.uk/learn/histories/1066-and-the-norman-conquest/build-a-norman-castle/
6. Rodgers & Noer, p. 335.
7. Susan Abernethy, *Herleva of Falaise, Mother of William the Conqueror*, www.medievalists.net/2014/07/herleva-falaise-mother-william-conqueror/
8. History Roadshow, *Matilda of Flanders Timeline of a Conquering Queen*, www.youtube.com/watch?v=c_zxZ3rCk9Y
9. The People's Profiles, *William the Conqueror: First Norman King of England Documentary*, www.youtube.com/watch?v=8kBHUez2mKY&t=2533s
10. Dr Kristine Tanton, *The Bayeux Tapestry*, www.khanacademy.org/humanities/ap-art-history/early-europe-and-colonial-americas/medieval-europe-islamic-world/a/bayeux-tapestry
11. Mark Cartwright, *The Impact of the Norman Conquest of England*, www.worldhistory.org/article/1323/the-impact-of-the-norman-conquest-of-england/
12. Michael Wood, *William the Conqueror: A Thorough Revolutionary*, www.bbc.co.uk/history/trail/conquest/norman/william_the_conqueror_04.shtml
13. Parry This, *Robert II Curthrose, Duke of Normandy: Crusades History*, www.youtube.com/watch?v=mFdEfuIbPS4
14. *Odo, Earl of Kent*, www.englishmonarchs.co.uk/normans_12.html
15. Miriam Bibby, *William the Conqueror's Exploding Corpse*, www.historic-uk.com/HistoryUK/HistoryofEngland/William-The-Conqueror-Exploding-Corpse/

Chapter 18
1. History Profiles, *The Last Viking | Magnus Strife Lover*, www.youtube.com/watch?v=Ms2BJvy7JqQ
2. History Profiles, *Sigurd the Crusader | The Viking Crusade*, www.youtube.com/watch?v=OaGESuyJKH8&t=768s

Bibliography

Abernethy, Susan, *Herleva of Falaise, Mother of William the Conqueror*, www.medievalists.net/2014/07/herleva-falaise-mother-william-conqueror/

Begadon, Paul, *The Layman's Havamal: A Modern Interpretation of Viking Age Wisdom*, Paul Begadon, 2021.

Bibby, Miriam, *William the Conqueror's Exploding Corpse*, www.historic-uk.com/HistoryUK/HistoryofEngland/William-The-Conqueror-Exploding-Corpse/

Browning, Robert, *Andrea del Sarto*, www.poetryfoundation.org/poems/43745/andrea-del-sarto

Build A Norman Castle, www.english-heritage.org.uk/learn/histories/1066-and-the-norman-conquest/build-a-norman-castle/

Burial Mound of Bjorn Ironside, https://paganplaces.com/places/burial-mound-of-bjorn-ironside/

Canute The Great (r. 1016–1035), www.royal.uk/canute-great-r-1016-1035

Cartwright, Mark, *The Impact of the Norman Conquest of England*, www.worldhistory.org/article/1323/the-impact-of-the-norman-conquest-of-england/

Christys, Anne, *Vikings in the South: Voyages to Iberia and the Mediterranean*, www.bloomsburycollections.com/book/vikings-in-the-south-voyages-to-iberia-and-the-mediterranean/ch1-introduction-don-teudo-rico-defeats-a-viking-raid

Clover, Carol J., 'The Politics of Scarcity: Notes on the Sex Ratio in Early Scandinavia' in *Norse Values and Society* (Scandinavian Studies) (Spring), University of Illinois Press, 1988.

Crawford, Jackson, *Drengr: The Ultimate Viking Compliment*, www.youtube.com/watch?v=z0xSbY1lQLY

Crawford, Jackson, *How Odin Got the Mead of Poetry*, www.wondriumdaily.com/how-odin-got-the-mead-of-poetry/

Crawford, Jackson, (translation), *The Saga of The Volsungs with the Saga of Ragnar Lothbrok*, Hackett Classics, 2017.

Crawford, Jackson, *The Varangian Guard*, www.youtube.com/watch?v=J0iT1-eEqVI

Erik the Red, https://visitgreenland.com/about-greenland/erik-the-red/

Eiriksson, Leifur, Scudder, Bernard et al., *Egil's Saga*, Penguin Classics, 2004.

Farley, Adam, *The Viking Berserkers Were Norse Warriors Who Entered a Trance-Like Rage During Battle*, https://allthatsinteresting.com/berserker

Frank, Roberta, *Viking atrocity and Skaldic verse: The rite of the Blood-Eagle*, https://academic.oup.com/ehr/article/XCIX/CCCXCI/332/389819

Fridriksdottir, Katrin Johanna, *Valkyrie: The Women of The Viking World*, Bloomsbury Academic, 2021.

Grammaticus, Saxo, *Gesta Danorum of Saxo Grammaticus*, Kindle, 2012.
Gritton, Jim, *Ynvgars saga vidforla and the Ingvar Runestones: A Question of Evidence*, file:///Users/jamieryder/Downloads/Yngvars_saga_vidforla_and_the_Ingvar_Run.pdf
Gurevich, Elena, *Skaldic Praise Poetry and Macrologia: some observations on Olafr Thordarson's use of his sources*, www.sagaconference.org/SC11/SC11_Gurevich.pdf
Hakon The Good's Saga, www.sacred-texts.com/neu/heim/05hakon.htm
Hansley, Keith C., *The Dramatic Celestial Dating Debate Over the Battle Of Stiklestad*, https://thehistorianshut.com/2023/04/19/the-dramatic-celestial-dating-debate-over-the-battle-of-stiklestad/
Heide, Eldar, *Viking – 'rower shifting'? An entymological contribution*, https://web.archive.org/web/20140714233409/http://eldar-heide.net/Publikasjonar%20til%20heimesida/viking%20rowshift.pdf
History Profiles, *Sigurd the Crusader | The Viking Crusade*, www.youtube.com/watch?v=OaGESuyJKH8&t=768s
History Profiles, *The Greatest Viking King | Canute the Great | Vikings Valhalla*, www.youtube.com/watch?v=Z_ocWb5nO1A
History Profiles, *The Last Viking | Magnus Strife Lover*, www.youtube.com/watch?v=Ms2BJvy7JqQ
History Profiles, *The True Story of Emma of Normandy |Vikings Valhalla*, www.youtube.com/watch?v=PaNQ7_aGFJo
History Roadshow, *Matilda of Flanders Timeline of a Conquering Queen*, www.youtube.com/watch?v=c_zxZ3rCk9Y
History Time, *Sviatoslav 'the brave': Grand Prince of Kiev 945–972*, www.youtube.com/watch?v=KlAFetvDH1E
History Time, *The Real Bjorn Ironside // Vikings in Spain & the Mediterranean*, www.youtube.com/watch?v=UgKQJ3WGJBk&t=2293s
Holmgang and Einvigi: Scandinavian Forms of the Duel, www.vikinganswerlady.com/holmgang.shtml
Hollway, Don, *The Last Viking: The True Story of King Harald Hardrada*, Osprey Publishing, 2021.
Jarman, Cat, *River Kings: The Vikings from Scandinavia to the Silk Roads*, William Collins, 2021.
Johnson, Alex, *Olga of Kiev: The One Saint You Don't Want to Mess With*, https://museumhack.com/olga-of-kiev/
L'Anse aux Meadows, http://viking.archeurope.com/settlement/vinland/lanse-aux-meadows/
Lambert, Tim, *A Brief History of Greenland*, https://localhistories.org/a-brief-history-of-greenland/
Lockett, Charles J., *The Varangian Guard: Who Were the Vikings of Byzantium?*, www.thecollector.com/varangian-guard-byzantine-empire/
Making a Viking Ship, https://regia.org/research/ships/Ships1.htm
Markussen, Jonas Lau, *The Ingvar Expedition*, https://jonaslaumarkussen.com/article/the-ingvar-expedition/

McCoy, Dan, *Helm of Awe*, https://norse-mythology.org/symbols/helm-of-awe/
McCoy, Dan, *Outlawry in The Viking Age*, https://norse-mythology.org/outlawry-viking-age/
McCoy, Dan, *The Aesir-Vanir War*, https://norse-mythology.org/tales/the-aesir-vanir-war/
McCoy, Dan, *Vegvisir*, https://norse-mythology.org/vegvisir/
Murphy, Luke John, Fuller, Heidi R., Willan, Peter L. T., Gates, Monte A., *An Anatomy of the Blood Eagle: The Practicalities of Viking Torture*, www.journals.uchicago.edu/doi/10.1086/717332
Normandy History, Family Crest & Coats of Arms, www.houseofnames.com/normandy-family-crest
Norman People, www.medievalchronicles.com/medieval-history/medieval-history-periods/the-normans/norman-people/
Odo, Earl of Kent, www.englishmonarchs.co.uk/normans_12.html
Parry This, *Robert II Curthose, Duke of Normandy – Crusades History*, www.youtube.com/watch?v=mFdEfuIbPS4
Potts, Debbie, *Skaldic Poetry: A Short Introduction*, www.asnc.cam.ac.uk/resources/mpvp/wp-content/uploads/2013/02/Introduction-to-Skaldic-Poetry_Debbie-Potts.pdf
Price, Neil, *The Children of Ash and Elm: A History of The Vikings*, Penguin History, 2021.
Risala: Ibn Fadlan's Account of the Rus, www.vikinganswerlady.com/ibn_fdln.shtml
Rodgers, David & Noer, Kurt, *Sons of Vikings: A Legendary History of the Viking Age*, Kindle, 2018.
Rouă, Victor, *The Norse Settlement of Greenland and the Mystery Behind Its Demise*, www.thedockyards.com/the-norse-settlement-of-greenland-and-the-mystery-behind-its-demise/
Schein, Seth, *The Mortal Hero: An Introduction to Homer's Iliad*, University of California Press, 1984.
Sharpe, John C., *The Viking Expansion: climate, population, plunder*, https://scholarworks.umt.edu/cgi/viewcontent.cgi?article=4881&context=etd
Sturluson, Snorri, *Heimskringla, or the Chronicle of the Kings of Norway*, Kindle, 2011.
Tanton, Dr Kristine, *The Bayeux Tapestry*, www.khanacademy.org/humanities/ap-art-history/early-europe-and-colonial-americas/medieval-europe-islamic-world/a/bayeux-tapestry
The coin that established Norway's monetary system, www.historiskmuseum.no/english/exhibitions/good-as-gold/the-coin-that-established-norways-monetary-system/
The Danish Conquest Part 11: The Battle of Sherston, https://aclerkofoxford.blogspot.com/2016/06/the-danish-conquest-part-11-battle-of.html
The Death of Baldr, www.hurstwic.org/history/articles/mythology/myths/text/baldr.htm
The Legendary Adventures of Thor in Norse Mythology, www.history.co.uk/articles/the-legendary-adventures-of-thor-in-norse-mythology
The People's Profiles, *William the Conqueror: First Norman King of England Documentary*, www.youtube.com/watch?v=8kBHUez2mKY&t=2533s

The Saga of Erik the Red, https://sagadb.org/eiriks_saga_rauda.en

The Tale of Thor's Wedding, https://asgard.scot/blogs/news/the-tale-of-thors-wedding

The Weapons of 1066, www.english-heritage.org.uk/learn/histories/1066-and-the-norman-conquest/the-weaponry-of-1066/

Tolkien, J. R. R., *Fellowship of The Ring*, Kindle, 2009.

Turner, James, *Harald Hardrada: Overthrowing of an Emperor*, www.medievalists.net/2022/08/harald-hardrada-overthrowing-emperor/

When Harold Met William in 1064; A Tale of Quicksand And Cunning, www.normandythenandnow.com/when-harold-met-william-in-1064/

Where Was Vinland?, http://viking.archeurope.com/settlement/vinland/where-was-vinland/

Who were the Dreaded Jomsvikings?, https://thevikingherald.com/article/who-were-the-dreaded-jomsvikings/20?utm_content=cmp-true

Wood, Michael, *William the Conqueror: A Thorough Revolutionary*, www.bbc.co.uk/history/trail/conquest/norman/william_the_conqueror_04.shtml

Woolf, Dr Alex, in-person interview.

Index

Aslaug, 15–16, 21–22, 24–26
Aud the Deep-Minded, 76–81

Baldr, xxiii–xxv
Berserker, 50
Bjorn Ironside, 29–30, 99–102
Blood eagle, 33–34
Brynhild (Volsung saga), 4, 6, 8–18, 109
Byzantine Empire, 83, 85–86, 91–93, 118–23

Christianity, xxv, 36–42, 51–53, 69, 77, 91, 101, 107–8, 124, 140, 152–60
Cnut, 44, 47–53, 116–17, 124, 133

Eric Bloodaxe, 37, 39, 41, 58, 63–66
Eriksdottir, Freydis, 105, 109–12
Erikson, Leif, 105, 107–12
Erik the Red, 103–7

Freyja, xxvii, xix, xxi, xxv–xxvi, xxxiii–xxxvi, 72, 105

Gudrun (Volsung saga), 10, 13–18

Hakon the Good, 36–42, 57, 66–67
Harald Finehair, 36–37, 42, 44, 58, 77
Harald Hardrada, 44, 113–38, 153
Heimdall, xxvi, xxix, xxxv

Igor of the Rus, 85–87
Ivar the Boneless, 25, 28–35
Ingvar the Well-Travelled, 95–98

Jomsviking, 48–50

Lodbrok, Ragnar, 19–27, 29–31, 101–2
Loki, xx, xxiii–xxxvi, 73, 76–77

Mjolnir, xx, xxi, xxiii, xxv–xxvi, 73, 158

Normans, 134, 137, 139–51
Norse gender identity, xxxiii, 12–13
Norse poetry 45, 54–75, 128, 135
Norse politics xvi–xvii, 46
Norse runes xviii, 9, 63, 65, 95–98
Norse travels
   British Isles, xii, 23, 25, 28–35, 36–37, 47–53, 65–66, 133–38, 153–54
   Iceland 5, 11, 41, 48, 56, 58–60, 65–66, 78–81, 97, 103–105, 111, 122, 131
   Greenland, 103–8
   Mediterranean, 99–103
   North America, 108–12
   The East, 82–94, 95–98, 116–23
Norse women
   as shield-maidens, 10–13, 46, 73, 113,
   as politicians, 43–46, 76–81

Odin, xviii–xxxvi, 6–9, 17, 34, 55–56, 71, 90, 96–97, 158
Olaf the Saint, 43–44, 52, 113–117, 122–23
Olafsdottir, Astrid, 43–46, 125
Olga, 88–94
Outlawry, xvi, 40, 104, 110

Poetic Edda, xxxvi, 5, 56–57,
Prose Edda, 56

Rus', 82–94, 117 - 118
Rurik, 82–85

Saga
   as a storytelling device, 5
   of Ragnar Lodbrok, 19–35
   of Harald Hardrada, 113–38

   of Egil Skallagrimsson, 5, 57–70
   Volsungs, 1–18
Sigurd the Crusader, 152–60
Sigurd the Dragon Slayer, 1–8
Skallagrimsson, Egil, 57–70
Sturluson, Snorri, 41, 45, 116, 120–21, 131
Sviatoslav the Brave, 88–94

Thor xx–xxxvi, 76–77
Thorkill the Tall, 48–50

Valkyries, xxxiv, 8–13, 28, 99

Varangian Guard, 83–84, 118–23, 130, 157
Vikings
   Meaning, xxiii–xiv
   as an occupation, xxiii–xiv, xv, 52

William the Conqueror, 53, 133–34, 137, 139–51, 152

Dear Reader,

We hope you have enjoyed this book, but why not share your views on social media? You can also follow our pages to see more about our other products: facebook.com/penandswordbooks or follow us on Twitter @penswordbooks

You can also view our products at www.pen-and-sword.co.uk (UK and ROW) or www.penandswordbooks.com (North America).

To keep up to date with our latest releases and online catalogues, please sign up to our newsletter at: www.pen-and-sword.co.uk/newsletter

If you would like a printed catalogue with our latest books, then please email: enquiries@pen-and-sword.co.uk or telephone: 01226 734555 (UK and ROW) or email: Uspen-and-sword@casematepublishers.com or telephone: (610) 853-9131 (North America).

We respect your privacy and we will only use personal information to send you information about our products.

Thank you!